SUPERGIRL and the LEGION of SUPER-HEROES

Dominator War

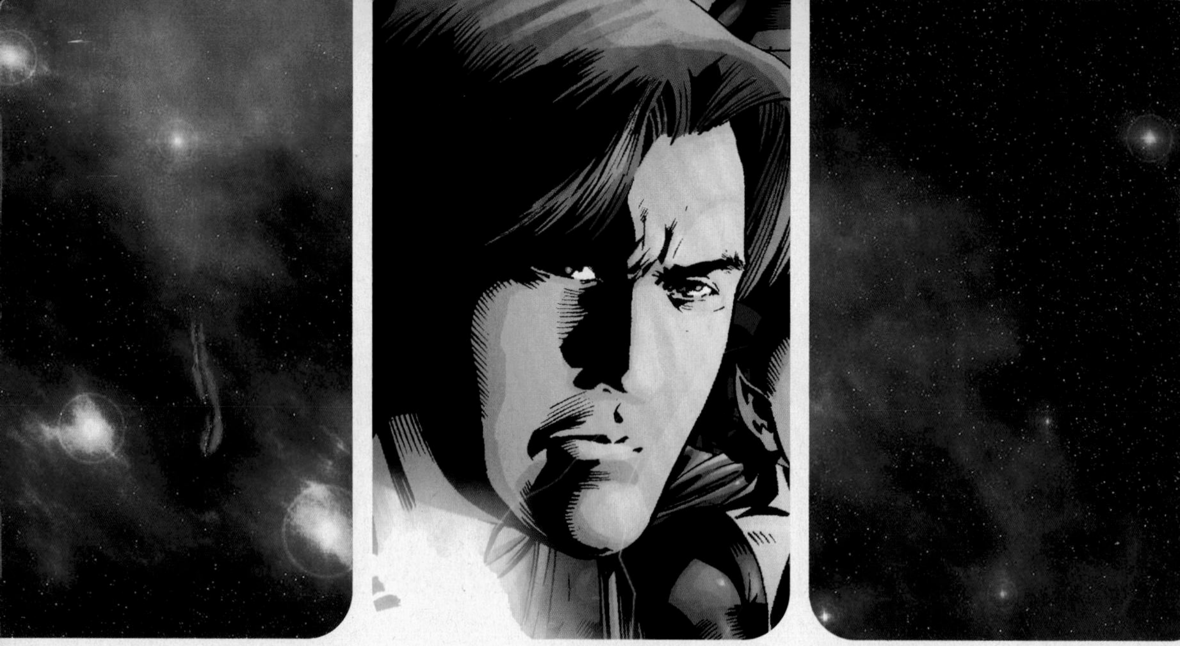

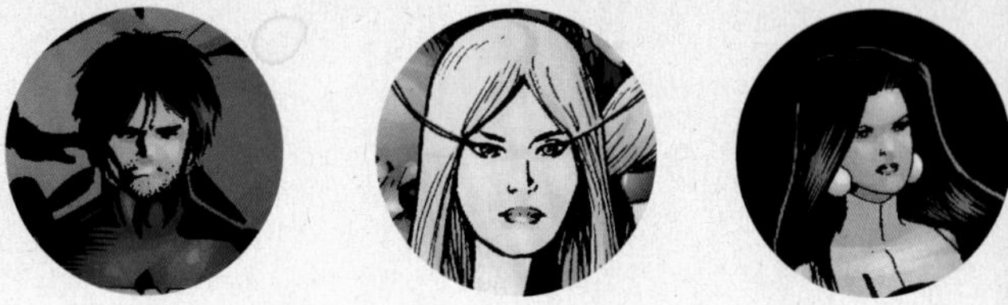

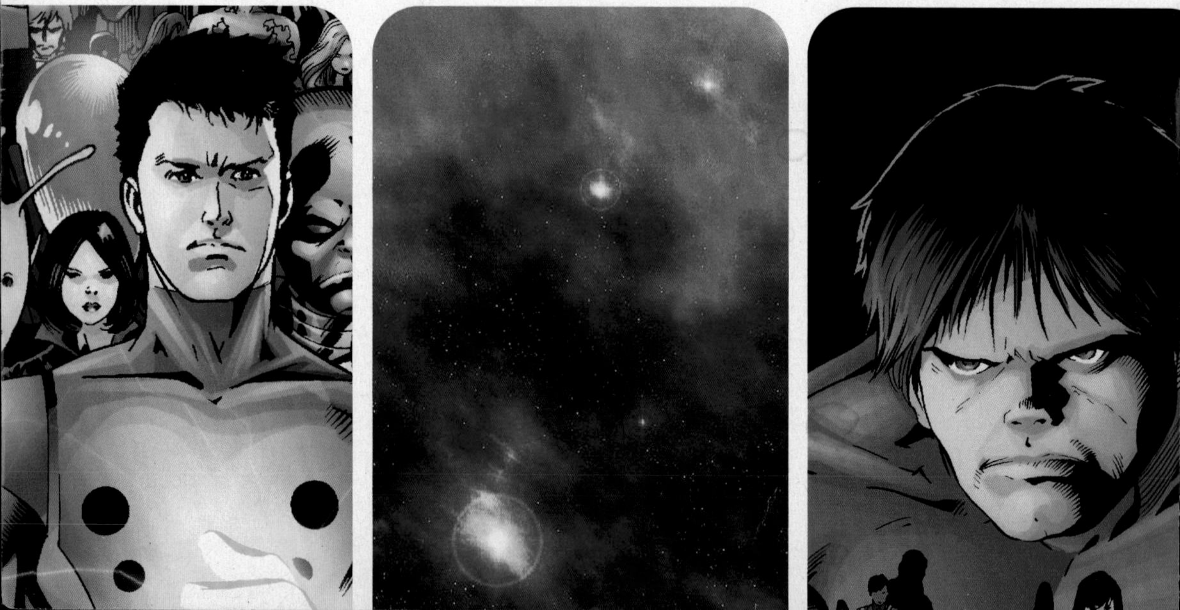

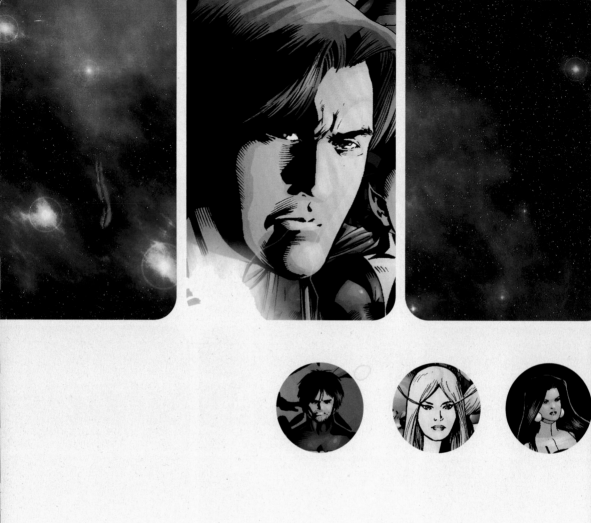

SUPERGIRL and the LEGION of SUPER-HEROES
Dominator War

WRITERS
Mark Waid
WITH
Tony Bedard

PENCILS
Barry Kitson
WITH
Kevin Sharpe

INKS
Mick Gray
WITH
Jimmy Palmiotti
Mark McKenna
Jack Purcell

COLORS
Nathan Eyring

LETTERS
Travis Lanham
Jared K. Fletcher
Pat Brosseau
Phil Balsman

Dan DiDio
Senior VP-Executive Editor

Mike Marts
Editor-original series

Jeanine Schaefer
Associate Editor-original series

Harvey Richards
Assistant Editor-original series

Bob Joy
Editor-collected edition

Robbin Brosterman
Senior Art Director

Paul Levitz
President & Publisher

Georg Brewer
VP-Design & DC Direct Creative

Richard Bruning
Senior VP-Creative Director

Patrick Caldon
Executive VP-Finance & Operations

Chris Caramalis
VP-Finance

John Cunningham
VP-Marketing

Terri Cunningham
VP-Managing Editor

Alison Gill
VP-Manufacturing

Hank Kanalz
VP-General Manager, WildStorm

Jim Lee
Editorial Director-WildStorm

Paula Lowitt
Senior VP-Business & Legal Affairs

MaryEllen McLaughlin
VP-Advertising & Custom Publishing

John Nee
VP-Business Development

Gregory Noveck
Senior VP-Creative Affairs

Sue Pohja
Senior VP-Book Trade Sales

Cheryl Rubin
Senior VP-Brand Management

Jeff Trojan
VP-Business Development, DC Direct

Bob Wayne
VP-Sales

Cover art by Barry Kitson with Nathan Eyring

**SUPERGIRL AND THE LEGION OF
SUPER-HEROES: DOMINATOR WAR**

DC Comics, 1700 Broadway, New York, NY 10019
A Warner Bros. Entertainment Company
Printed in Canada. Second printing.
ISBN: 978-1-4012-1442-5

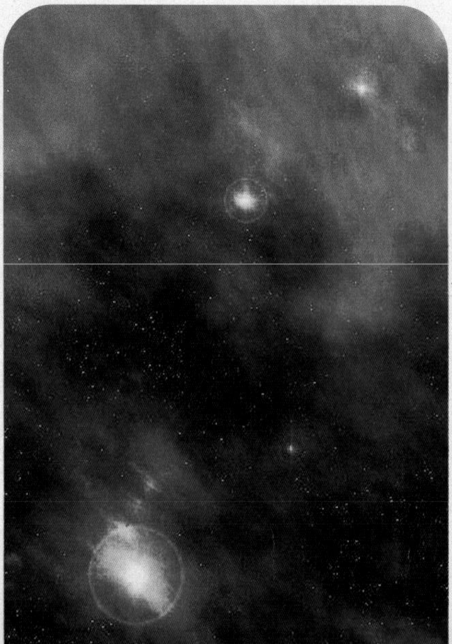

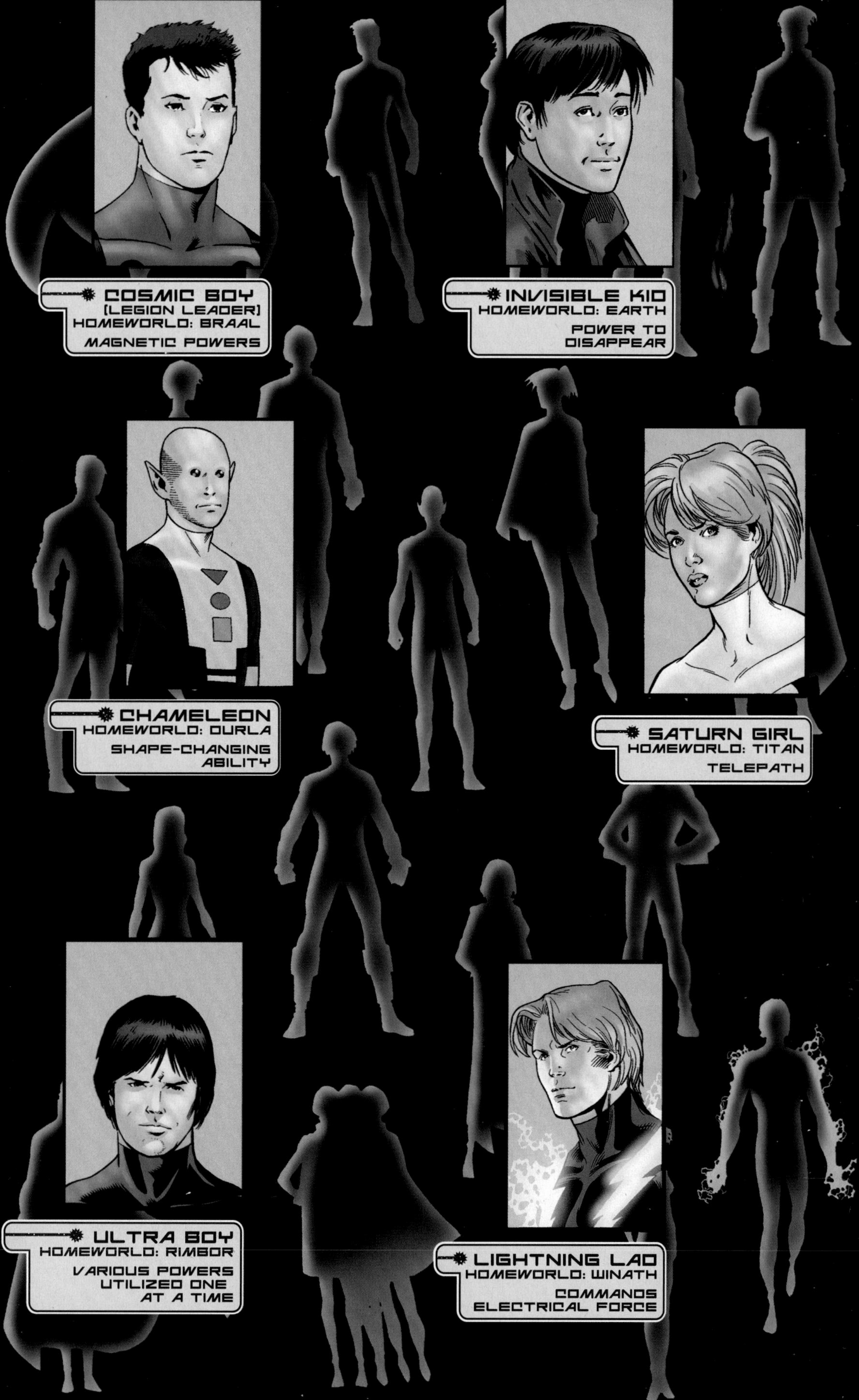

COSMIC BOY
[LEGION LEADER]
HOMEWORLD: BRAAL
MAGNETIC POWERS
INVISIBLE KID
HOMEWORLD: EARTH
POWER TO DISAPPEAR
CHAMELEON
HOMEWORLD: DURLA
SHAPE-CHANGING ABILITY
SATURN GIRL
HOMEWORLD: TITAN
TELEPATH
ULTRA BOY
HOMEWORLD: RIMBOR
VARIOUS POWERS UTILIZED ONE AT A TIME
LIGHTNING LAD
HOMEWORLD: WINATH
COMMANDS ELECTRICAL FORCE

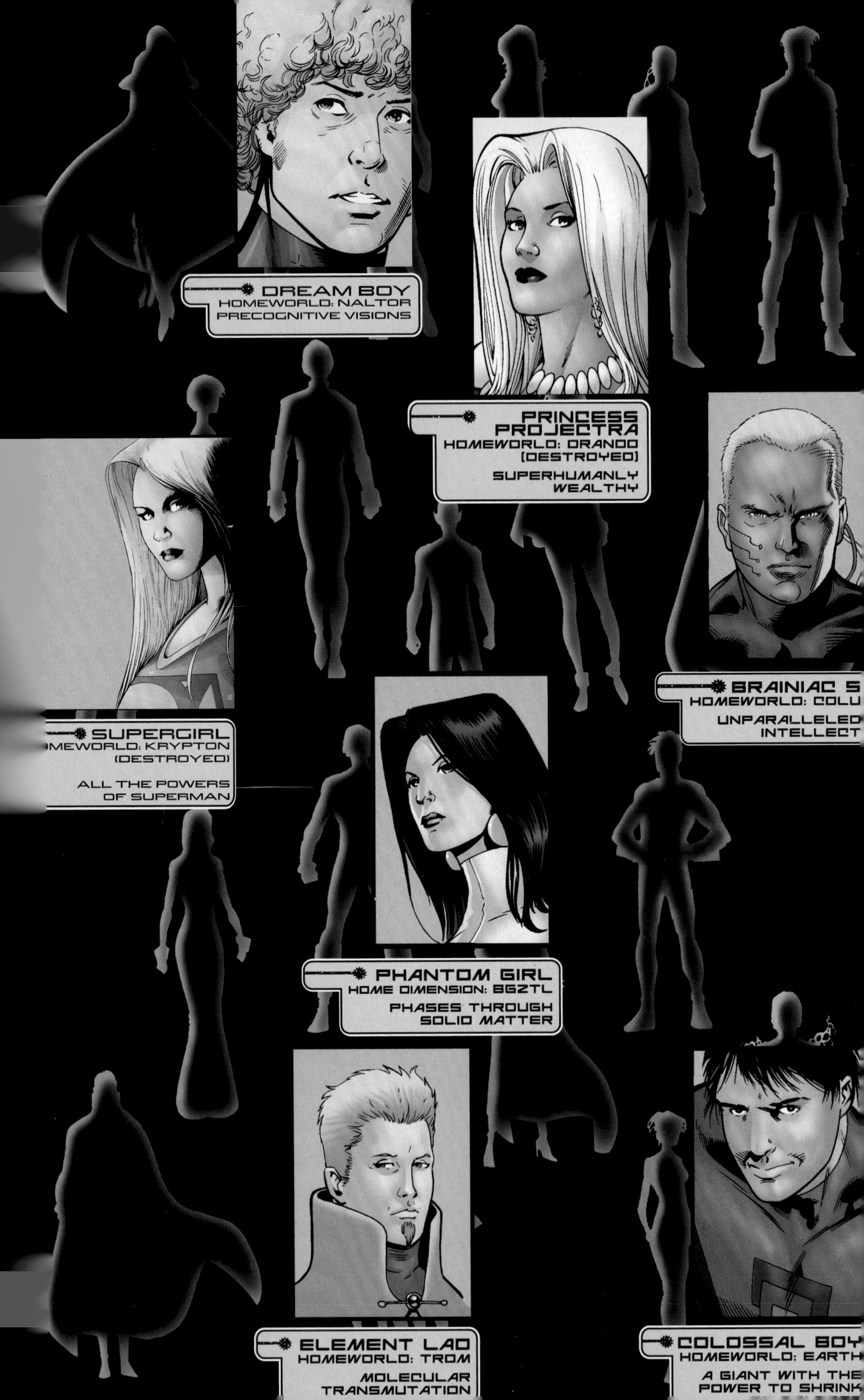
DREAM BOY
HOMEWORLD: NALTOR
PRECOGNITIVE VISIONS
PRINCESS PROJECTRA
HOMEWORLD: ORANDO (DESTROYED)
SUPERHUMANLY WEALTHY
SUPERGIRL
MEWORLD: KRYPTON (DESTROYED)
ALL THE POWERS OF SUPERMAN
BRAINIAC 5
HOMEWORLD: COLU
UNPARALLELED INTELLECT
PHANTOM GIRL
HOME DIMENSION: BGZTL
PHASES THROUGH SOLID MATTER
ELEMENT LAD
HOMEWORLD: TROM
MOLECULAR TRANSMUTATION
COLOSSAL BOY
HOMEWORLD: EARTH
A GIANT WITH THE POWER TO SHRINK

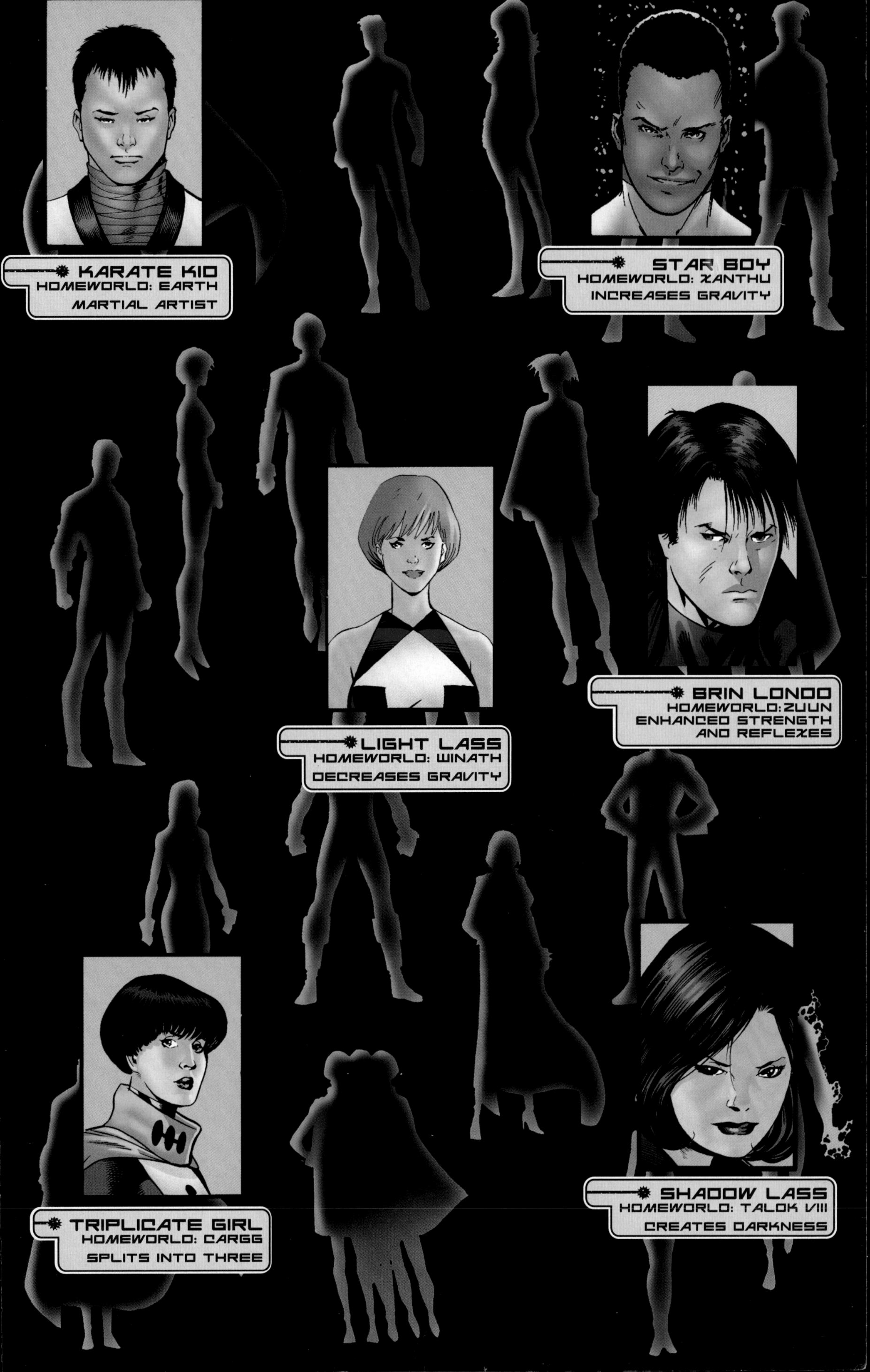
KARATE KID
HOMEWORLD: EARTH
MARTIAL ARTIST
STAR BOY
HOMEWORLD: XANTHU
INCREASES GRAVITY
BRIN LONDO
HOMEWORLD:ZUUN
ENHANCED STRENGTH
AND REFLEXES
LIGHT LASS
HOMEWORLD: WINATH
DECREASES GRAVITY
TRIPLICATE GIRL
HOMEWORLD: CARGG
SPLITS INTO THREE
SHADOW LASS
HOMEWORLD: TALOK VIII
CREATES DARKNESS

DREAM GIRL
[DECEASED?]
HOMEWORLD: NALTOR
PRECOGNITIVE VISIONS

THEENA
HOMEWORLD: BOXTOR
HOST TO
SYMBIOTIC TRACKER

MON-EL
PHANTOM ZONE REFUGEE
SUPER-STRENGTH

SUN BOY
[RESIGNED]
HOMEWORLD: EARTH
HEAT GENERATION

P R E V I O U S L Y . . .

With no headquarters, equipment or money, the core members of the galaxy's greatest team of teen adventurers, the Legion of Super-Heroes, affiliated themselves with the intergalactic government United Planets, in an act of desperation to keep the team together. The formerly rebellious Legionnaires received full funding and pardons for past offenses, in exchange for supplying the UP with much needed help in policing the galaxy. However, to the thousands of Legion members across the galaxy, this was viewed as a betrayal.

At the same time, Braniac Five and a small group of Legionnaires covertly executed Brainy's plan to resurrect deceased member Dream Girl. The scenario ended with the disappearance of Dream Girl's body. The discouraged team headed back to Earth, unaware Brainy was keeping a secret… He is still in contact with Dream Girl… or, at least, he thinks he is.

Meanwhile, the Wanderers, a team of super-powered teens secretly working outside the law, discover a plot that threatens the universe. A race of "superior" beings known as the Dominators is planning to attack the UP. The Dominators attacked Earth a thousand years ago, and were defeated. They returned to their home planet where they have had a peaceful though non-communicative co-existence with the rest of the galaxy. Knowing the truth, the Wanderers have been transporting heroes, including Legionnaires, to join their side in the inevitable war.

The rest of the members of the Legion discovered and rescued a young man named Mon-El, who has been trapped in the limbo realm known as the Phantom Zone. As powerful as Supergirl, the youth was dying due to exposure to his one mortal weakness: lead. Braniac released him from the zone and cured his disease, but then the Wanderers suddenly kidnapped Mon-El.

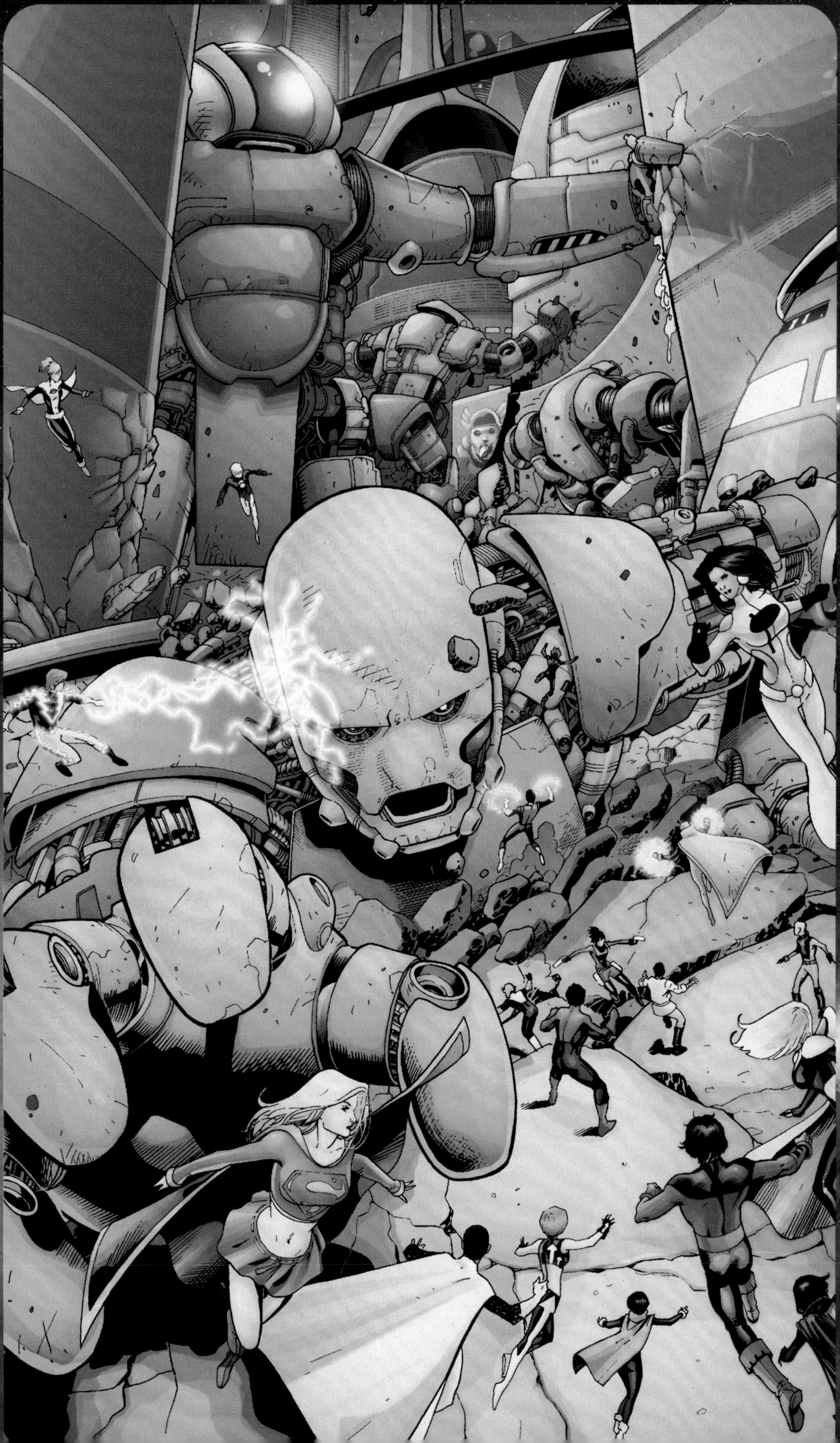

CHAPTER 1

Mark Waid Writer
Barry Kitson Penciller
Mick Gray Inker
Barry Kitson & **Nathan Eyring** Cover

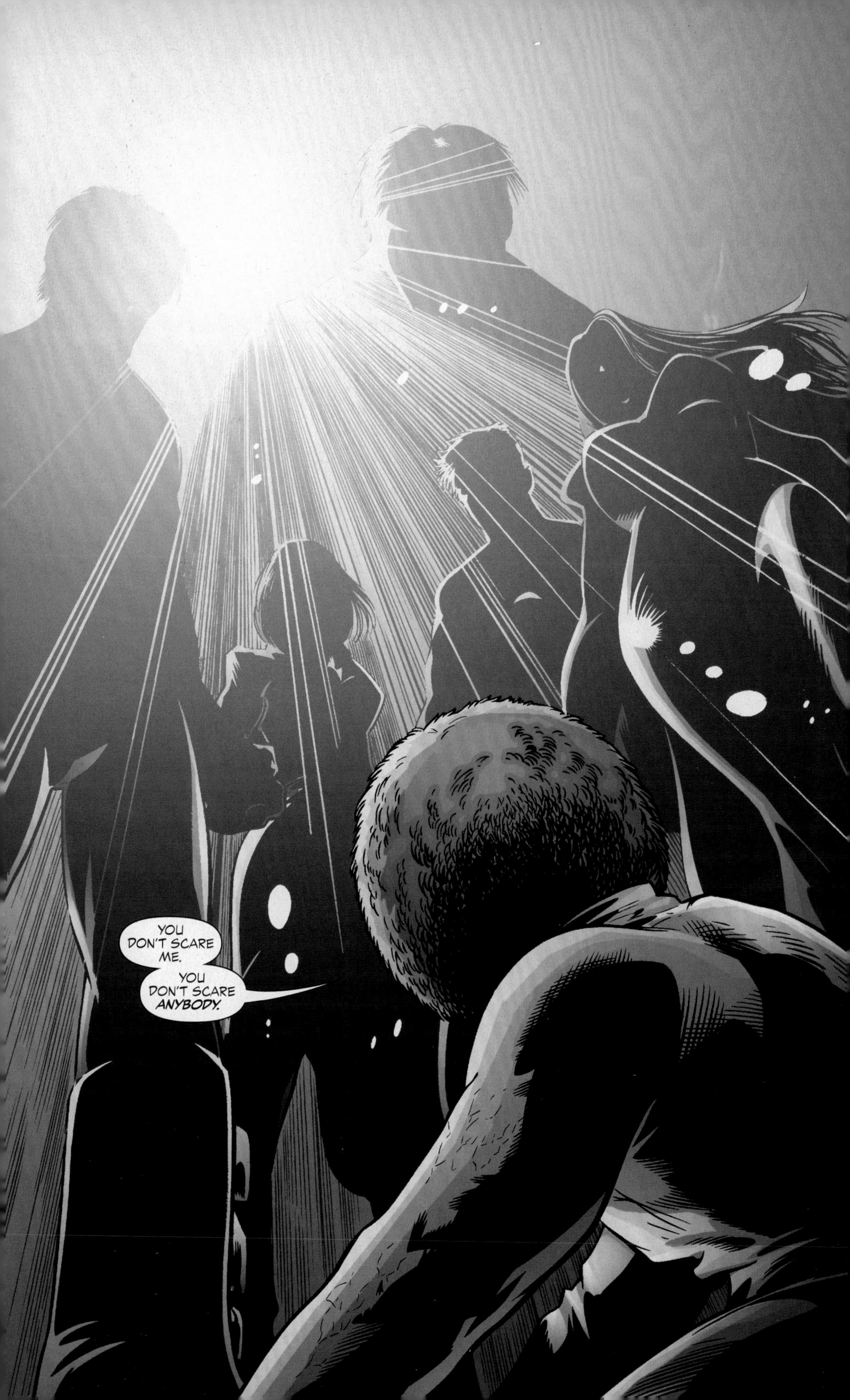
YOU DON'T SCARE ME.
YOU DON'T SCARE *ANYBODY.*

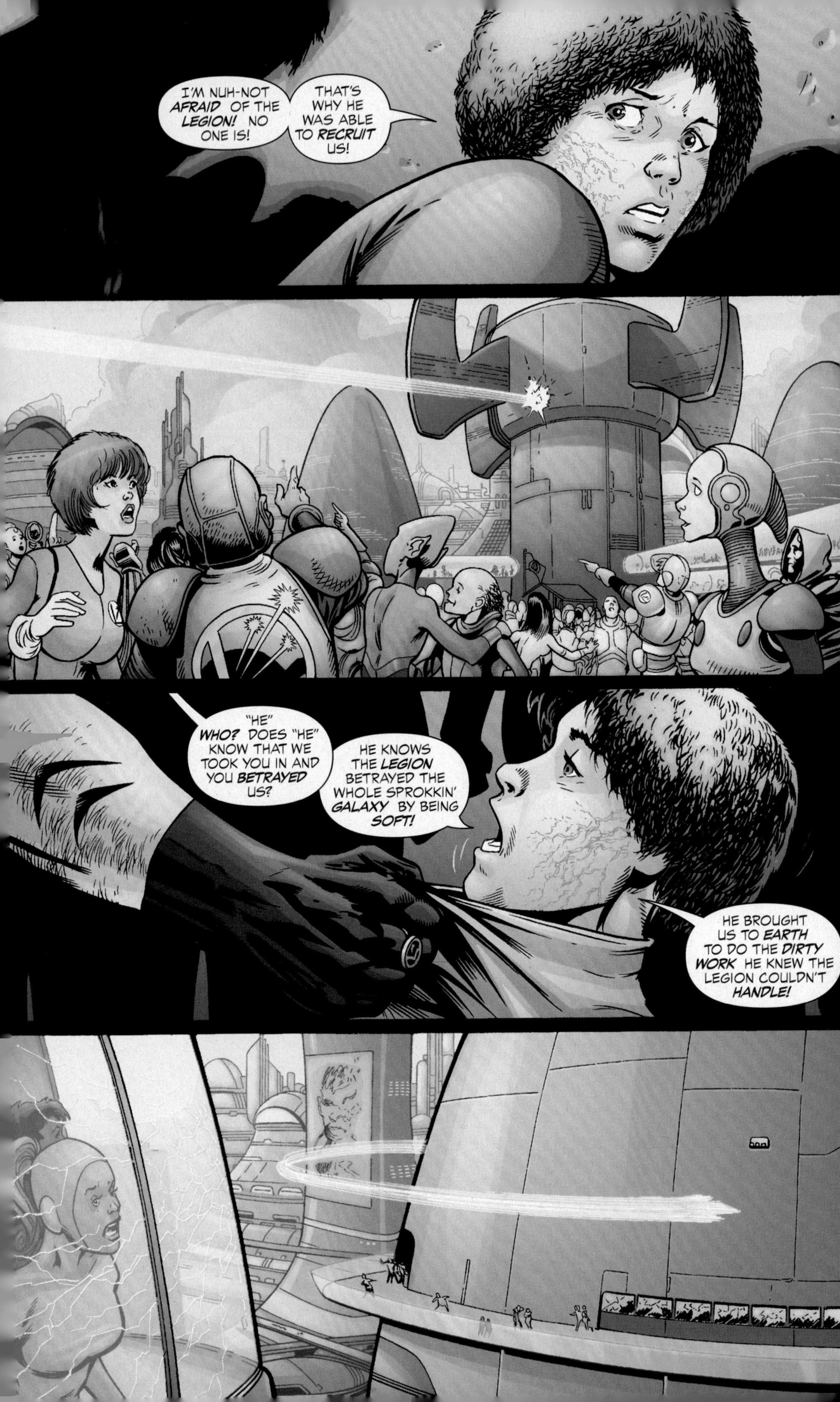
I'M NUH-NOT AFRAID OF THE LEGION! NO ONE IS!
THAT'S WHY HE WAS ABLE TO RECRUIT US!
"HE" WHO? DOES "HE" KNOW THAT WE TOOK YOU IN AND YOU BETRAYED US?
HE KNOWS THE LEGION BETRAYED THE WHOLE SPROKKIN' GALAXY BY BEING SOFT!
HE BROUGHT US TO EARTH TO DO THE DIRTY WORK HE KNEW THE LEGION COULDN'T HANDLE!

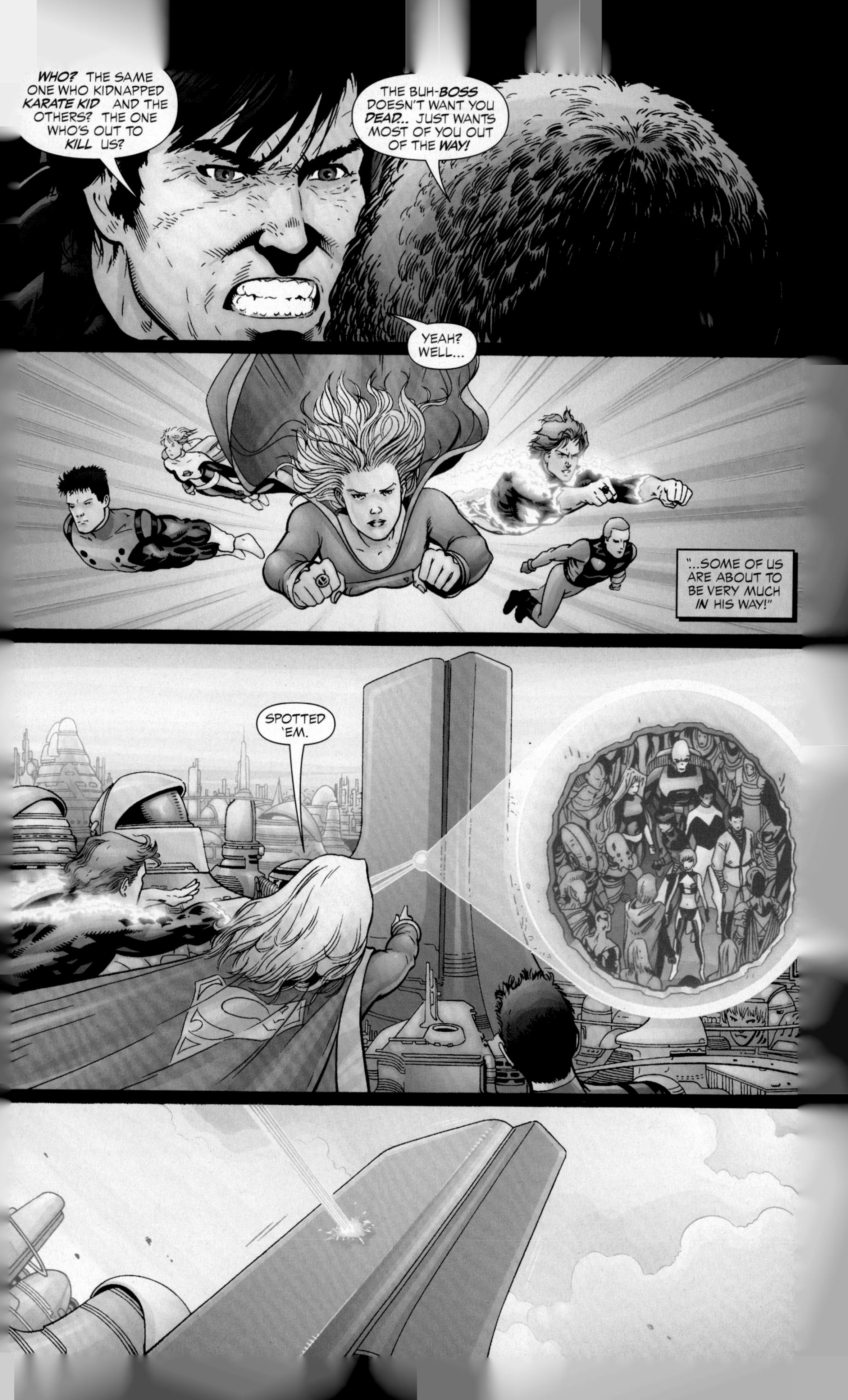
WHO? THE SAME ONE WHO KIDNAPPED KARATE KID AND THE OTHERS? THE ONE WHO'S OUT TO KILL US?
THE BUH-BOSS DOESN'T WANT YOU DEAD... JUST WANTS MOST OF YOU OUT OF THE WAY!
YEAH? WELL...
"...SOME OF US ARE ABOUT TO BE VERY MUCH IN HIS WAY!"
SPOTTED 'EM.

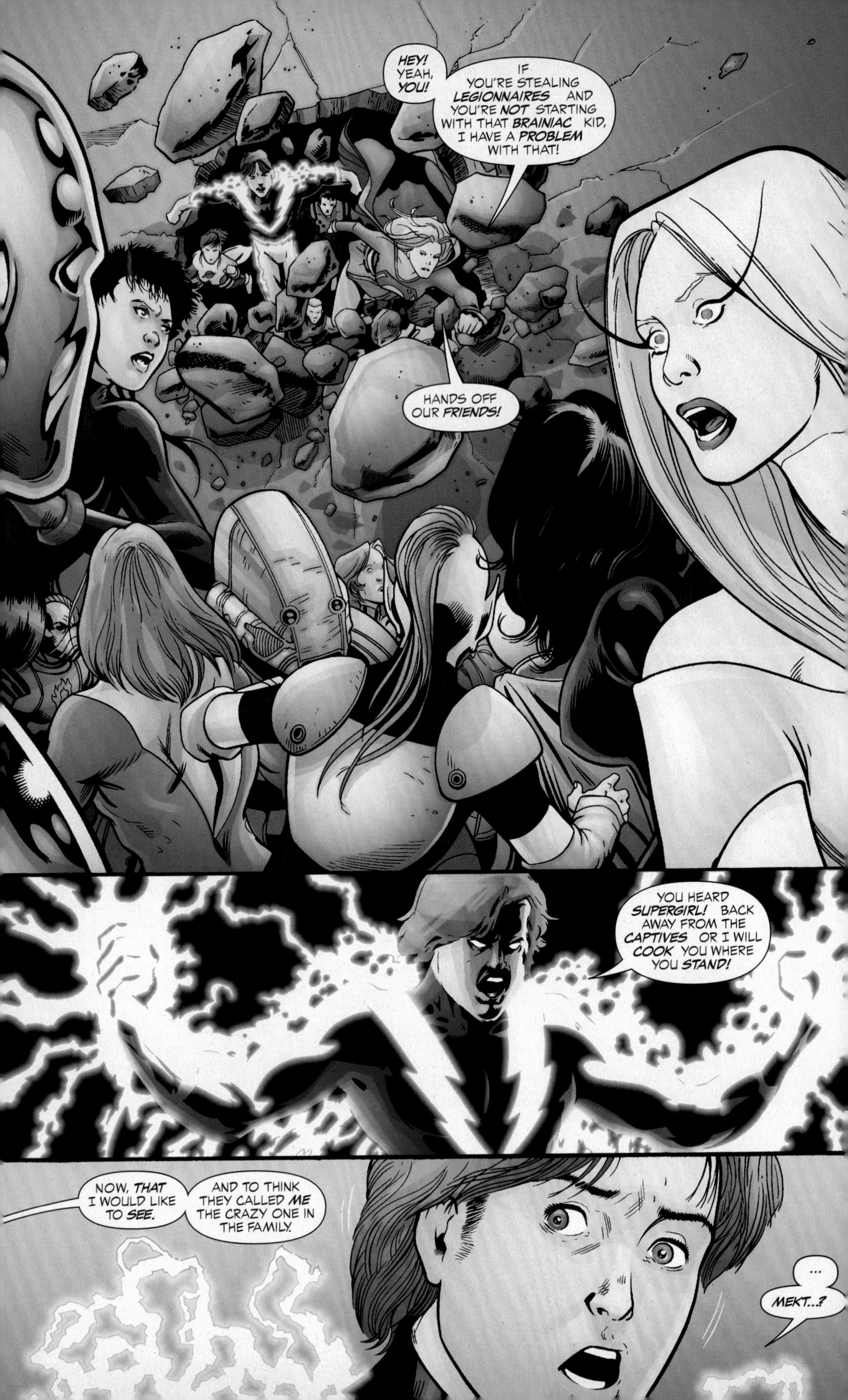
HEY! YEAH, YOU!
IF YOU'RE STEALING LEGIONNAIRES AND YOU'RE NOT STARTING WITH THAT BRAINIAC KID, I HAVE A PROBLEM WITH THAT!
HANDS OFF OUR FRIENDS!
YOU HEARD SUPERGIRL! BACK AWAY FROM THE CAPTIVES OR I WILL COOK YOU WHERE YOU STAND!
NOW, THAT I WOULD LIKE TO SEE.
AND TO THINK THEY CALLED ME THE CRAZY ONE IN THE FAMILY.
... MEKT...?

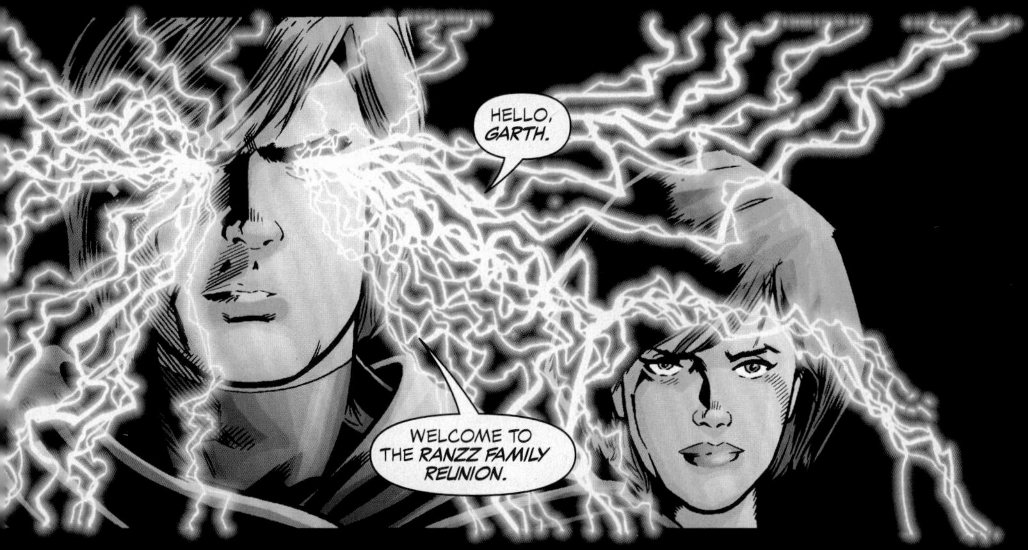
HELLO, GARTH.
WELCOME TO THE RANZZ FAMILY REUNION.

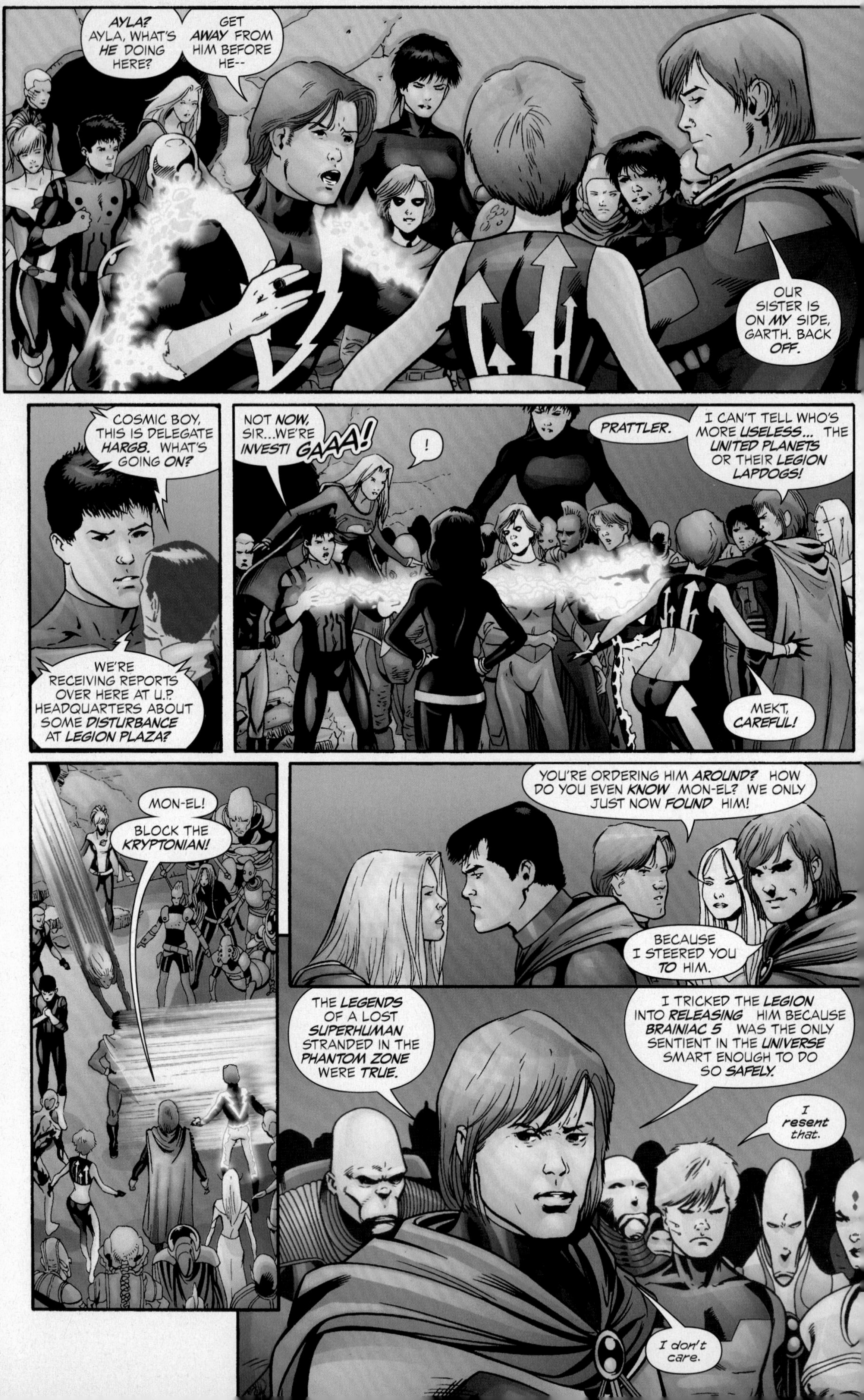
AYLA? AYLA, WHAT'S HE DOING HERE?
GET AWAY FROM HIM BEFORE HE--
OUR SISTER IS ON MY SIDE, GARTH. BACK OFF.
COSMIC BOY, THIS IS DELEGATE HARG8. WHAT'S GOING ON?
WE'RE RECEIVING REPORTS OVER HERE AT U.P. HEADQUARTERS ABOUT SOME DISTURBANCE AT LEGION PLAZA?
NOT NOW, SIR...WE'RE INVESTI GAAA!
!
PRATTLER.
I CAN'T TELL WHO'S MORE USELESS... THE UNITED PLANETS OR THEIR LEGION LAPDOGS!
MEKT, CAREFUL!
MON-EL!
BLOCK THE KRYPTONIAN!
YOU'RE ORDERING HIM AROUND? HOW DO YOU EVEN KNOW MON-EL? WE ONLY JUST NOW FOUND HIM!
BECAUSE I STEERED YOU TO HIM.
THE LEGENDS OF A LOST SUPERHUMAN STRANDED IN THE PHANTOM ZONE WERE TRUE.
I TRICKED THE LEGION INTO RELEASING HIM BECAUSE BRAINIAC 5 WAS THE ONLY SENTIENT IN THE UNIVERSE SMART ENOUGH TO DO SO SAFELY.
I resent that.
I don't care.

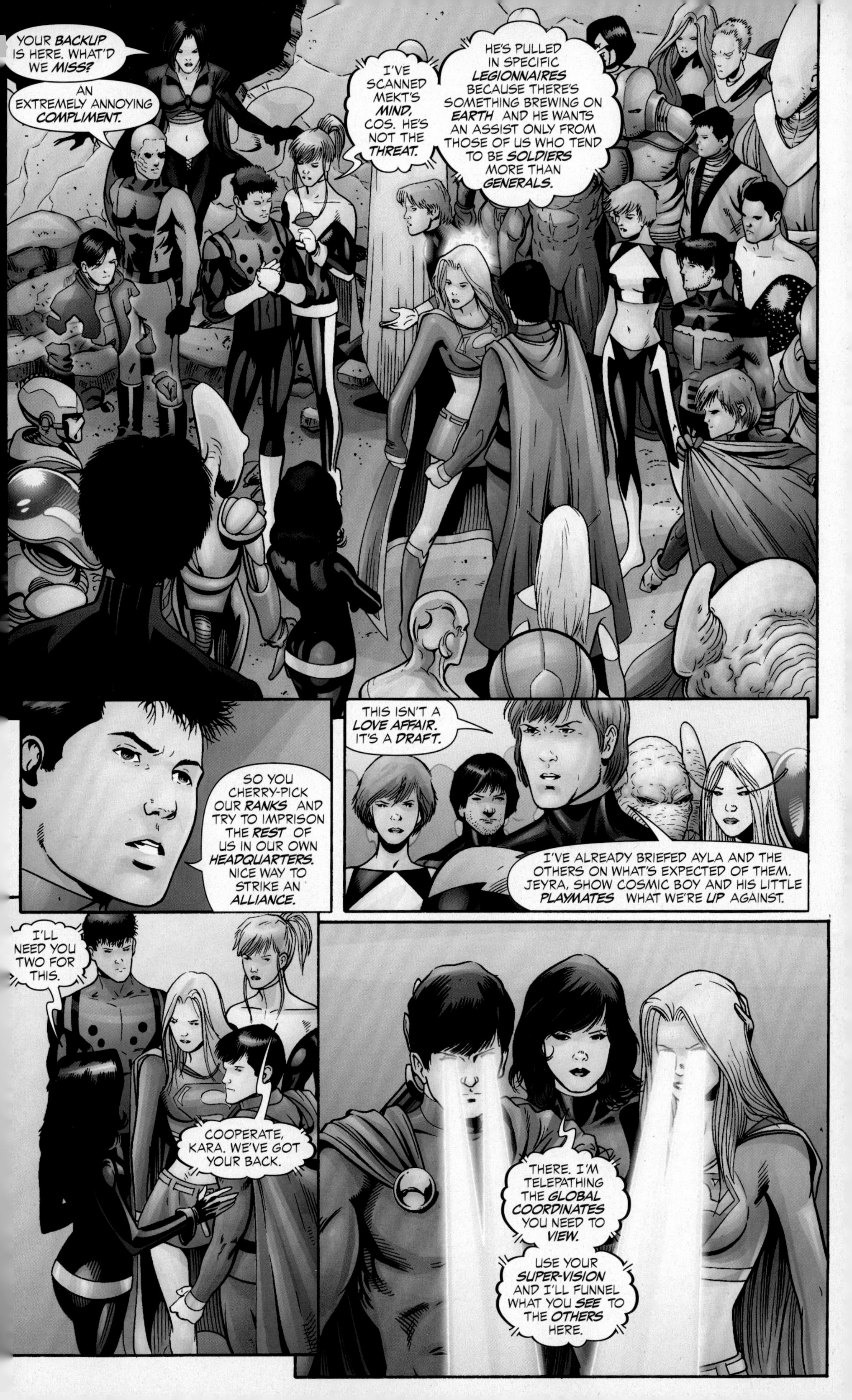
YOUR BACKUP IS HERE. WHAT'D WE MISS?
AN EXTREMELY ANNOYING COMPLIMENT.
I'VE SCANNED MEKT'S MIND, COS. HE'S NOT THE THREAT.
HE'S PULLED IN SPECIFIC LEGIONNAIRES BECAUSE THERE'S SOMETHING BREWING ON EARTH AND HE WANTS AN ASSIST ONLY FROM THOSE OF US WHO TEND TO BE SOLDIERS MORE THAN GENERALS.
SO YOU CHERRY-PICK OUR RANKS AND TRY TO IMPRISON THE REST OF US IN OUR OWN HEADQUARTERS. NICE WAY TO STRIKE AN ALLIANCE.
THIS ISN'T A LOVE AFFAIR. IT'S A DRAFT.
I'VE ALREADY BRIEFED AYLA AND THE OTHERS ON WHAT'S EXPECTED OF THEM. JEYRA, SHOW COSMIC BOY AND HIS LITTLE PLAYMATES WHAT WE'RE UP AGAINST.
I'LL NEED YOU TWO FOR THIS.
COOPERATE, KARA. WE'VE GOT YOUR BACK.
THERE. I'M TELEPATHING THE GLOBAL COORDINATES YOU NEED TO VIEW.
USE YOUR SUPER-VISION AND I'LL FUNNEL WHAT YOU SEE TO THE OTHERS HERE.

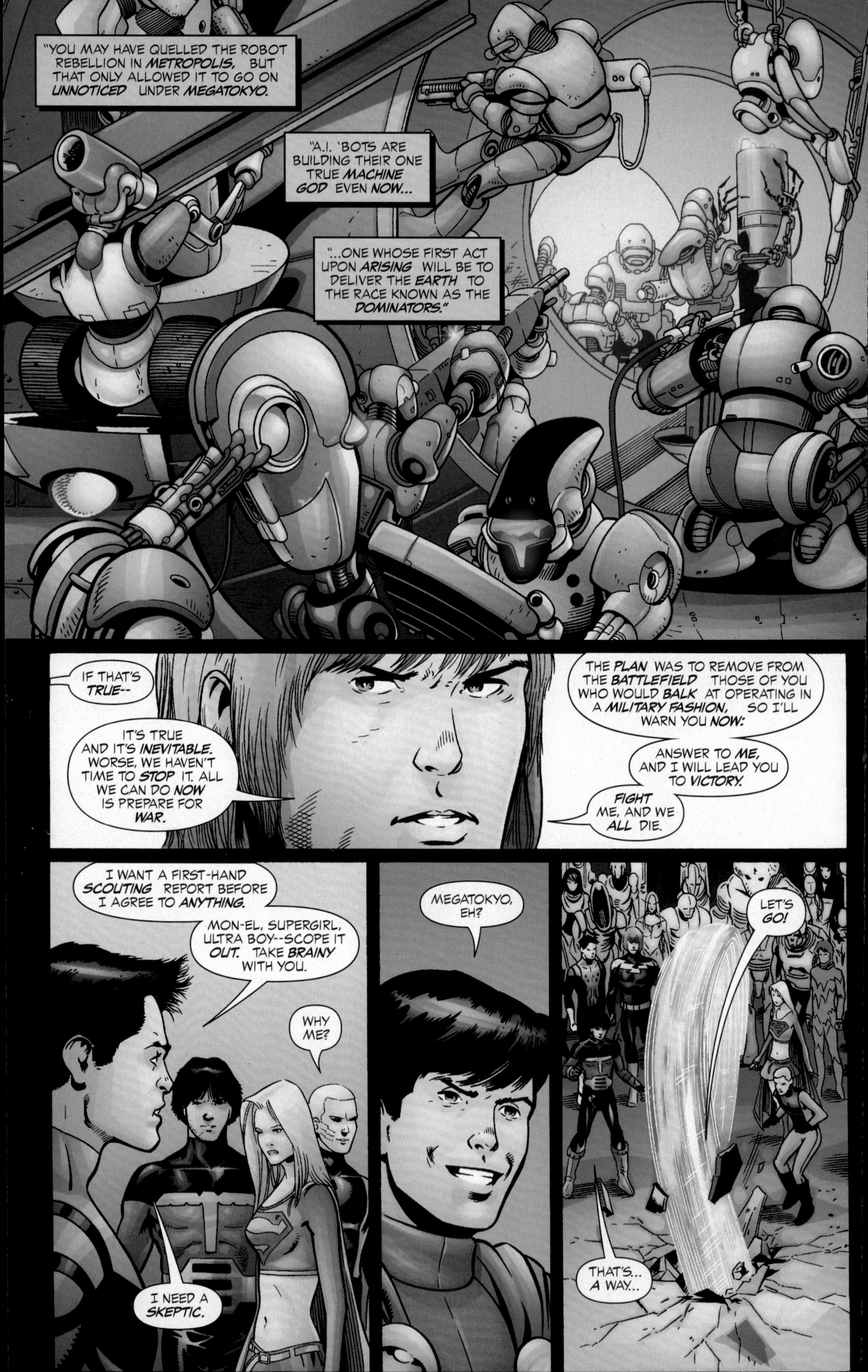
"YOU MAY HAVE QUELLED THE ROBOT REBELLION IN METROPOLIS, BUT THAT ONLY ALLOWED IT TO GO ON UNNOTICED UNDER MEGATOKYO.
"A.I. 'BOTS ARE BUILDING THEIR ONE TRUE MACHINE GOD EVEN NOW...
"...ONE WHOSE FIRST ACT UPON ARISING WILL BE TO DELIVER THE EARTH TO THE RACE KNOWN AS THE DOMINATORS."
IF THAT'S TRUE--
IT'S TRUE AND IT'S INEVITABLE. WORSE, WE HAVEN'T TIME TO STOP IT. ALL WE CAN DO NOW IS PREPARE FOR WAR.
THE PLAN WAS TO REMOVE FROM THE BATTLEFIELD THOSE OF YOU WHO WOULD BALK AT OPERATING IN A MILITARY FASHION, SO I'LL WARN YOU NOW:
ANSWER TO ME, AND I WILL LEAD YOU TO VICTORY.
FIGHT ME, AND WE ALL DIE.
I WANT A FIRST-HAND SCOUTING REPORT BEFORE I AGREE TO ANYTHING.
MON-EL, SUPERGIRL, ULTRA BOY--SCOPE IT OUT. TAKE BRAINY WITH YOU.
WHY ME?
I NEED A SKEPTIC.
MEGATOKYO, EH?
LET'S GO!
THAT'S... A WAY...

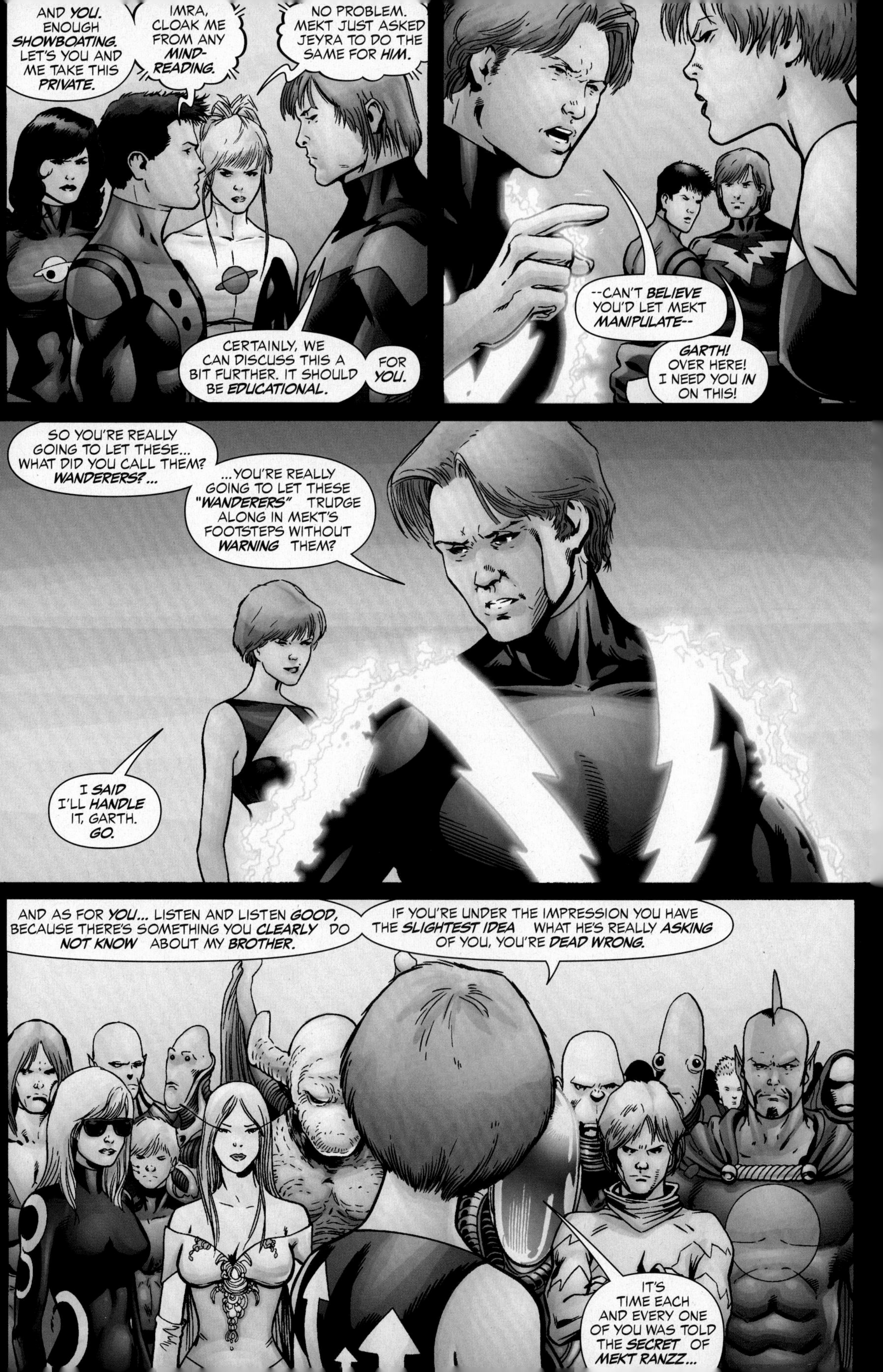
AND YOU. ENOUGH SHOWBOATING. LET'S YOU AND ME TAKE THIS PRIVATE.
IMRA, CLOAK ME FROM ANY MIND-READING.
NO PROBLEM. MEKT JUST ASKED JEYRA TO DO THE SAME FOR HIM.
CERTAINLY, WE CAN DISCUSS THIS A BIT FURTHER. IT SHOULD BE EDUCATIONAL.
FOR YOU.
--CAN'T BELIEVE YOU'D LET MEKT MANIPULATE--
GARTH! OVER HERE! I NEED YOU IN ON THIS!
SO YOU'RE REALLY GOING TO LET THESE... WHAT DID YOU CALL THEM? WANDERERS?...
...YOU'RE REALLY GOING TO LET THESE "WANDERERS" TRUDGE ALONG IN MEKT'S FOOTSTEPS WITHOUT WARNING THEM?
I SAID I'LL HANDLE IT, GARTH. GO.
AND AS FOR YOU... LISTEN AND LISTEN GOOD, BECAUSE THERE'S SOMETHING YOU CLEARLY DO NOT KNOW ABOUT MY BROTHER.
IF YOU'RE UNDER THE IMPRESSION YOU HAVE THE SLIGHTEST IDEA WHAT HE'S REALLY ASKING OF YOU, YOU'RE DEAD WRONG.
IT'S TIME EACH AND EVERY ONE OF YOU WAS TOLD THE SECRET OF MEKT RANZZ...

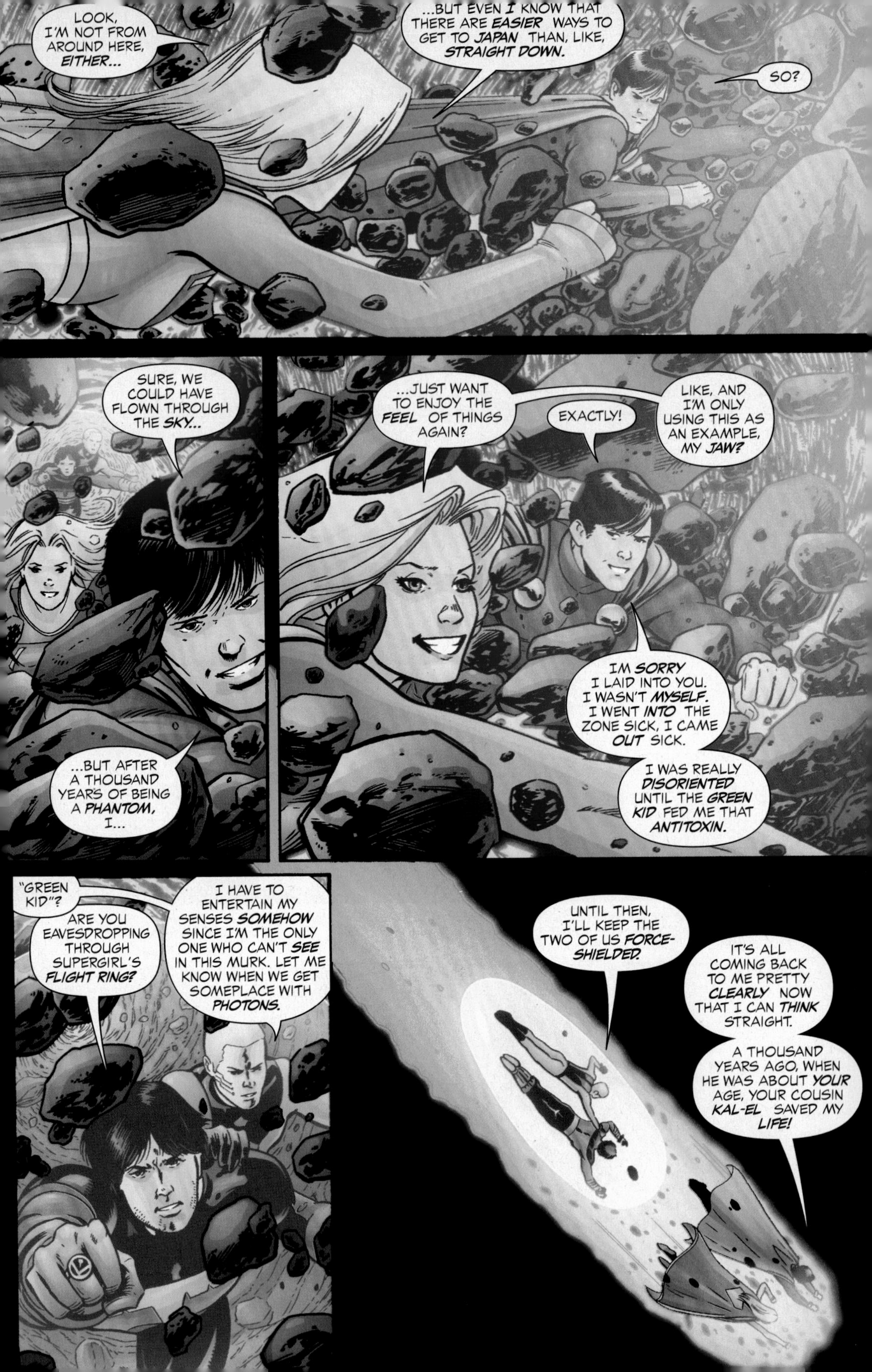
LOOK, I'M NOT FROM AROUND HERE, EITHER...
...BUT EVEN I KNOW THAT THERE ARE EASIER WAYS TO GET TO JAPAN THAN, LIKE, STRAIGHT DOWN.
SO?
SURE, WE COULD HAVE FLOWN THROUGH THE SKY...
...BUT AFTER A THOUSAND YEARS OF BEING A PHANTOM, I...
...JUST WANT TO ENJOY THE FEEL OF THINGS AGAIN?
EXACTLY!
LIKE, AND I'M ONLY USING THIS AS AN EXAMPLE, MY JAW?
IM SORRY I LAID INTO YOU. I WASN'T MYSELF. I WENT INTO THE ZONE SICK, I CAME OUT SICK.
I WAS REALLY DISORIENTED UNTIL THE GREEN KID FED ME THAT ANTITOXIN.
"GREEN KID"? ARE YOU EAVESDROPPING THROUGH SUPERGIRL'S FLIGHT RING?
I HAVE TO ENTERTAIN MY SENSES SOMEHOW SINCE I'M THE ONLY ONE WHO CAN'T SEE IN THIS MURK. LET ME KNOW WHEN WE GET SOMEPLACE WITH PHOTONS.
UNTIL THEN, I'LL KEEP THE TWO OF US FORCE-SHIELDED.
IT'S ALL COMING BACK TO ME PRETTY CLEARLY NOW THAT I CAN THINK STRAIGHT.
A THOUSAND YEARS AGO, WHEN HE WAS ABOUT YOUR AGE, YOUR COUSIN KAL-EL SAVED MY LIFE!

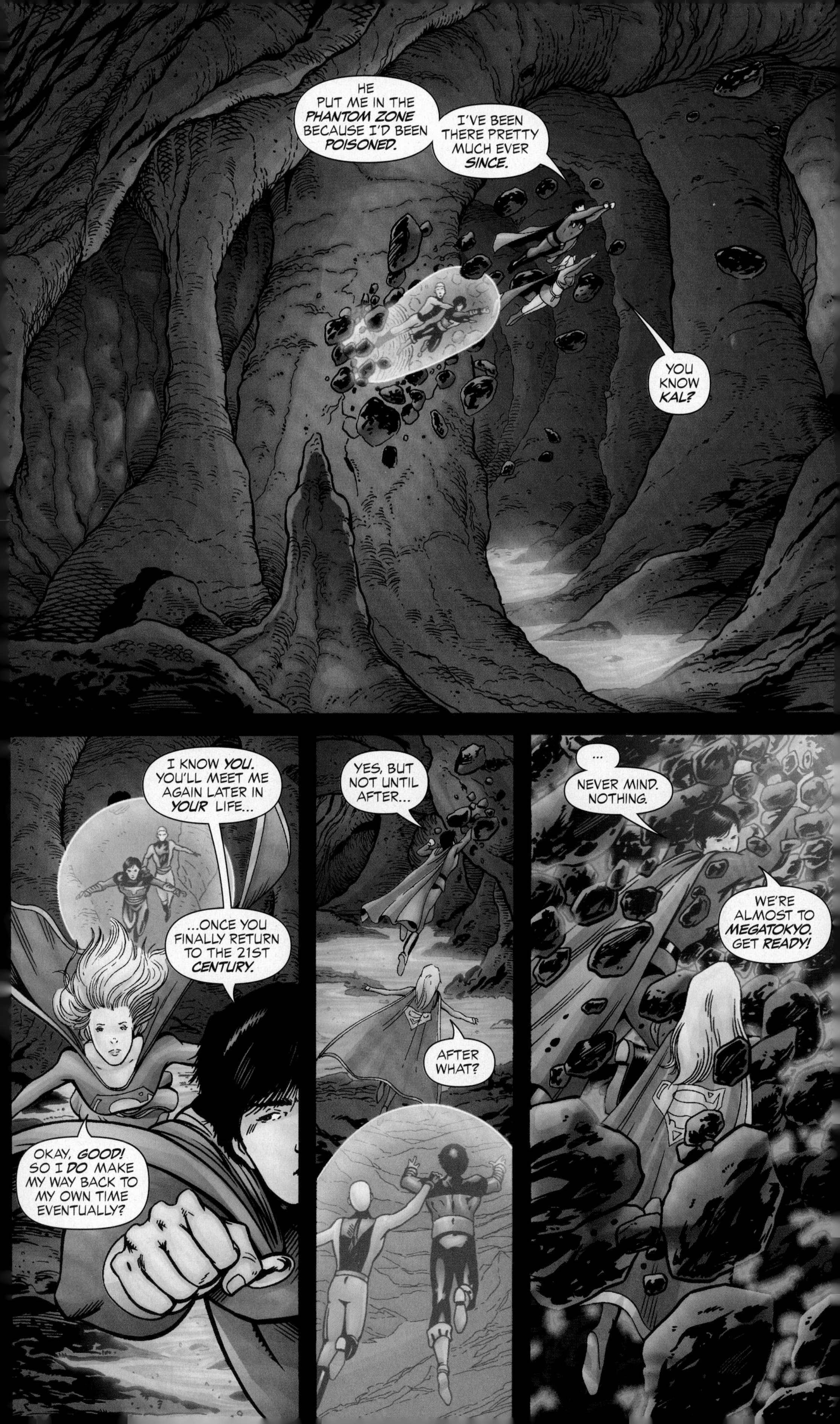
HE PUT ME IN THE PHANTOM ZONE BECAUSE I'D BEEN POISONED.
I'VE BEEN THERE PRETTY MUCH EVER SINCE.
YOU KNOW KAL?
I KNOW YOU. YOU'LL MEET ME AGAIN LATER IN YOUR LIFE...
...ONCE YOU FINALLY RETURN TO THE 21ST CENTURY.
OKAY, GOOD! SO I DO MAKE MY WAY BACK TO MY OWN TIME EVENTUALLY?
YES, BUT NOT UNTIL AFTER...
AFTER WHAT?
...
NEVER MIND. NOTHING.
WE'RE ALMOST TO MEGATOKYO. GET READY!

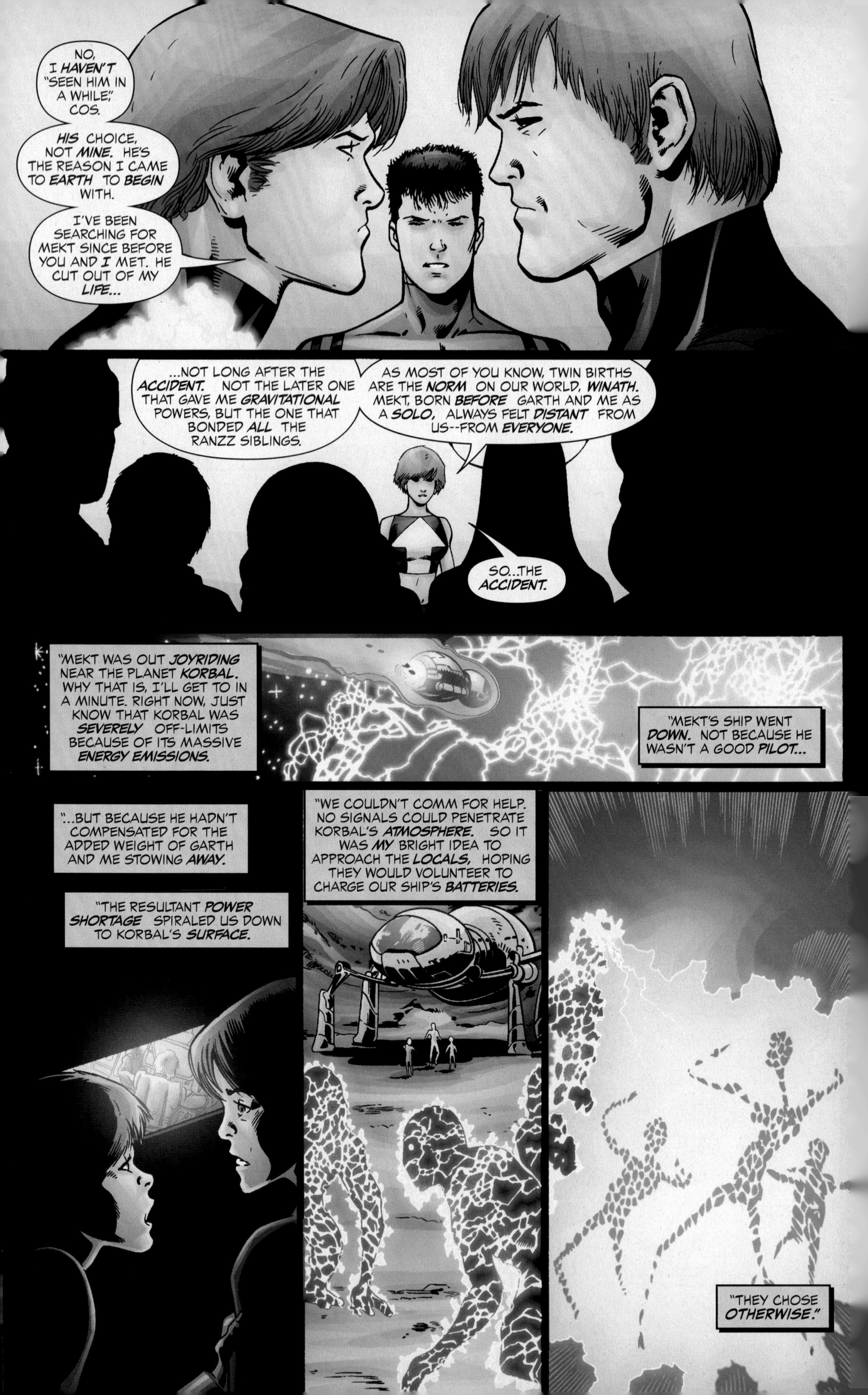

NO, I HAVEN'T "SEEN HIM IN A WHILE," COS.
HIS CHOICE, NOT MINE. HE'S THE REASON I CAME TO EARTH TO BEGIN WITH.
I'VE BEEN SEARCHING FOR MEKT SINCE BEFORE YOU AND I MET. HE CUT OUT OF MY LIFE...
...NOT LONG AFTER THE ACCIDENT. NOT THE LATER ONE THAT GAVE ME GRAVITATIONAL POWERS, BUT THE ONE THAT BONDED ALL THE RANZZ SIBLINGS.
AS MOST OF YOU KNOW, TWIN BIRTHS ARE THE NORM ON OUR WORLD, WINATH. MEKT, BORN BEFORE GARTH AND ME AS A SOLO, ALWAYS FELT DISTANT FROM US--FROM EVERYONE.
SO...THE ACCIDENT.
"MEKT WAS OUT JOYRIDING NEAR THE PLANET KORBAL. WHY THAT IS, I'LL GET TO IN A MINUTE. RIGHT NOW, JUST KNOW THAT KORBAL WAS SEVERELY OFF-LIMITS BECAUSE OF ITS MASSIVE ENERGY EMISSIONS.
"MEKT'S SHIP WENT DOWN. NOT BECAUSE HE WASN'T A GOOD PILOT...
"...BUT BECAUSE HE HADN'T COMPENSATED FOR THE ADDED WEIGHT OF GARTH AND ME STOWING AWAY.
"THE RESULTANT POWER SHORTAGE SPIRALED US DOWN TO KORBAL'S SURFACE.
"WE COULDN'T COMM FOR HELP. NO SIGNALS COULD PENETRATE KORBAL'S ATMOSPHERE. SO IT WAS MY BRIGHT IDEA TO APPROACH THE LOCALS, HOPING THEY WOULD VOLUNTEER TO CHARGE OUR SHIP'S BATTERIES.
"THEY CHOSE OTHERWISE."

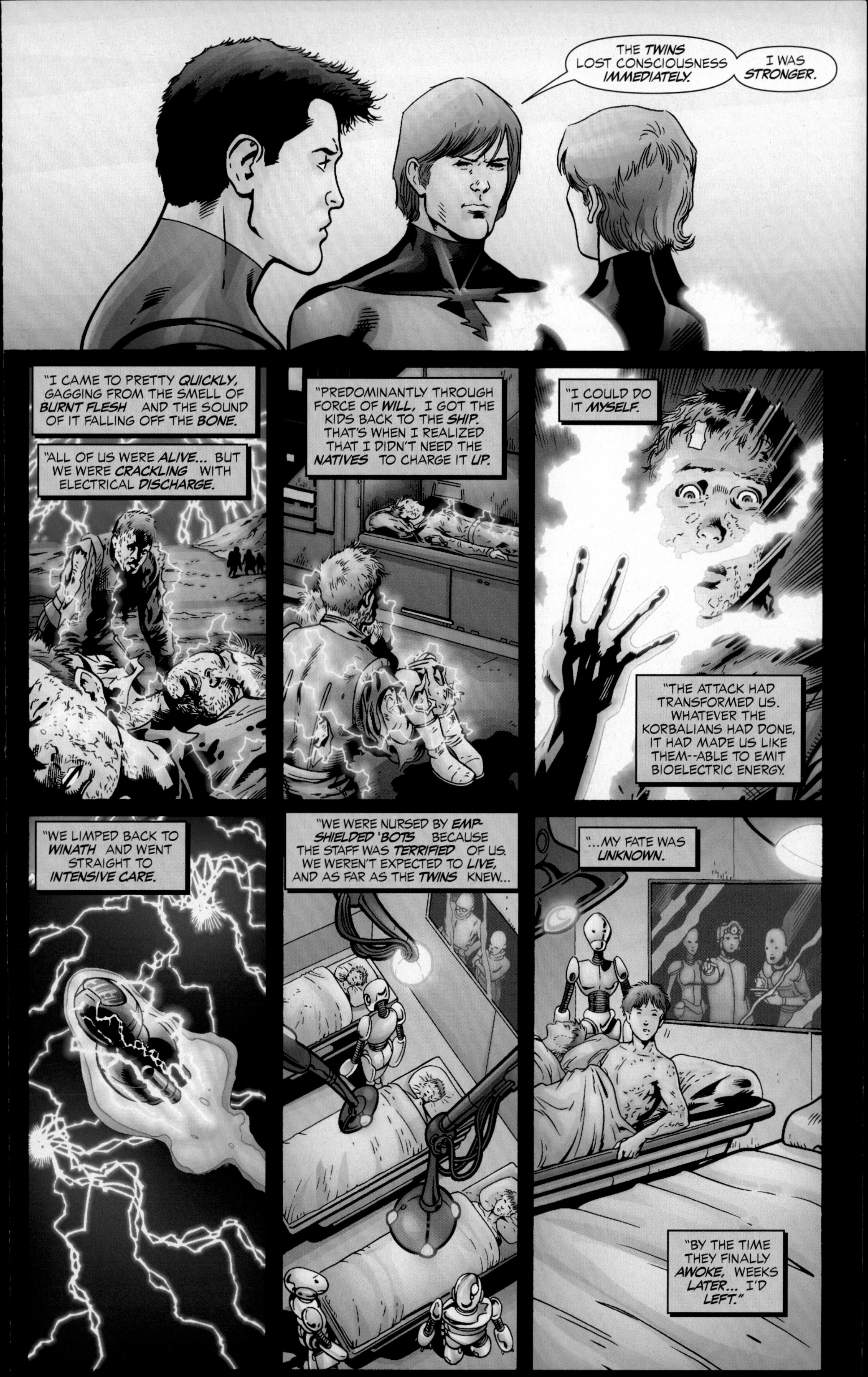
THE TWINS LOST CONSCIOUSNESS IMMEDIATELY.
I WAS STRONGER.
"I CAME TO PRETTY QUICKLY, GAGGING FROM THE SMELL OF BURNT FLESH AND THE SOUND OF IT FALLING OFF THE BONE.
"ALL OF US WERE ALIVE... BUT WE WERE CRACKLING WITH ELECTRICAL DISCHARGE.
"PREDOMINANTLY THROUGH FORCE OF WILL, I GOT THE KIDS BACK TO THE SHIP. THAT'S WHEN I REALIZED THAT I DIDN'T NEED THE NATIVES TO CHARGE IT UP.
"I COULD DO IT MYSELF.
"THE ATTACK HAD TRANSFORMED US. WHATEVER THE KORBALIANS HAD DONE, IT HAD MADE US LIKE THEM--ABLE TO EMIT BIOELECTRIC ENERGY.
"WE LIMPED BACK TO WINATH AND WENT STRAIGHT TO INTENSIVE CARE.
"WE WERE NURSED BY EMP-SHIELDED 'BOTS BECAUSE THE STAFF WAS TERRIFIED OF US. WE WEREN'T EXPECTED TO LIVE, AND AS FAR AS THE TWINS KNEW...
"...MY FATE WAS UNKNOWN.
"BY THE TIME THEY FINALLY AWOKE, WEEKS LATER... I'D LEFT."

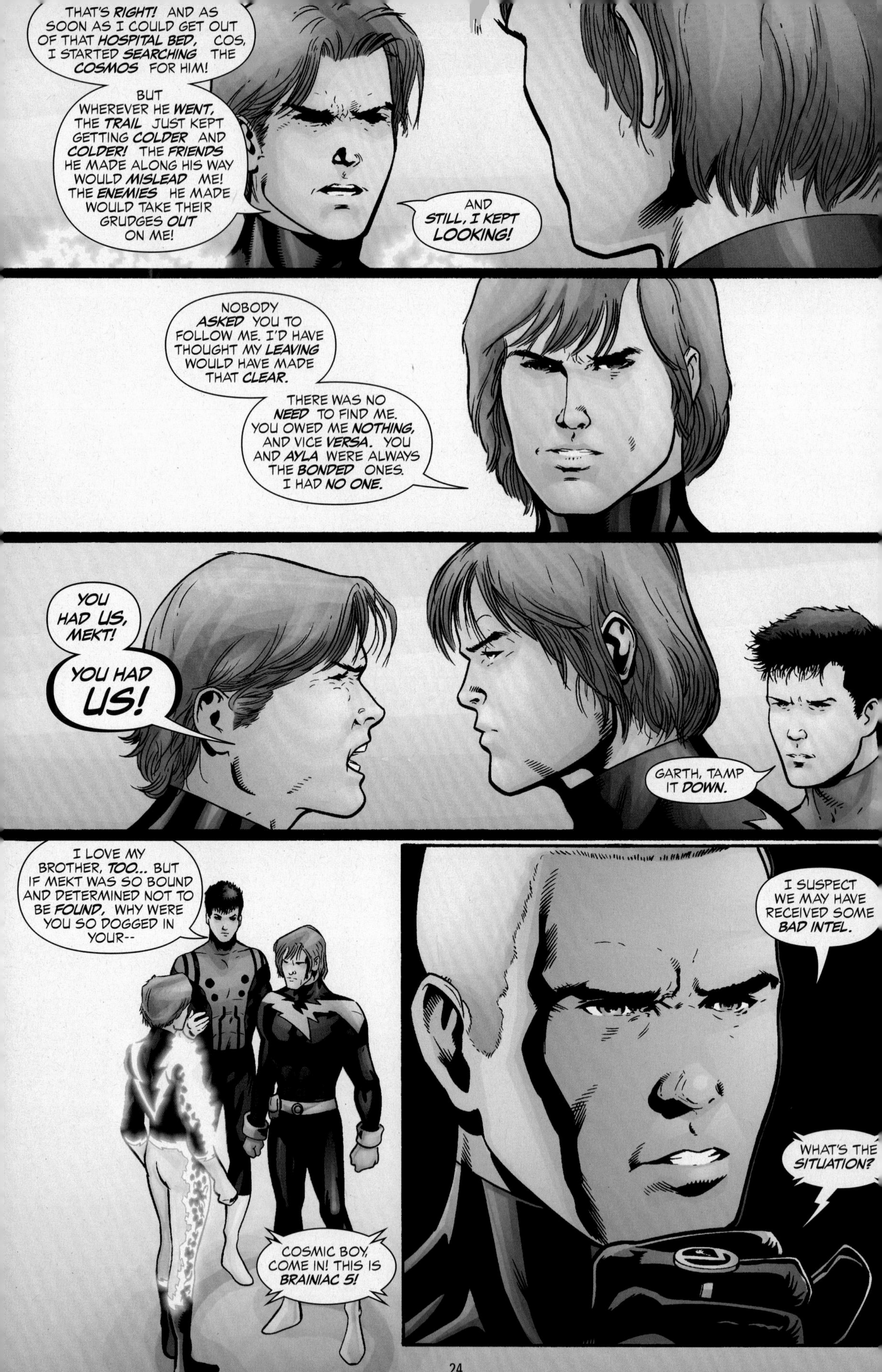
THAT'S RIGHT! AND AS SOON AS I COULD GET OUT OF THAT HOSPITAL BED, COS, I STARTED SEARCHING THE COSMOS FOR HIM!
BUT WHEREVER HE WENT, THE TRAIL JUST KEPT GETTING COLDER AND COLDER! THE FRIENDS HE MADE ALONG HIS WAY WOULD MISLEAD ME! THE ENEMIES HE MADE WOULD TAKE THEIR GRUDGES OUT ON ME!
AND STILL, I KEPT LOOKING!
NOBODY ASKED YOU TO FOLLOW ME. I'D HAVE THOUGHT MY LEAVING WOULD HAVE MADE THAT CLEAR.
THERE WAS NO NEED TO FIND ME. YOU OWED ME NOTHING, AND VICE VERSA. YOU AND AYLA WERE ALWAYS THE BONDED ONES. I HAD NO ONE.
YOU HAD US, MEKT!
YOU HAD US!
GARTH, TAMP IT DOWN.
I LOVE MY BROTHER, TOO... BUT IF MEKT WAS SO BOUND AND DETERMINED NOT TO BE FOUND, WHY WERE YOU SO DOGGED IN YOUR--
COSMIC BOY, COME IN! THIS IS BRAINIAC 5!
I SUSPECT WE MAY HAVE RECEIVED SOME BAD INTEL.
WHAT'S THE SITUATION?

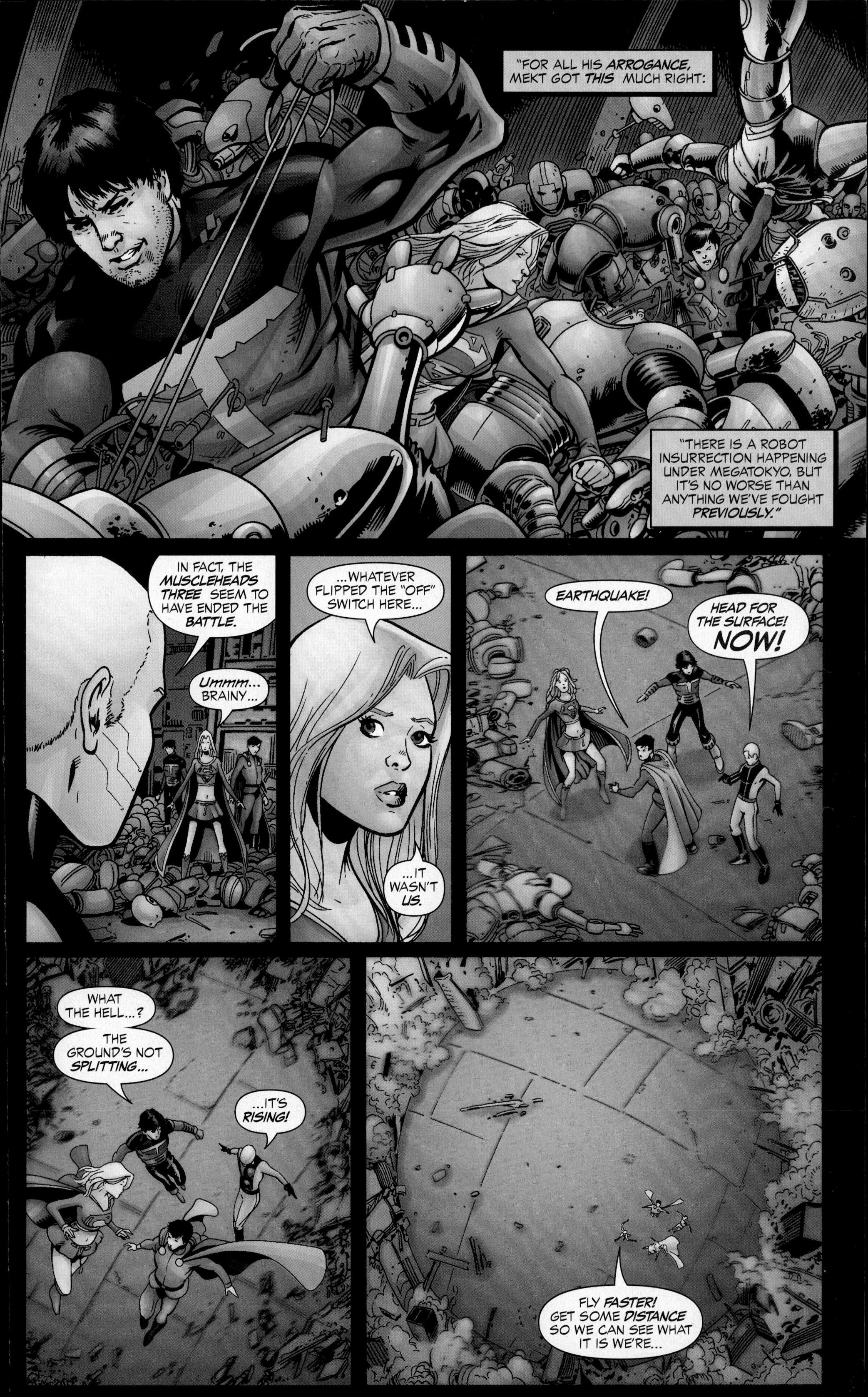
"FOR ALL HIS ARROGANCE, MEKT GOT THIS MUCH RIGHT:
"THERE IS A ROBOT INSURRECTION HAPPENING UNDER MEGATOKYO, BUT IT'S NO WORSE THAN ANYTHING WE'VE FOUGHT PREVIOUSLY."
IN FACT, THE MUSCLEHEADS THREE SEEM TO HAVE ENDED THE BATTLE.
Ummm... BRAINY...
...WHATEVER FLIPPED THE "OFF" SWITCH HERE...
...IT WASN'T US.
EARTHQUAKE!
HEAD FOR THE SURFACE! NOW!
WHAT THE HELL...?
THE GROUND'S NOT SPLITTING...
...IT'S RISING!
FLY FASTER! GET SOME DISTANCE SO WE CAN SEE WHAT IT IS WE'RE...

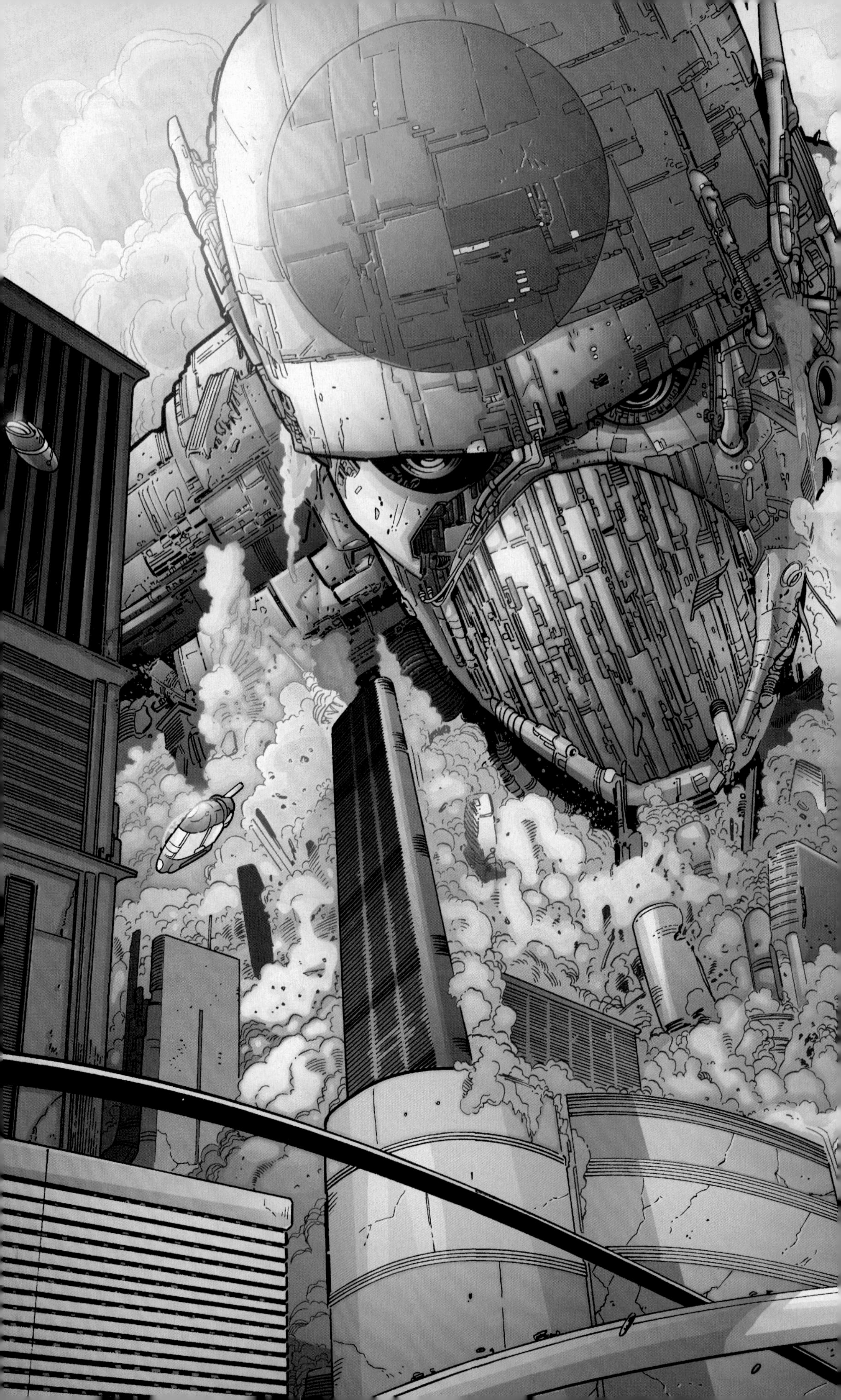

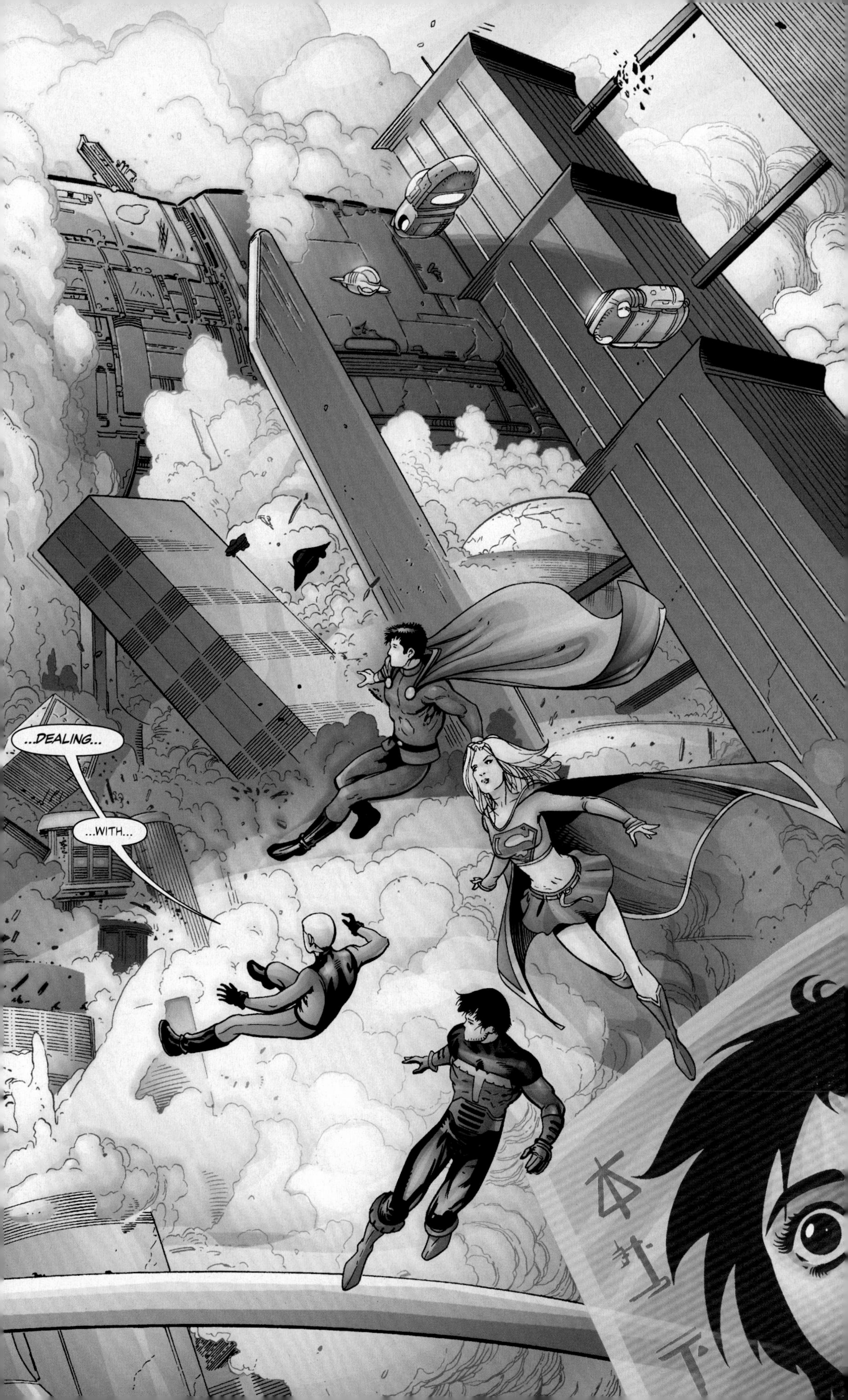
...DEALING...
...WITH...

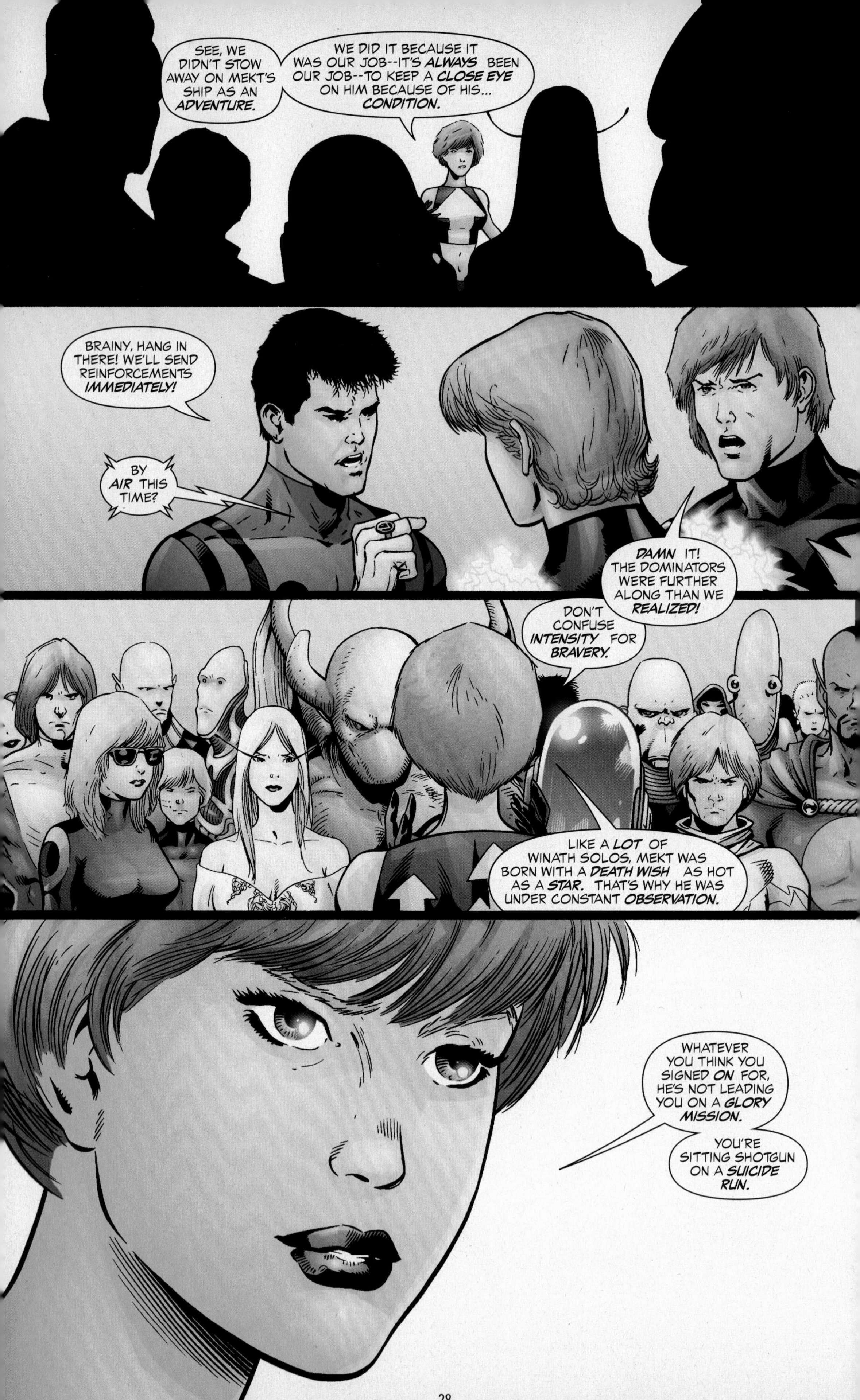
SEE, WE DIDN'T STOW AWAY ON MEKT'S SHIP AS AN *ADVENTURE*.
WE DID IT BECAUSE IT WAS OUR JOB--IT'S *ALWAYS* BEEN OUR JOB--TO KEEP A *CLOSE EYE* ON HIM BECAUSE OF HIS... *CONDITION*.
BRAINY, HANG IN THERE! WE'LL SEND REINFORCEMENTS *IMMEDIATELY!*
BY *AIR* THIS TIME?
DAMN IT! THE DOMINATORS WERE FURTHER ALONG THAN WE *REALIZED!*
DON'T CONFUSE *INTENSITY* FOR *BRAVERY*.
LIKE A *LOT* OF WINATH SOLOS, MEKT WAS BORN WITH A *DEATH WISH* AS HOT AS A *STAR*. THAT'S WHY HE WAS UNDER CONSTANT *OBSERVATION*.
WHATEVER YOU THINK YOU SIGNED *ON* FOR, HE'S NOT LEADING YOU ON A *GLORY MISSION*.
YOU'RE SITTING SHOTGUN ON A *SUICIDE RUN*.

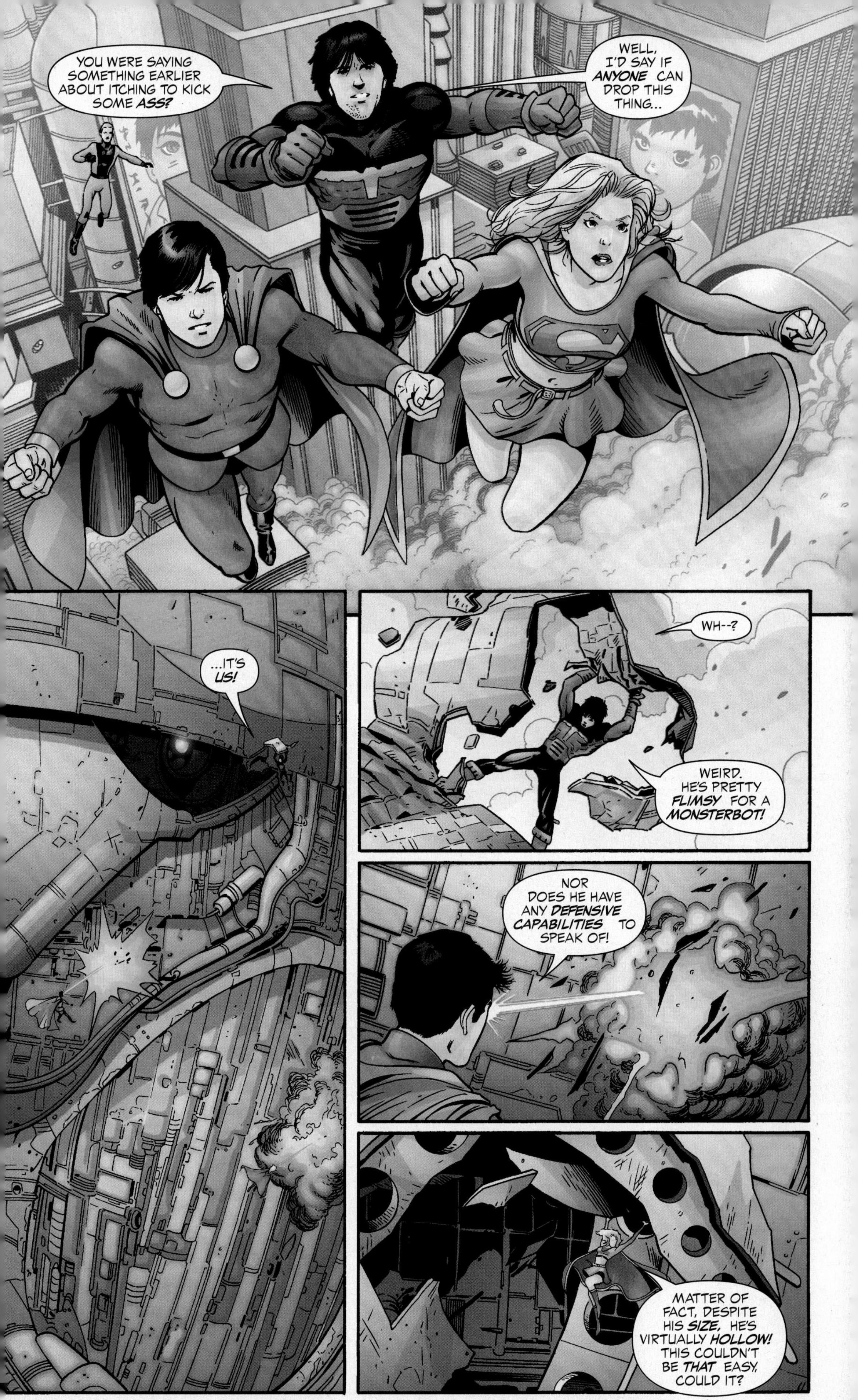

YOU WERE SAYING SOMETHING EARLIER ABOUT ITCHING TO KICK SOME ASS?
WELL, I'D SAY IF ANYONE CAN DROP THIS THING...
...IT'S US!
WH--?
WEIRD. HE'S PRETTY FLIMSY FOR A MONSTERBOT!
NOR DOES HE HAVE ANY DEFENSIVE CAPABILITIES TO SPEAK OF!
MATTER OF FACT, DESPITE HIS SIZE, HE'S VIRTUALLY HOLLOW! THIS COULDN'T BE THAT EASY, COULD IT?

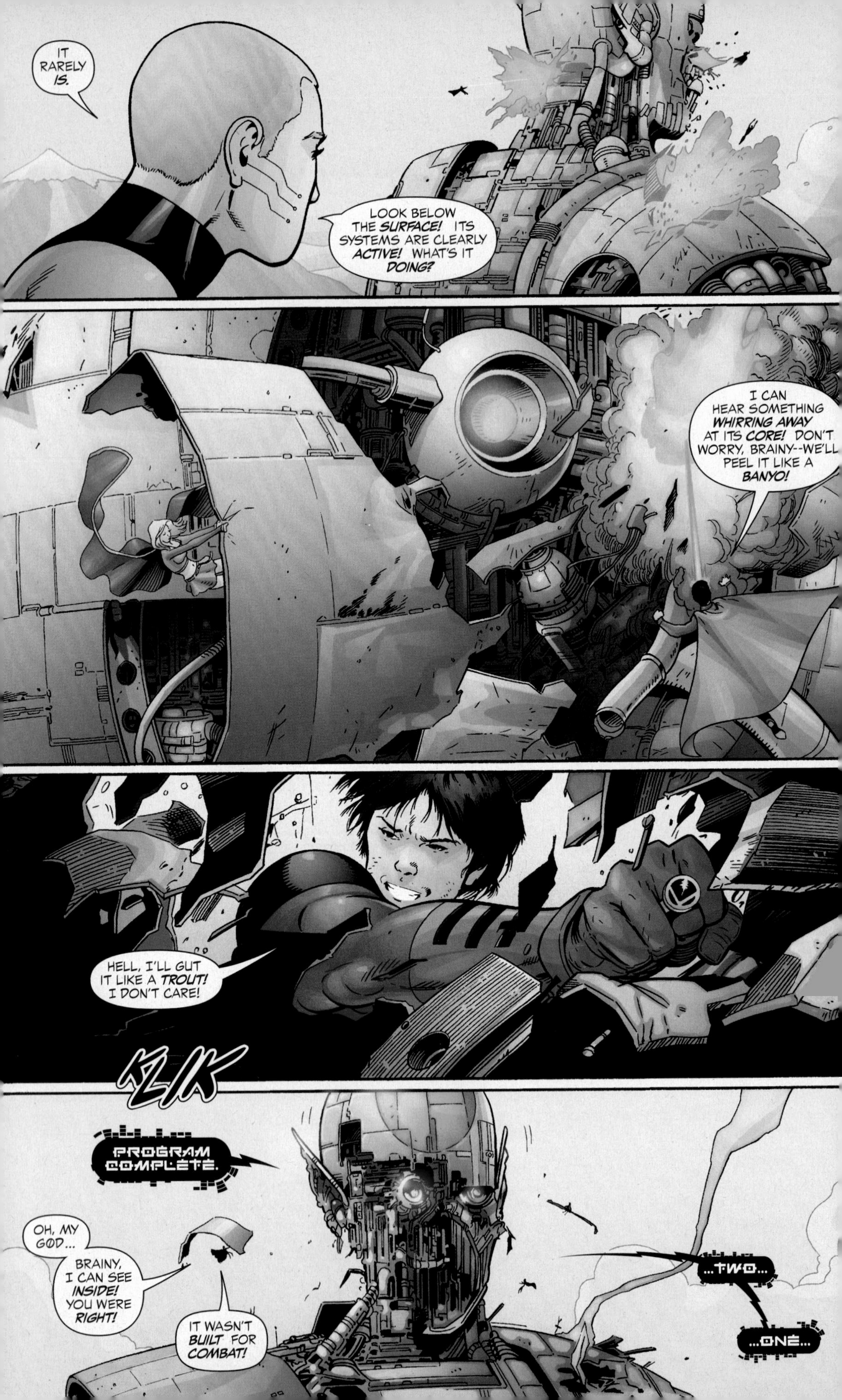
IT RARELY IS.
LOOK BELOW THE SURFACE! ITS SYSTEMS ARE CLEARLY ACTIVE! WHAT'S IT DOING?
I CAN HEAR SOMETHING WHIRRING AWAY AT ITS CORE! DON'T WORRY, BRAINY--WE'LL PEEL IT LIKE A BANYO!
HELL, I'LL GUT IT LIKE A TROUT! I DON'T CARE!
KLIK
PROGRAM COMPLETE.
OH, MY GOD...
BRAINY, I CAN SEE INSIDE! YOU WERE RIGHT!
IT WASN'T BUILT FOR COMBAT!
...TWO...
...ONE...

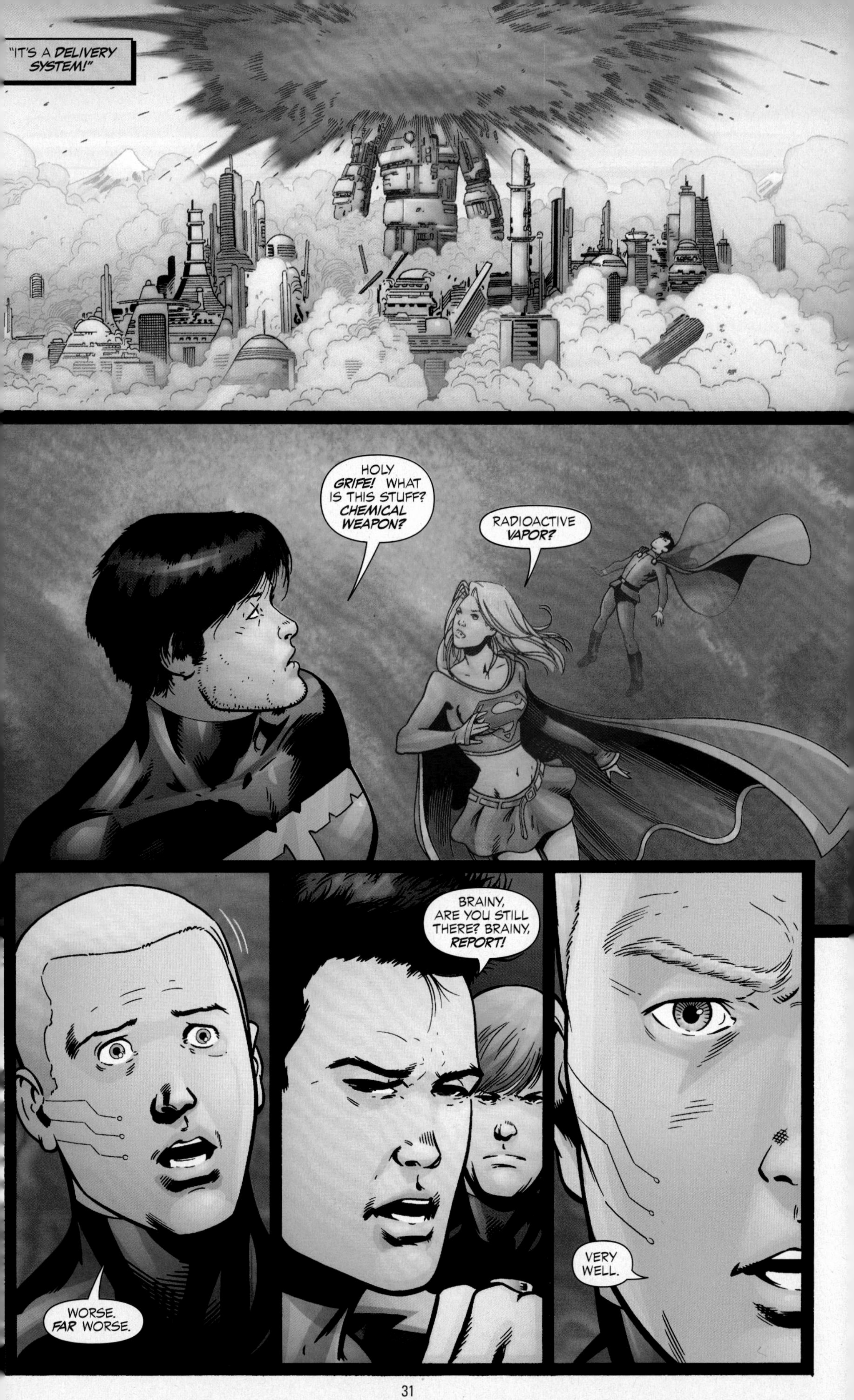
"IT'S A DELIVERY SYSTEM!"
HOLY GRIFE! WHAT IS THIS STUFF? CHEMICAL WEAPON?
RADIOACTIVE VAPOR?
WORSE. FAR WORSE.
BRAINY, ARE YOU STILL THERE? BRAINY, REPORT!
VERY WELL.

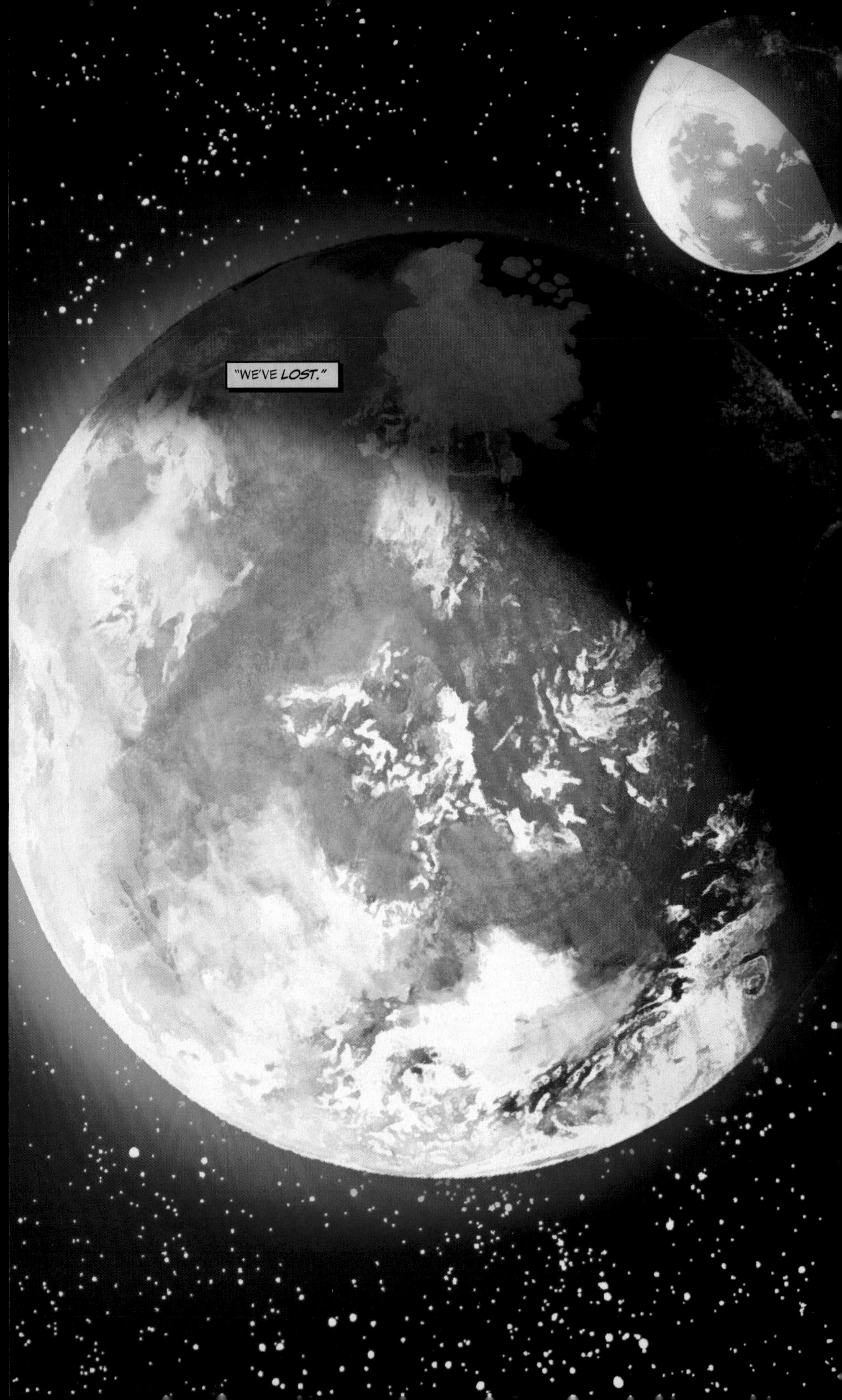
"WE'VE LOST."

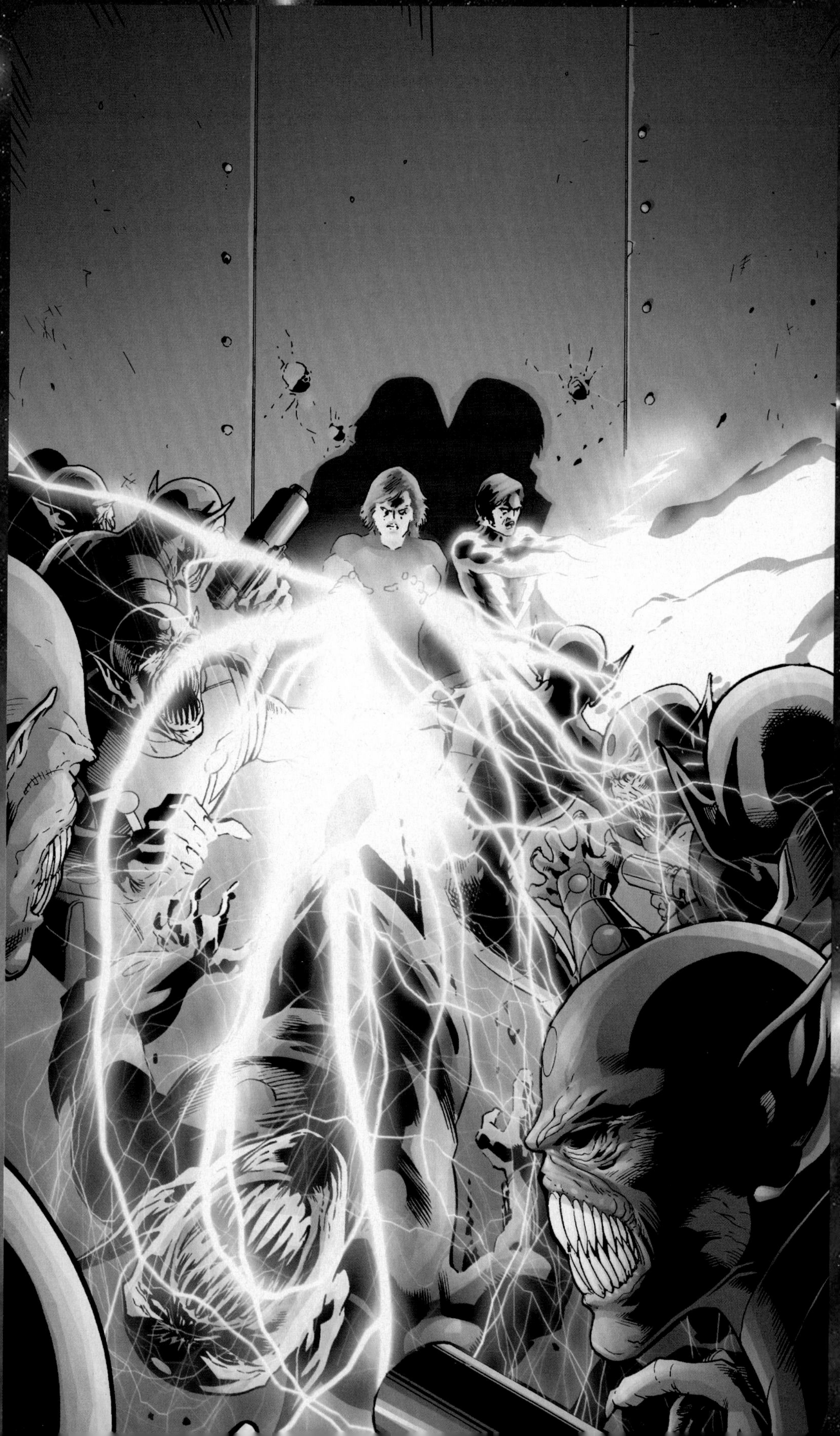

CHAPTER 2

Mark Waid Writer
Barry Kitson Penciller
Mick Gray Inker
Barry Kitson & **Nathan Eyring** Cover

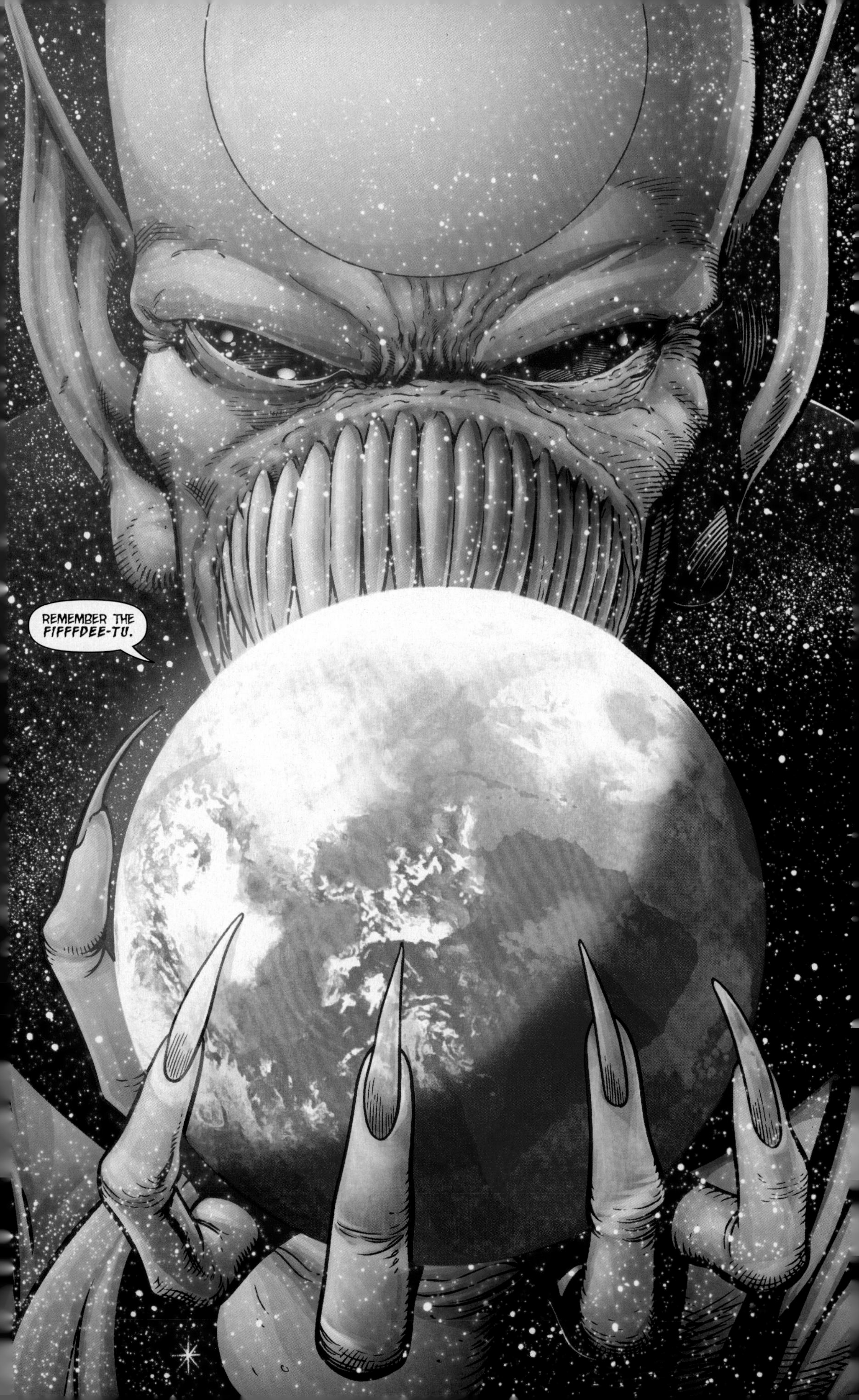
REMEMBER THE *FIFFFDEE-TU.*

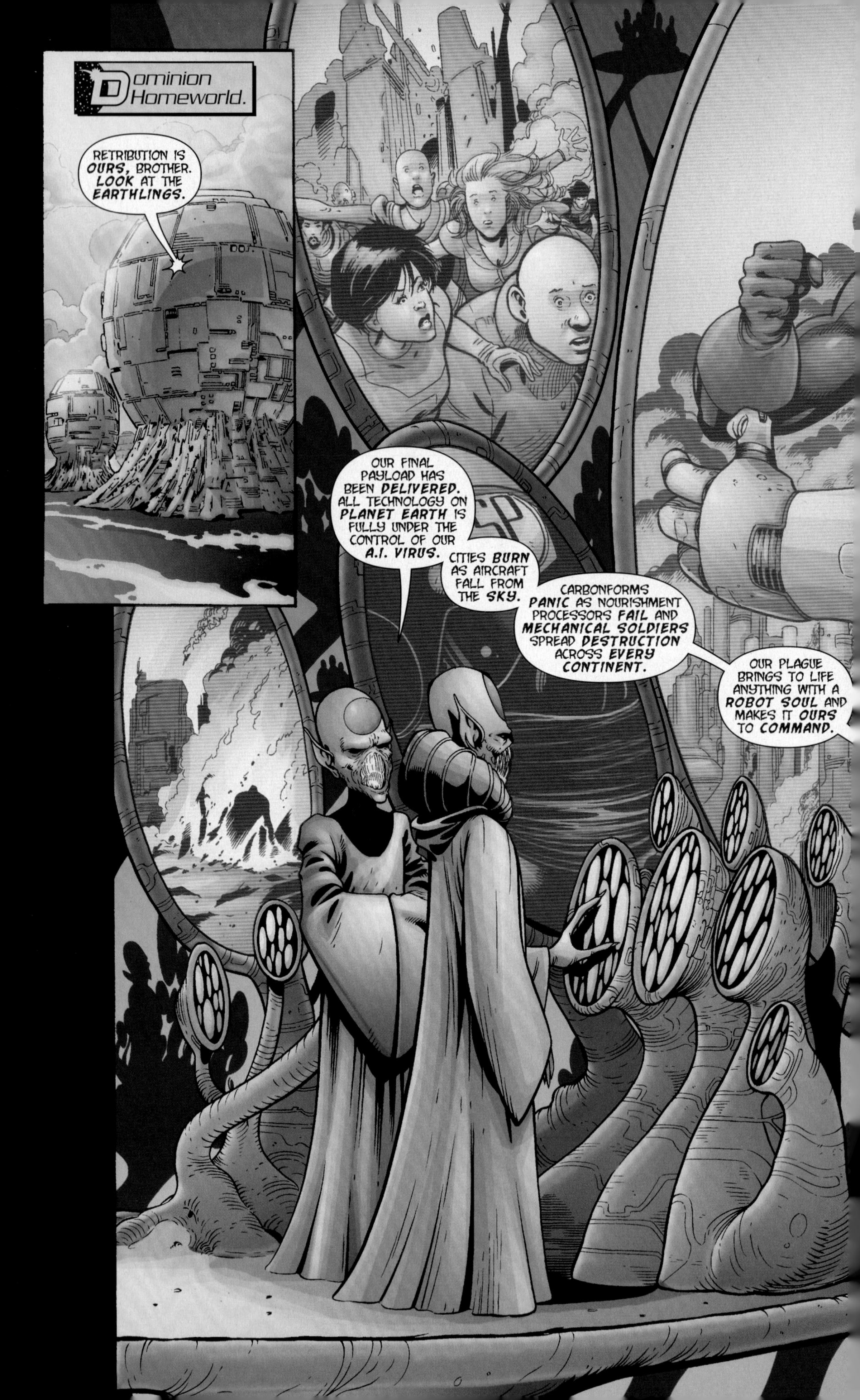
Dominion Homeworld.
RETRIBUTION IS OURS, BROTHER. LOOK AT THE EARTHLINGS.
OUR FINAL PAYLOAD HAS BEEN DELIVERED. ALL TECHNOLOGY ON PLANET EARTH IS FULLY UNDER THE CONTROL OF OUR A.I. VIRUS.
CITIES BURN AS AIRCRAFT FALL FROM THE SKY.
CARBONFORMS PANIC AS NOURISHMENT PROCESSORS FAIL AND MECHANICAL SOLDIERS SPREAD DESTRUCTION ACROSS EVERY CONTINENT.
OUR PLAGUE BRINGS TO LIFE ANYTHING WITH A ROBOT SOUL AND MAKES IT OURS TO COMMAND.

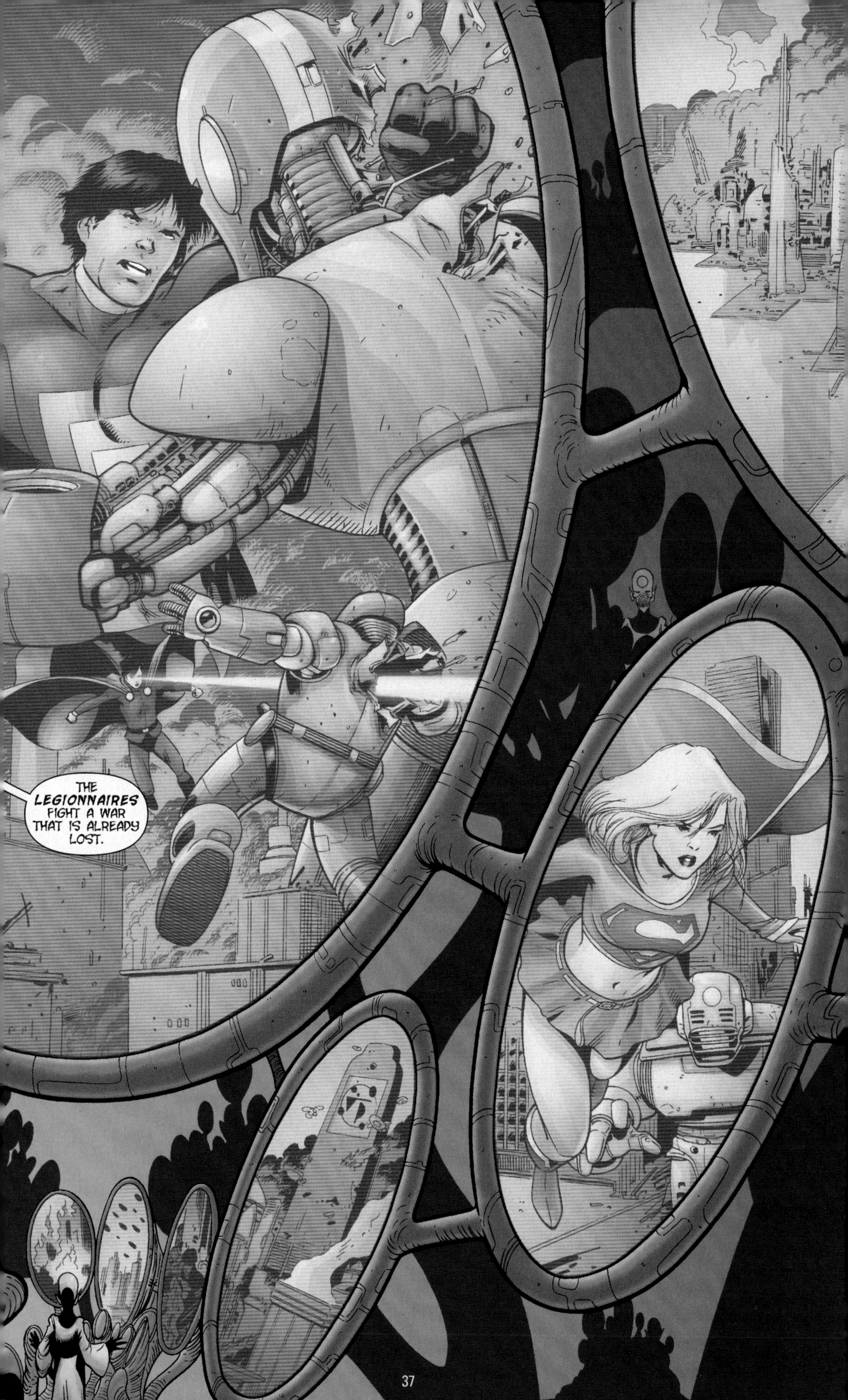
THE LEGIONNAIRES FIGHT A WAR THAT IS ALREADY LOST.

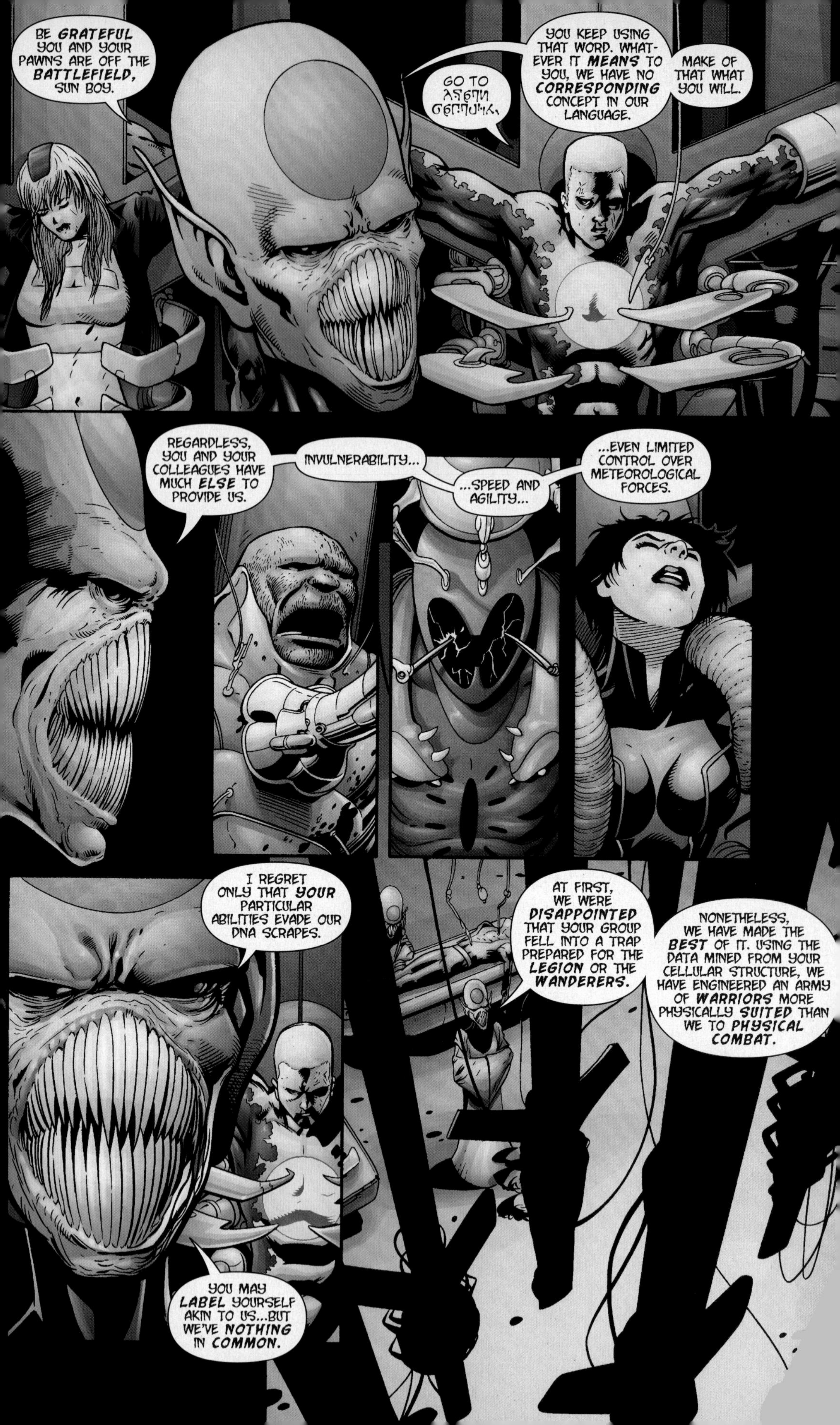

BE GRATEFUL YOU AND YOUR PAWNS ARE OFF THE BATTLEFIELD, SUN BOY.
GO TO
YOU KEEP USING THAT WORD. WHAT-EVER IT MEANS TO YOU, WE HAVE NO CORRESPONDING CONCEPT IN OUR LANGUAGE.
MAKE OF THAT WHAT YOU WILL.
REGARDLESS, YOU AND YOUR COLLEAGUES HAVE MUCH ELSE TO PROVIDE US.
INVULNERABILITY...
...SPEED AND AGILITY...
...EVEN LIMITED CONTROL OVER METEOROLOGICAL FORCES.
I REGRET ONLY THAT YOUR PARTICULAR ABILITIES EVADE OUR DNA SCRAPES.
YOU MAY LABEL YOURSELF AKIN TO US...BUT WE'VE NOTHING IN COMMON.
AT FIRST, WE WERE DISAPPOINTED THAT YOUR GROUP FELL INTO A TRAP PREPARED FOR THE LEGION OR THE WANDERERS.
NONETHELESS, WE HAVE MADE THE BEST OF IT. USING THE DATA MINED FROM YOUR CELLULAR STRUCTURE, WE HAVE ENGINEERED AN ARMY OF WARRIORS MORE PHYSICALLY SUITED THAN WE TO PHYSICAL COMBAT.

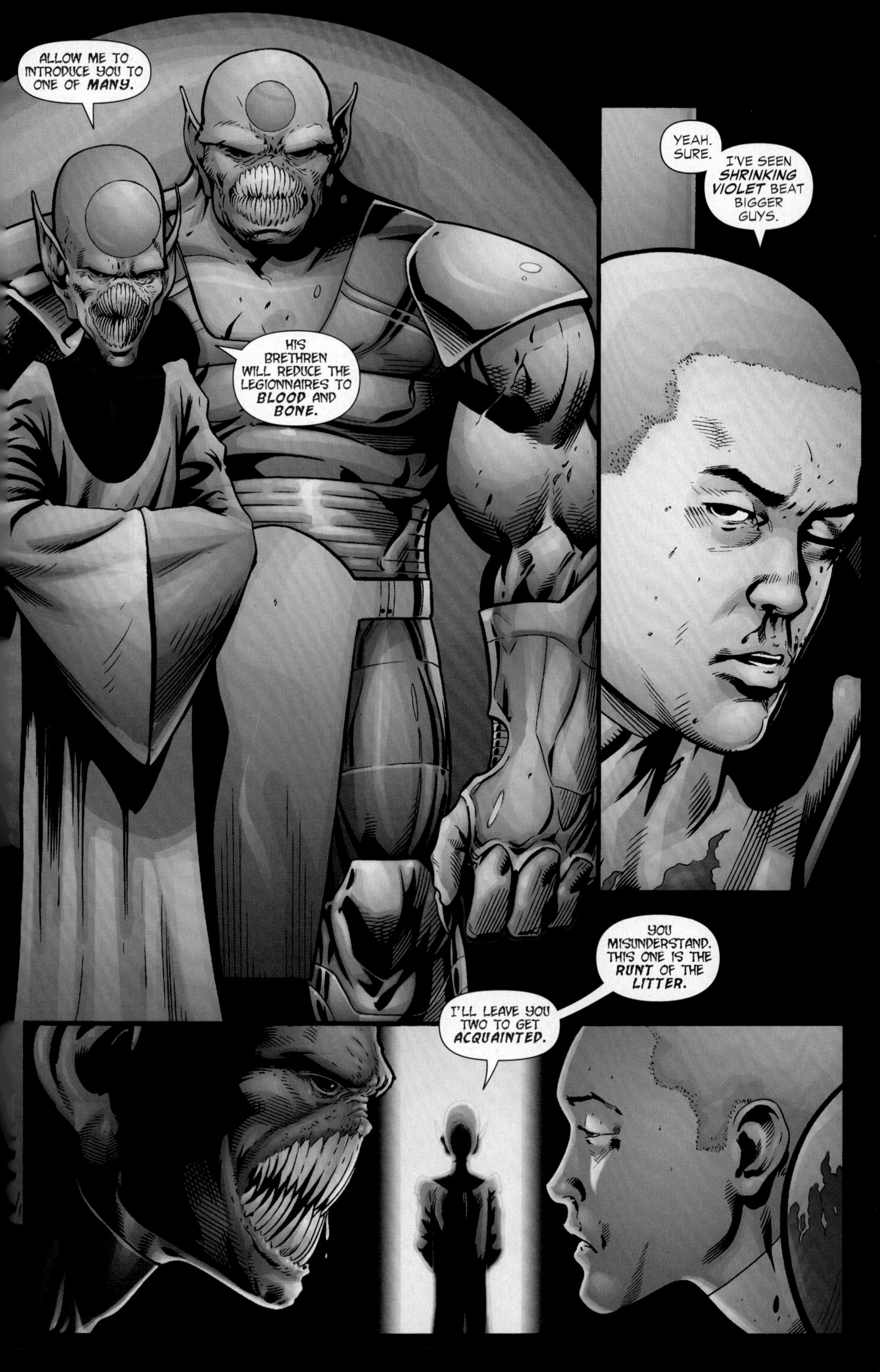
ALLOW ME TO INTRODUCE YOU TO ONE OF MANY.
HIS BRETHREN WILL REDUCE THE LEGIONNAIRES TO BLOOD AND BONE.
YEAH. SURE.
I'VE SEEN SHRINKING VIOLET BEAT BIGGER GUYS.
YOU MISUNDERSTAND. THIS ONE IS THE RUNT OF THE LITTER.
I'LL LEAVE YOU TWO TO GET ACQUAINTED.

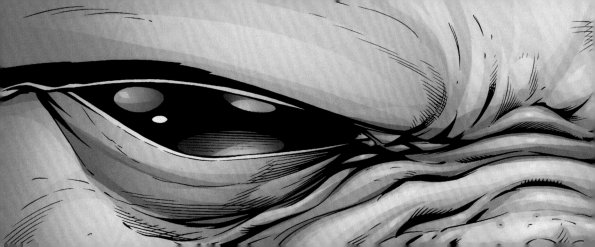

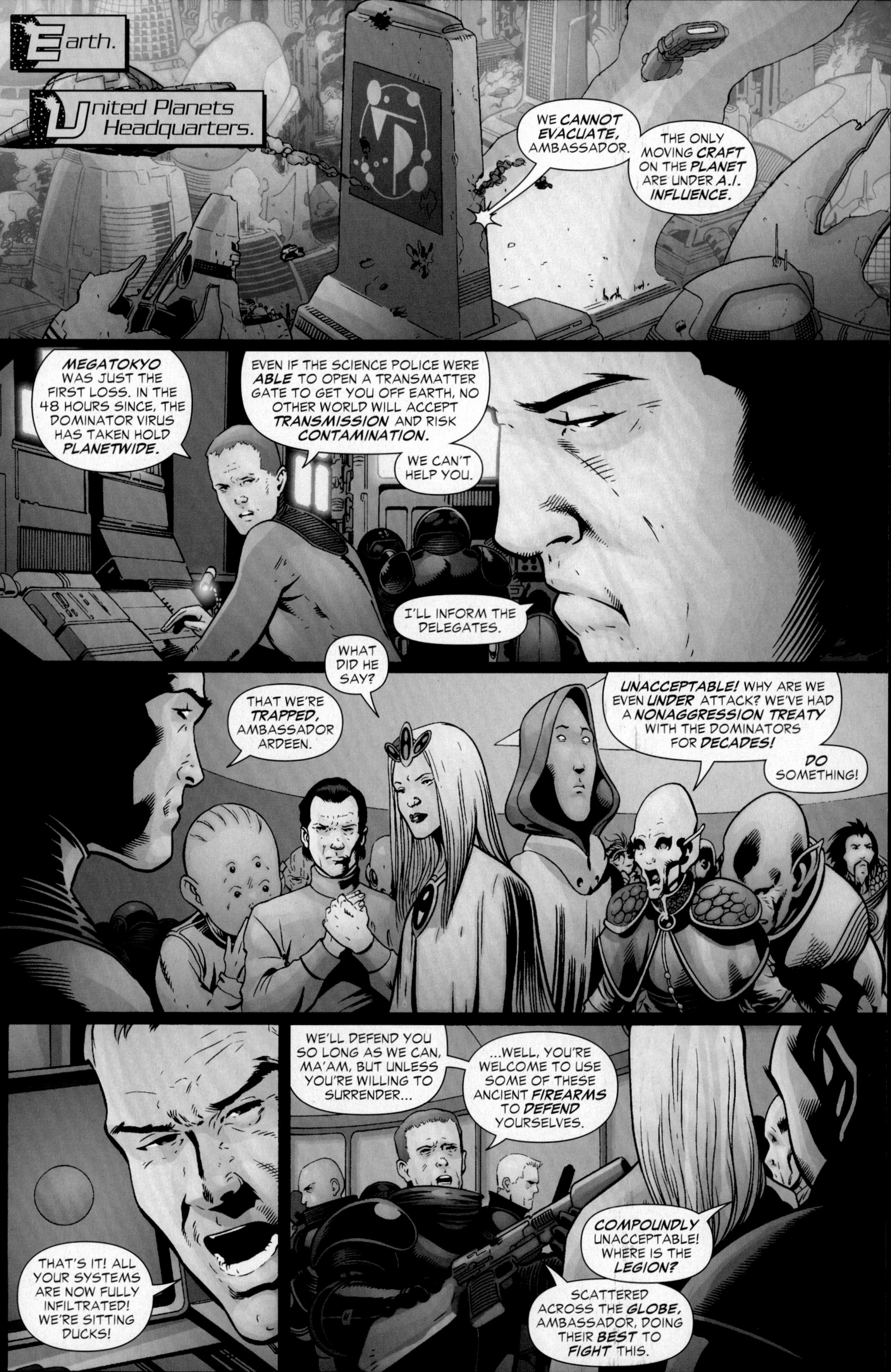
Earth.
United Planets Headquarters.
WE CANNOT EVACUATE, AMBASSADOR.
THE ONLY MOVING CRAFT ON THE PLANET ARE UNDER A.I. INFLUENCE.
MEGATOKYO WAS JUST THE FIRST LOSS. IN THE 48 HOURS SINCE, THE DOMINATOR VIRUS HAS TAKEN HOLD PLANETWIDE.
EVEN IF THE SCIENCE POLICE WERE ABLE TO OPEN A TRANSMATTER GATE TO GET YOU OFF EARTH, NO OTHER WORLD WILL ACCEPT TRANSMISSION AND RISK CONTAMINATION.
WE CAN'T HELP YOU.
I'LL INFORM THE DELEGATES.
WHAT DID HE SAY?
THAT WE'RE TRAPPED, AMBASSADOR ARDEEN.
UNACCEPTABLE! WHY ARE WE EVEN UNDER ATTACK? WE'VE HAD A NONAGGRESSION TREATY WITH THE DOMINATORS FOR DECADES!
DO SOMETHING!
THAT'S IT! ALL YOUR SYSTEMS ARE NOW FULLY INFILTRATED! WE'RE SITTING DUCKS!
WE'LL DEFEND YOU SO LONG AS WE CAN, MA'AM, BUT UNLESS YOU'RE WILLING TO SURRENDER...
...WELL, YOU'RE WELCOME TO USE SOME OF THESE ANCIENT FIREARMS TO DEFEND YOURSELVES.
COMPOUNDLY UNACCEPTABLE! WHERE IS THE LEGION?
SCATTERED ACROSS THE GLOBE, AMBASSADOR, DOING THEIR BEST TO FIGHT THIS.

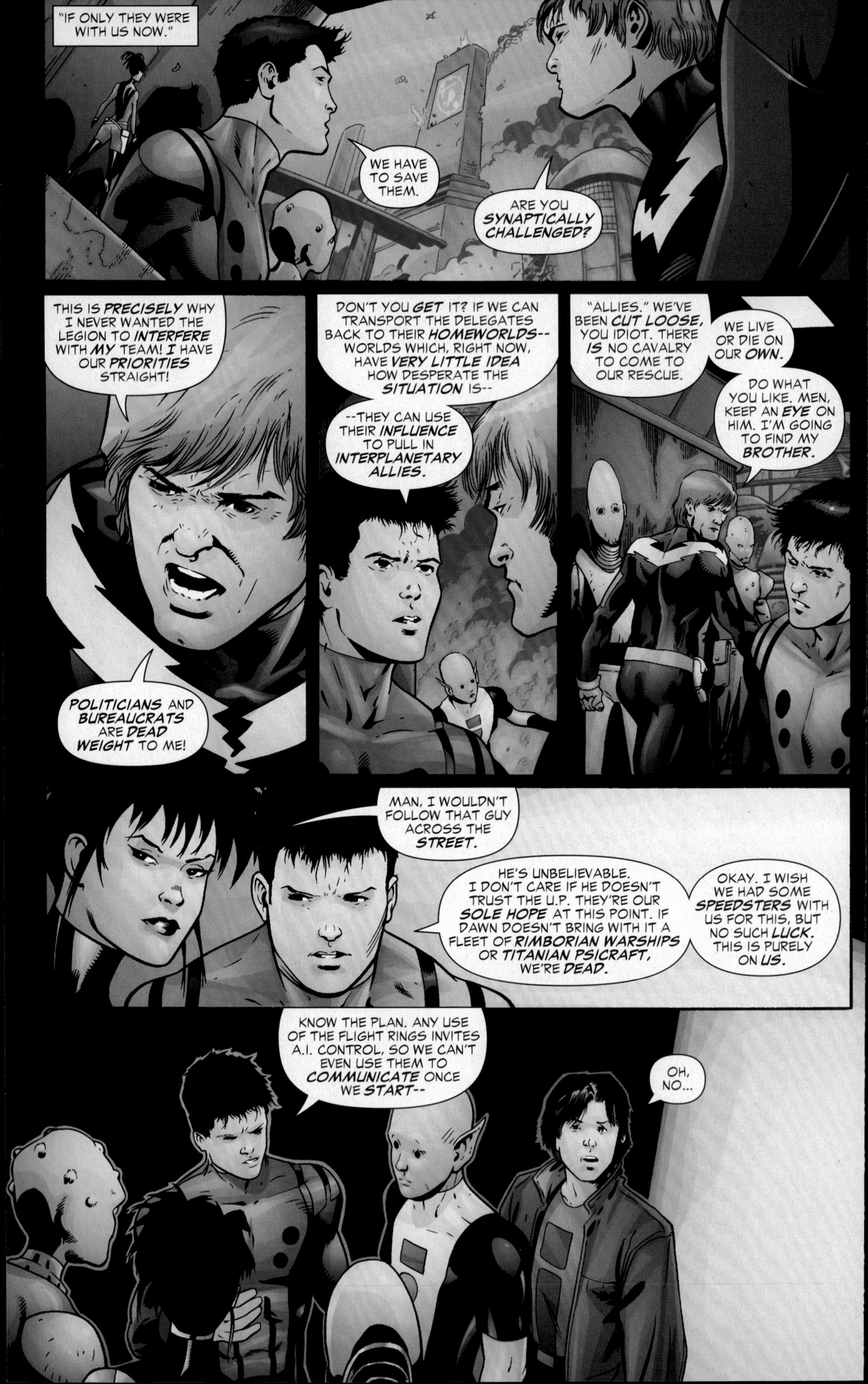
"IF ONLY THEY WERE WITH US NOW."
WE HAVE TO SAVE THEM.
ARE YOU SYNAPTICALLY CHALLENGED?
THIS IS PRECISELY WHY I NEVER WANTED THE LEGION TO INTERFERE WITH MY TEAM! I HAVE OUR PRIORITIES STRAIGHT!
POLITICIANS AND BUREAUCRATS ARE DEAD WEIGHT TO ME!
DON'T YOU GET IT? IF WE CAN TRANSPORT THE DELEGATES BACK TO THEIR HOMEWORLDS-- WORLDS WHICH, RIGHT NOW, HAVE VERY LITTLE IDEA HOW DESPERATE THE SITUATION IS--
--THEY CAN USE THEIR INFLUENCE TO PULL IN INTERPLANETARY ALLIES.
"ALLIES." WE'VE BEEN CUT LOOSE, YOU IDIOT. THERE IS NO CAVALRY TO COME TO OUR RESCUE.
WE LIVE OR DIE ON OUR OWN.
DO WHAT YOU LIKE. MEN, KEEP AN EYE ON HIM. I'M GOING TO FIND MY BROTHER.
MAN, I WOULDN'T FOLLOW THAT GUY ACROSS THE STREET.
HE'S UNBELIEVABLE. I DON'T CARE IF HE DOESN'T TRUST THE U.P. THEY'RE OUR SOLE HOPE AT THIS POINT. IF DAWN DOESN'T BRING WITH IT A FLEET OF RIMBORIAN WARSHIPS OR TITANIAN PSICRAFT, WE'RE DEAD.
OKAY. I WISH WE HAD SOME SPEEDSTERS WITH US FOR THIS, BUT NO SUCH LUCK. THIS IS PURELY ON US.
KNOW THE PLAN. ANY USE OF THE FLIGHT RINGS INVITES A.I. CONTROL, SO WE CAN'T EVEN USE THEM TO COMMUNICATE ONCE WE START--
OH, NO...

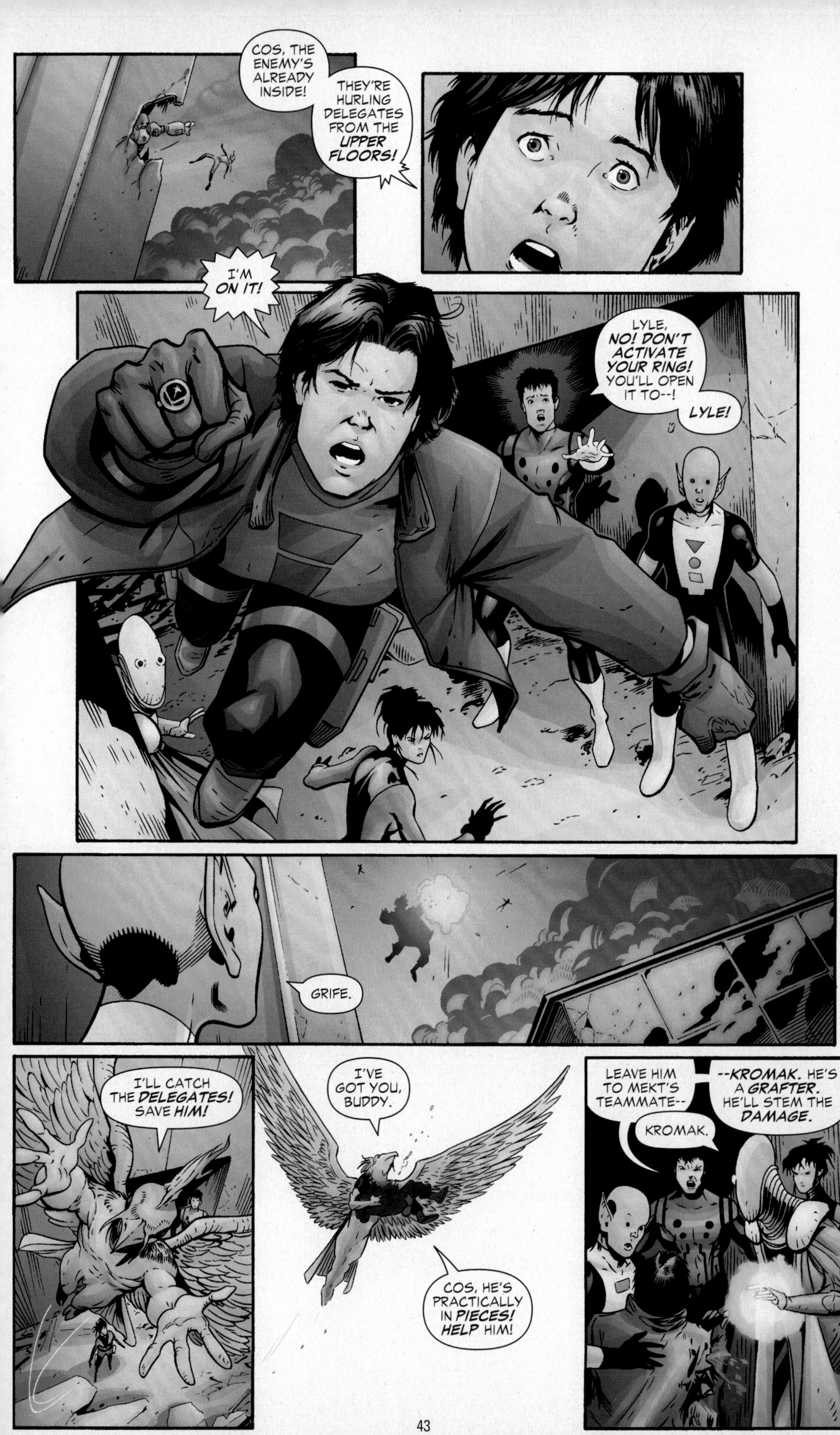
COS, THE ENEMY'S ALREADY INSIDE!
THEY'RE HURLING DELEGATES FROM THE *UPPER FLOORS!*
I'M *ON IT!*
LYLE, **NO! DON'T ACTIVATE YOUR RING!** YOU'LL OPEN IT TO--!
LYLE!
GRIFE.
I'LL CATCH THE ***DELEGATES!*** SAVE ***HIM!***
I'VE GOT YOU, BUDDY.
COS, HE'S PRACTICALLY IN ***PIECES! HELP*** HIM!
LEAVE HIM TO MEKT'S TEAMMATE--
KROMAK.
--***KROMAK.*** HE'S A ***GRAFTER.*** HE'LL STEM THE ***DAMAGE.***

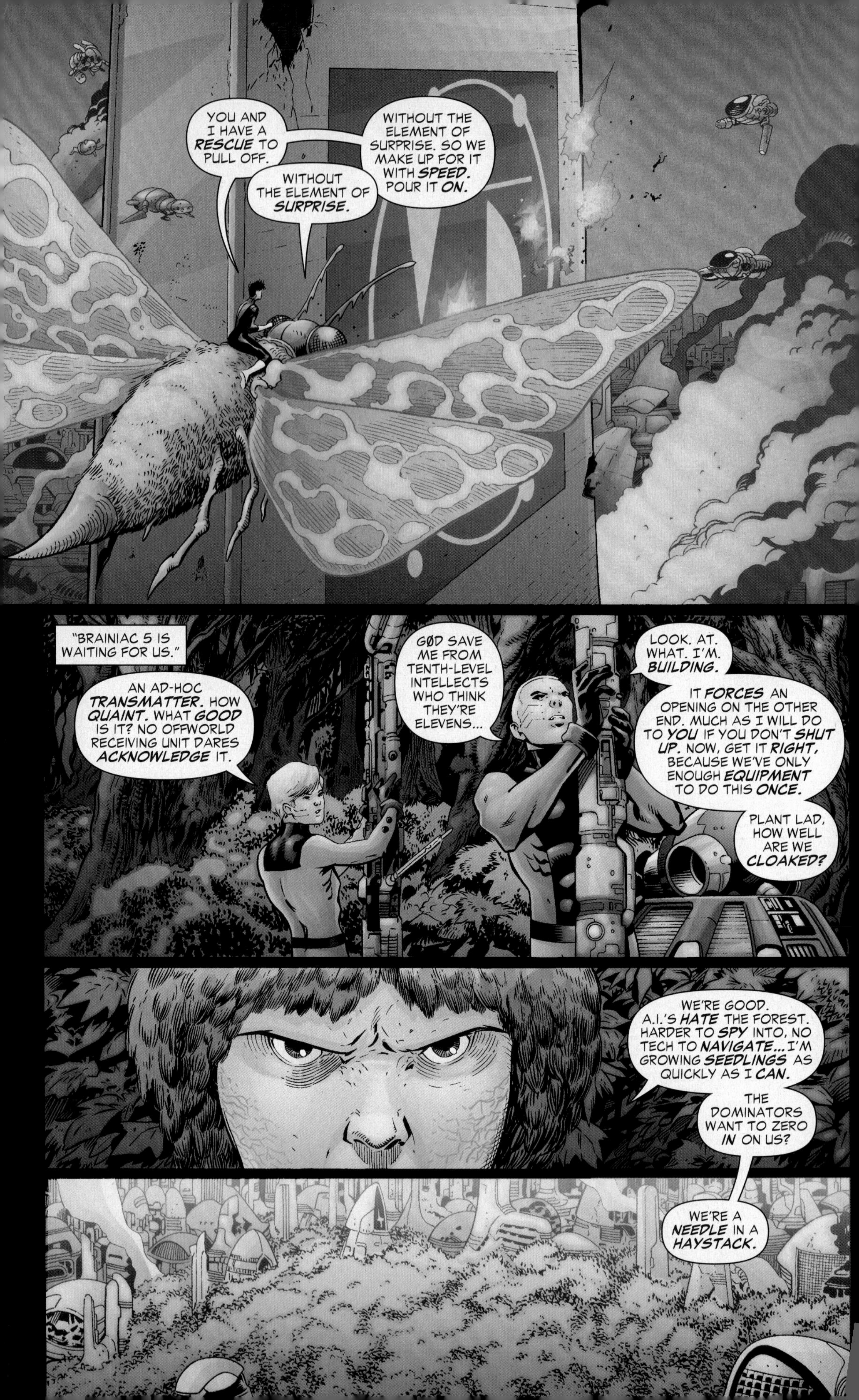
YOU AND I HAVE A RESCUE TO PULL OFF.
WITHOUT THE ELEMENT OF SURPRISE.
WITHOUT THE ELEMENT OF SURPRISE. SO WE MAKE UP FOR IT WITH SPEED. POUR IT ON.
"BRAINIAC 5 IS WAITING FOR US."
AN AD-HOC TRANSMATTER. HOW QUAINT. WHAT GOOD IS IT? NO OFFWORLD RECEIVING UNIT DARES ACKNOWLEDGE IT.
GØD SAVE ME FROM TENTH-LEVEL INTELLECTS WHO THINK THEY'RE ELEVENS...
LOOK. AT. WHAT. I'M. BUILDING.
IT FORCES AN OPENING ON THE OTHER END. MUCH AS I WILL DO TO YOU IF YOU DON'T SHUT UP. NOW, GET IT RIGHT, BECAUSE WE'VE ONLY ENOUGH EQUIPMENT TO DO THIS ONCE.
PLANT LAD, HOW WELL ARE WE CLOAKED?
WE'RE GOOD. A.I.'S HATE THE FOREST. HARDER TO SPY INTO, NO TECH TO NAVIGATE... I'M GROWING SEEDLINGS AS QUICKLY AS I CAN.
THE DOMINATORS WANT TO ZERO IN ON US?
WE'RE A NEEDLE IN A HAYSTACK.

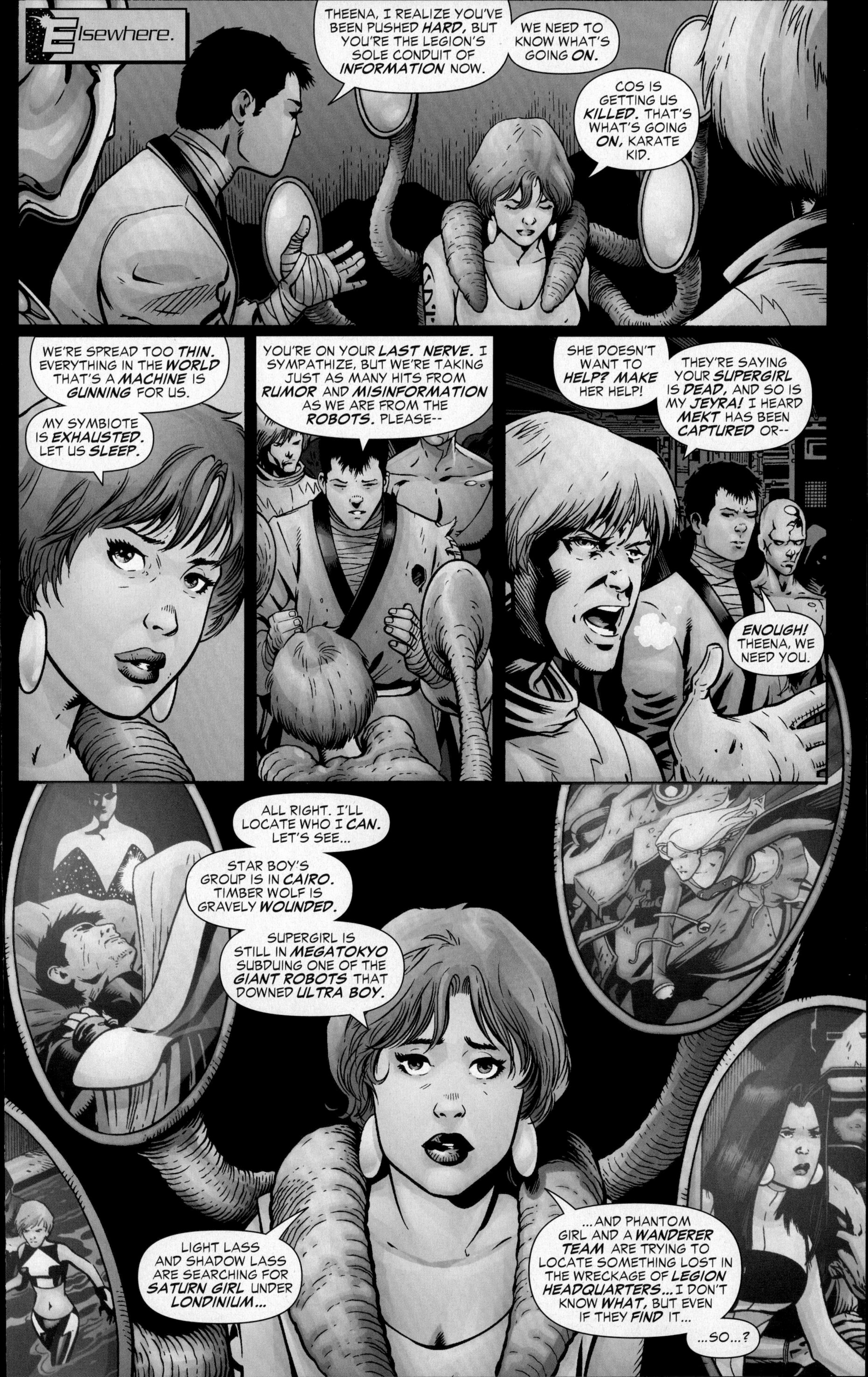
Elsewhere.
THEENA, I REALIZE YOU'VE BEEN PUSHED HARD, BUT YOU'RE THE LEGION'S SOLE CONDUIT OF INFORMATION NOW.
WE NEED TO KNOW WHAT'S GOING ON.
COS IS GETTING US KILLED. THAT'S WHAT'S GOING ON, KARATE KID.
WE'RE SPREAD TOO THIN. EVERYTHING IN THE WORLD THAT'S A MACHINE IS GUNNING FOR US.
MY SYMBIOTE IS EXHAUSTED. LET US SLEEP.
YOU'RE ON YOUR LAST NERVE. I SYMPATHIZE, BUT WE'RE TAKING JUST AS MANY HITS FROM RUMOR AND MISINFORMATION AS WE ARE FROM THE ROBOTS. PLEASE--
SHE DOESN'T WANT TO HELP? MAKE HER HELP!
THEY'RE SAYING YOUR SUPERGIRL IS DEAD, AND SO IS MY JEYRA! I HEARD MEKT HAS BEEN CAPTURED OR--
ENOUGH! THEENA, WE NEED YOU.
ALL RIGHT. I'LL LOCATE WHO I CAN. LET'S SEE...
STAR BOY'S GROUP IS IN CAIRO. TIMBER WOLF IS GRAVELY WOUNDED.
SUPERGIRL IS STILL IN MEGATOKYO SUBDUING ONE OF THE GIANT ROBOTS THAT DOWNED ULTRA BOY.
LIGHT LASS AND SHADOW LASS ARE SEARCHING FOR SATURN GIRL UNDER LONDINIUM...
...AND PHANTOM GIRL AND A WANDERER TEAM ARE TRYING TO LOCATE SOMETHING LOST IN THE WRECKAGE OF LEGION HEADQUARTERS... I DON'T KNOW WHAT, BUT EVEN IF THEY FIND IT...
...SO...?

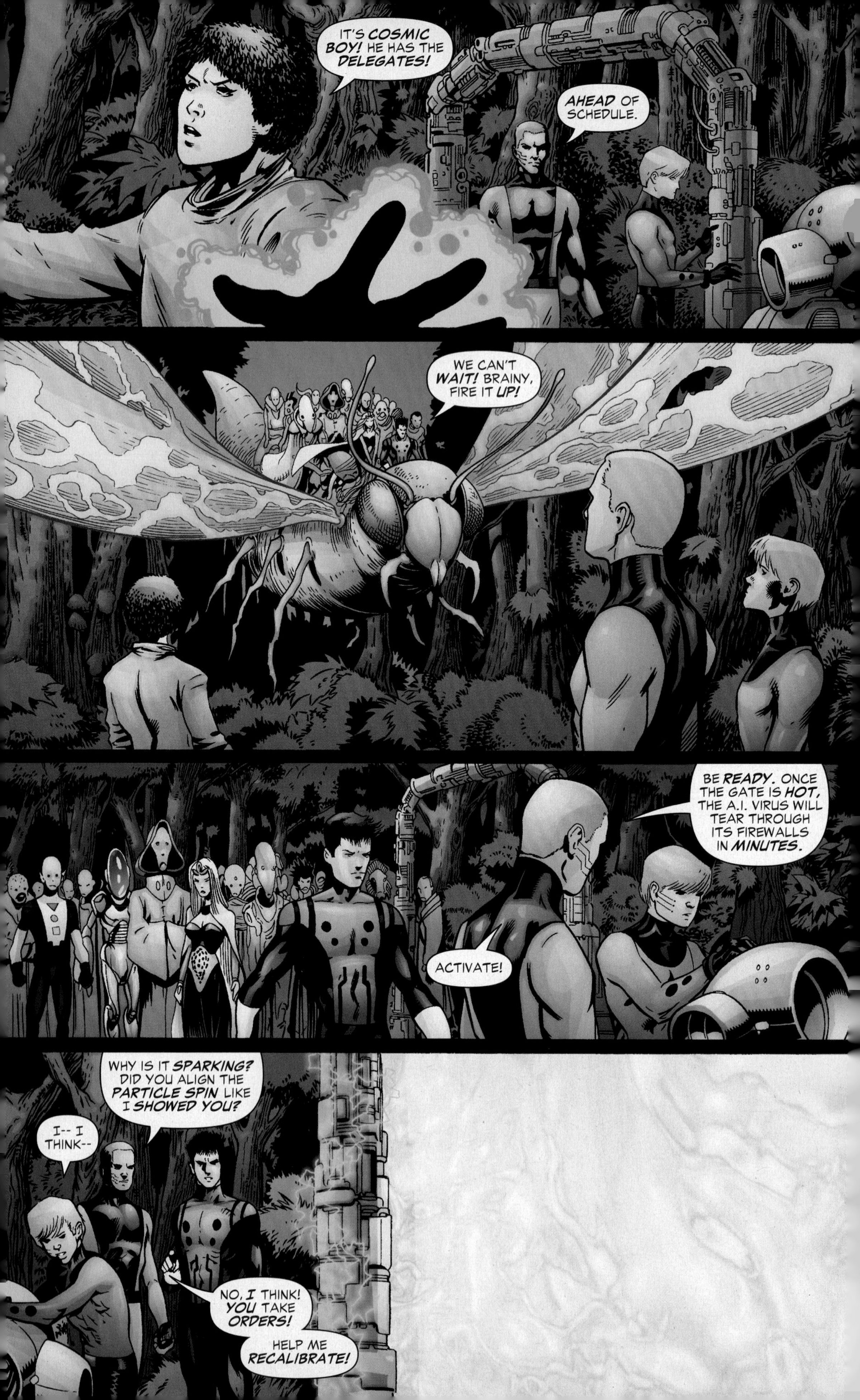
IT'S COSMIC BOY! HE HAS THE DELEGATES!
AHEAD OF SCHEDULE.
WE CAN'T WAIT! BRAINY, FIRE IT UP!
BE READY. ONCE THE GATE IS HOT, THE A.I. VIRUS WILL TEAR THROUGH ITS FIREWALLS IN MINUTES.
ACTIVATE!
WHY IS IT SPARKING? DID YOU ALIGN THE PARTICLE SPIN LIKE I SHOWED YOU?
I-- I THINK--
NO, I THINK! YOU TAKE ORDERS!
HELP ME RECALIBRATE!

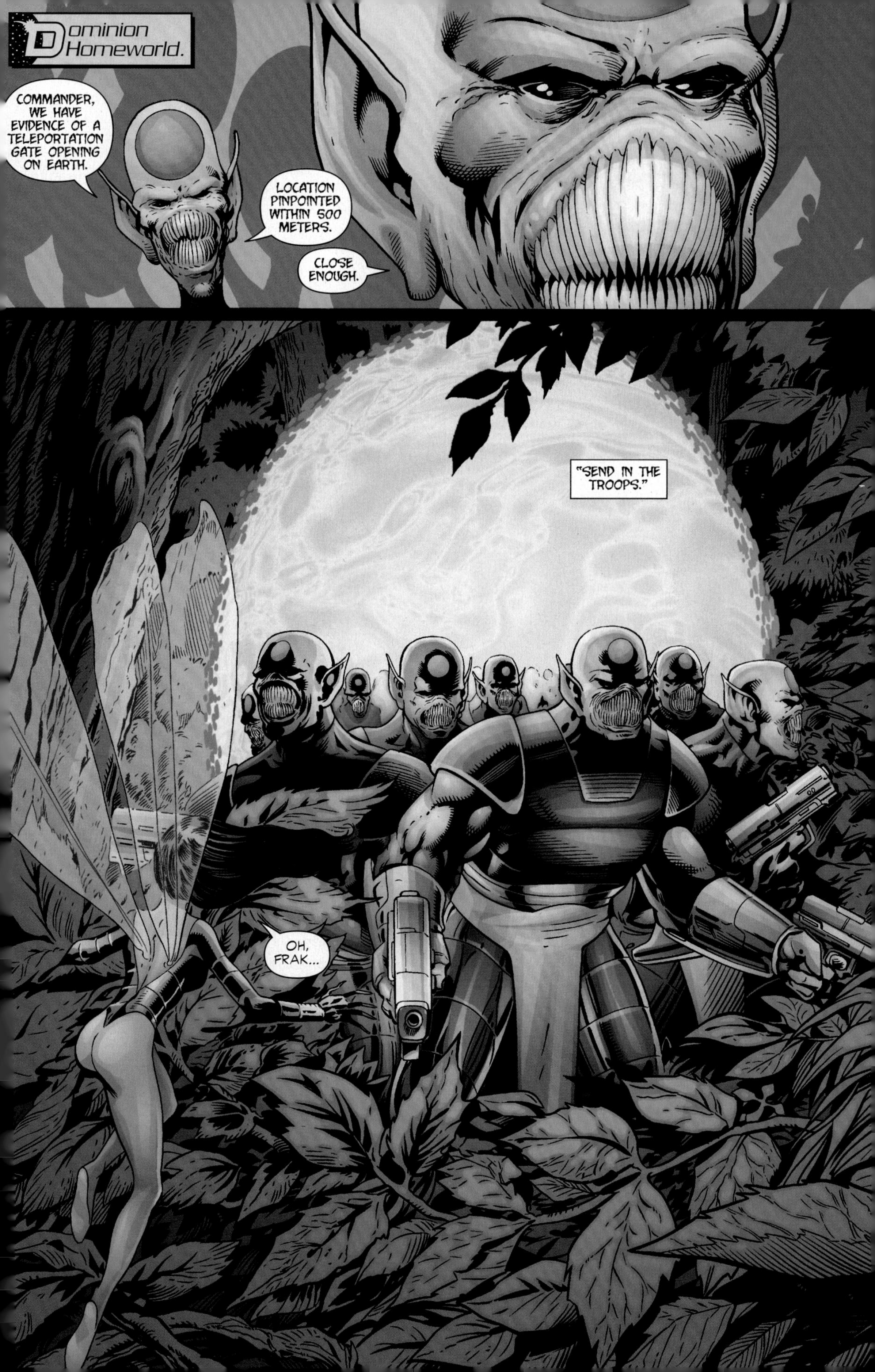
Dominion Homeworld.
COMMANDER, WE HAVE EVIDENCE OF A TELEPORTATION GATE OPENING ON EARTH.
LOCATION PINPOINTED WITHIN 500 METERS.
CLOSE ENOUGH.
"SEND IN THE TROOPS."
OH, FRAK...

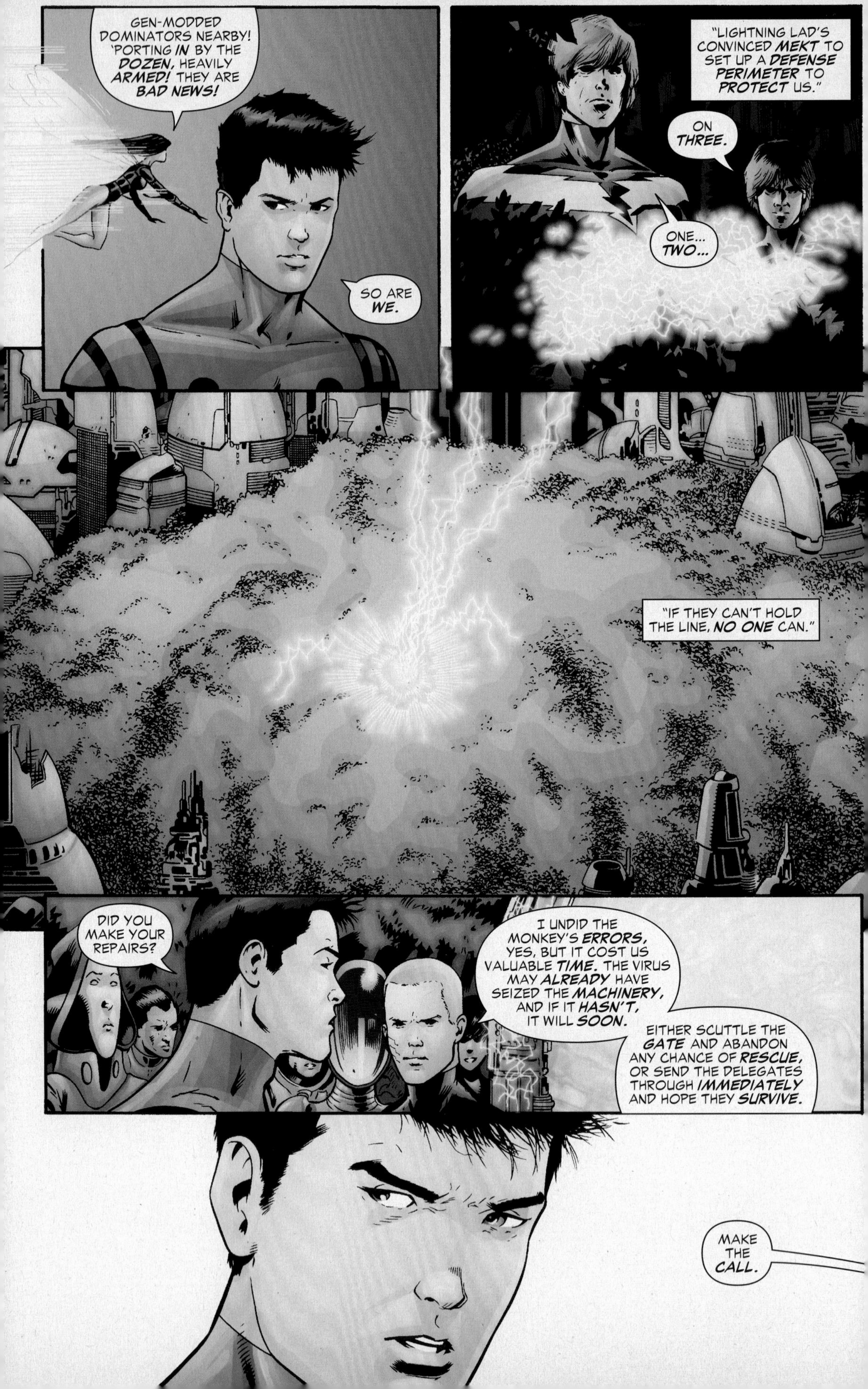
GEN-MODDED DOMINATORS NEARBY! 'PORTING IN BY THE DOZEN, HEAVILY ARMED! THEY ARE BAD NEWS!
SO ARE WE.
"LIGHTNING LAD'S CONVINCED MEKT TO SET UP A DEFENSE PERIMETER TO PROTECT US."
ON THREE.
ONE... TWO...
"IF THEY CAN'T HOLD THE LINE, NO ONE CAN."
DID YOU MAKE YOUR REPAIRS?
I UNDID THE MONKEY'S ERRORS, YES, BUT IT COST US VALUABLE TIME. THE VIRUS MAY ALREADY HAVE SEIZED THE MACHINERY, AND IF IT HASN'T, IT WILL SOON.
EITHER SCUTTLE THE GATE AND ABANDON ANY CHANCE OF RESCUE, OR SEND THE DELEGATES THROUGH IMMEDIATELY AND HOPE THEY SURVIVE.
MAKE THE CALL.

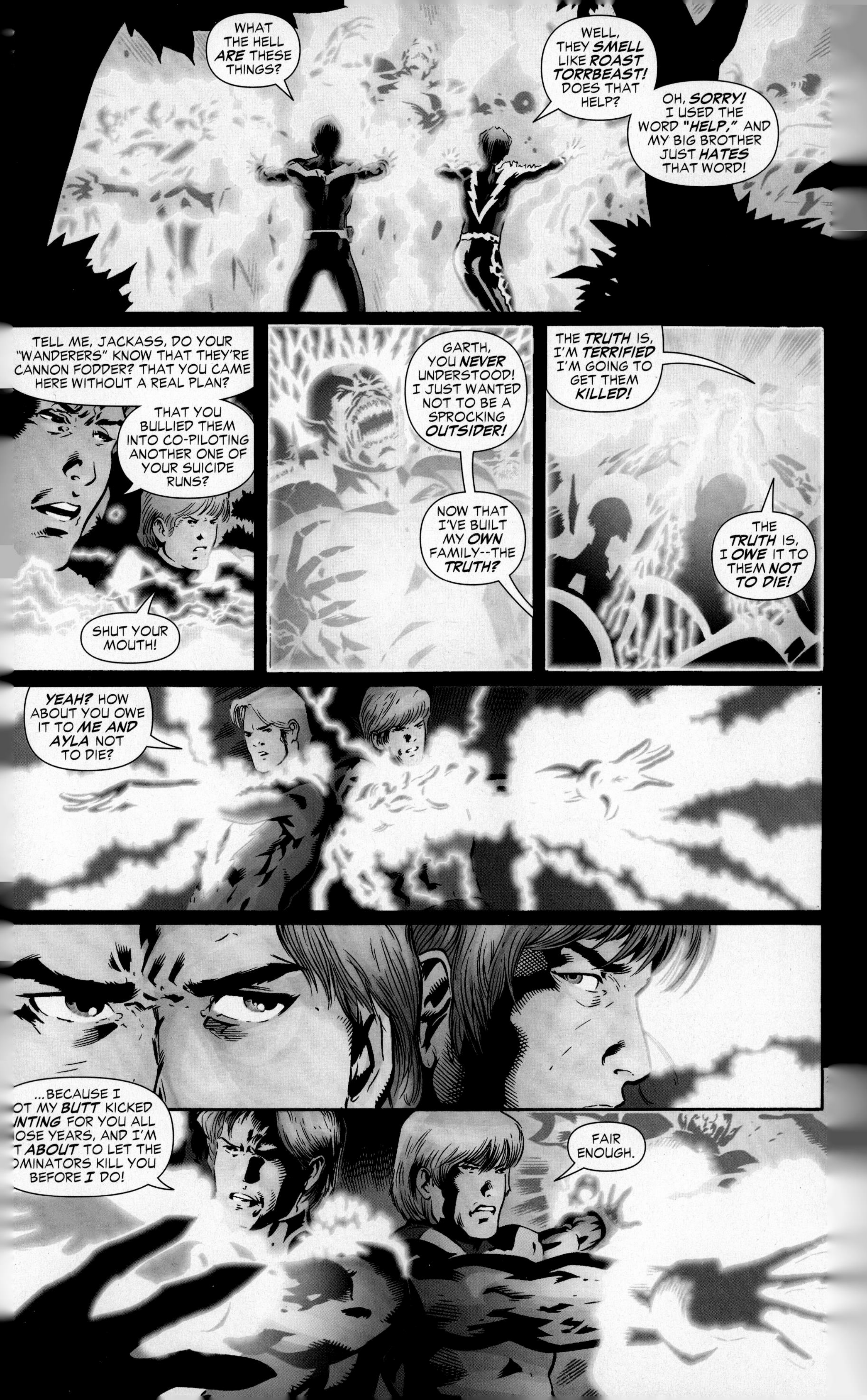
WHAT THE HELL ARE THESE THINGS?
WELL, THEY SMELL LIKE ROAST TORRBEAST! DOES THAT HELP?
OH, SORRY! I USED THE WORD "HELP," AND MY BIG BROTHER JUST HATES THAT WORD!
TELL ME, JACKASS, DO YOUR "WANDERERS" KNOW THAT THEY'RE CANNON FODDER? THAT YOU CAME HERE WITHOUT A REAL PLAN?
THAT YOU BULLIED THEM INTO CO-PILOTING ANOTHER ONE OF YOUR SUICIDE RUNS?
SHUT YOUR MOUTH!
GARTH, YOU NEVER UNDERSTOOD! I JUST WANTED NOT TO BE A SPROCKING OUTSIDER!
NOW THAT I'VE BUILT MY OWN FAMILY--THE TRUTH?
THE TRUTH IS, I'M TERRIFIED I'M GOING TO GET THEM KILLED!
THE TRUTH IS, I OWE IT TO THEM NOT TO DIE!
YEAH? HOW ABOUT YOU OWE IT TO ME AND AYLA NOT TO DIE?
...BECAUSE I OT MY BUTT KICKED NTING FOR YOU ALL OSE YEARS, AND I'M T ABOUT TO LET THE OMINATORS KILL YOU BEFORE I DO!
FAIR ENOUGH.

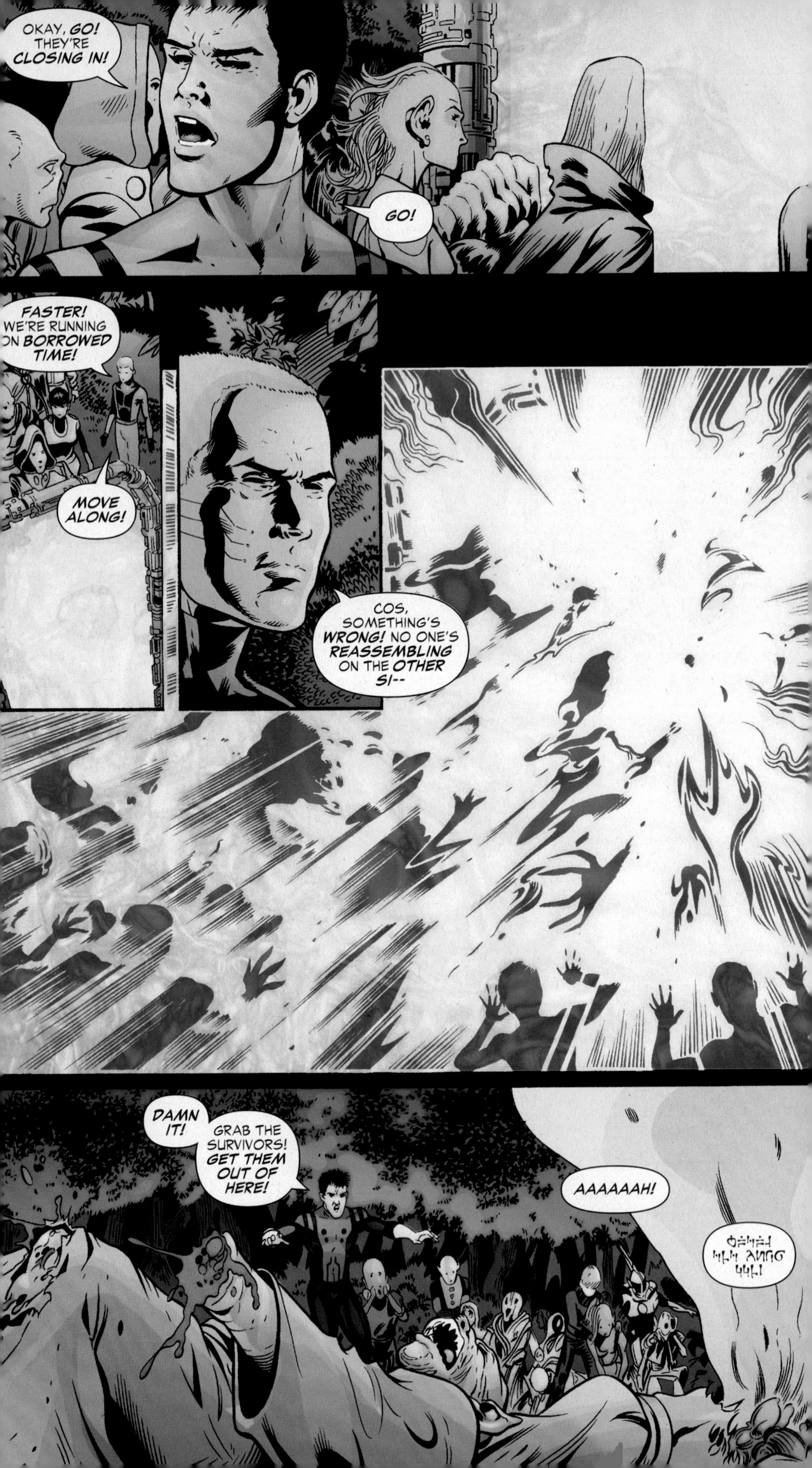
OKAY, GO! THEY'RE CLOSING IN!
GO!
FASTER! WE'RE RUNNING ON BORROWED TIME!
MOVE ALONG!
COS, SOMETHING'S WRONG! NO ONE'S REASSEMBLING ON THE OTHER SI--
DAMN IT!
GRAB THE SURVIVORS! GET THEM OUT OF HERE!
AAAAAAH!

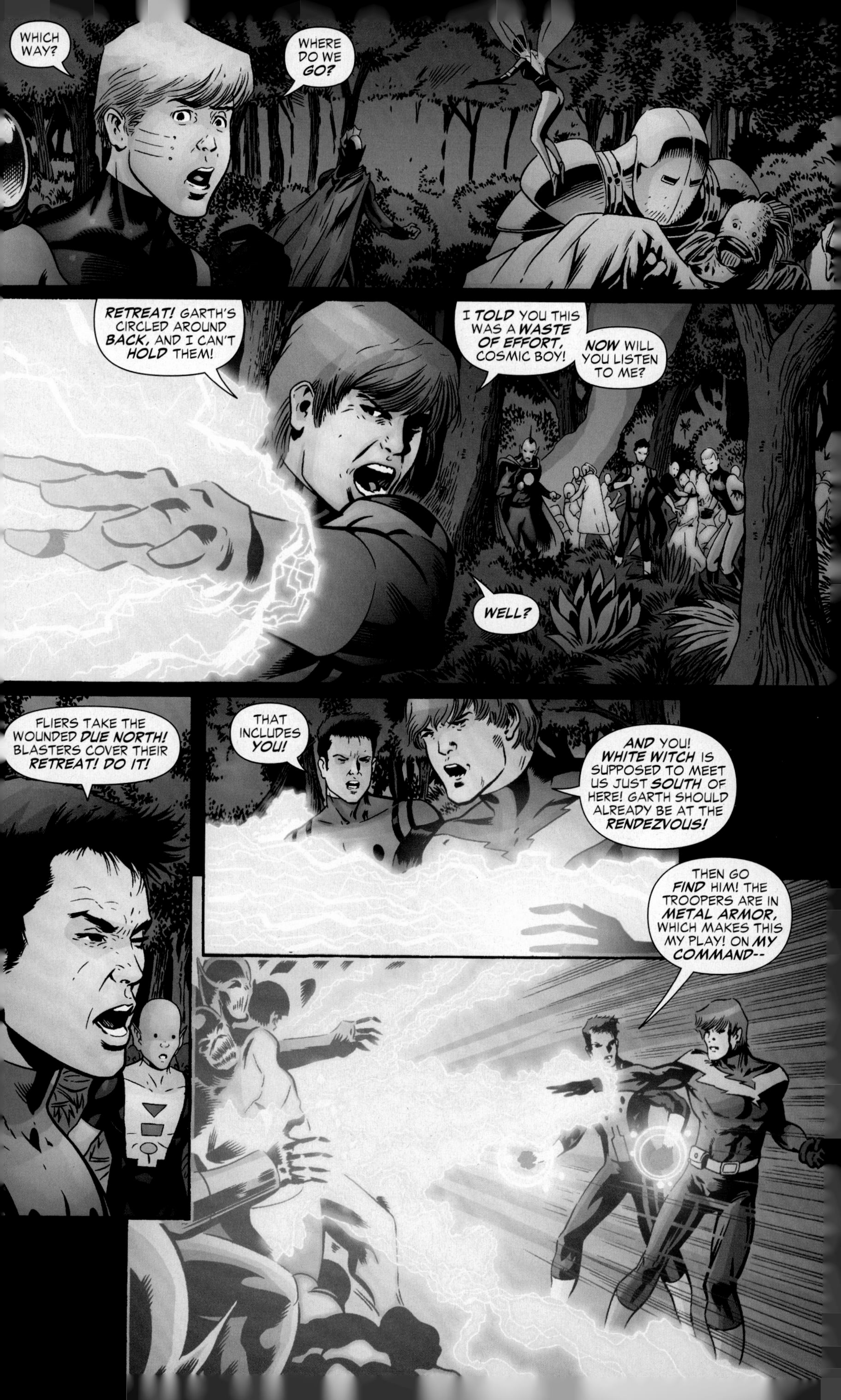
WHICH WAY?
WHERE DO WE GO?
RETREAT! GARTH'S CIRCLED AROUND BACK, AND I CAN'T HOLD THEM!
I TOLD YOU THIS WAS A WASTE OF EFFORT, COSMIC BOY!
NOW WILL YOU LISTEN TO ME?
WELL?
FLIERS TAKE THE WOUNDED DUE NORTH! BLASTERS COVER THEIR RETREAT! DO IT!
THAT INCLUDES YOU!
AND YOU! WHITE WITCH IS SUPPOSED TO MEET US JUST SOUTH OF HERE! GARTH SHOULD ALREADY BE AT THE RENDEZVOUS!
THEN GO FIND HIM! THE TROOPERS ARE IN METAL ARMOR, WHICH MAKES THIS MY PLAY! ON MY COMMAND--

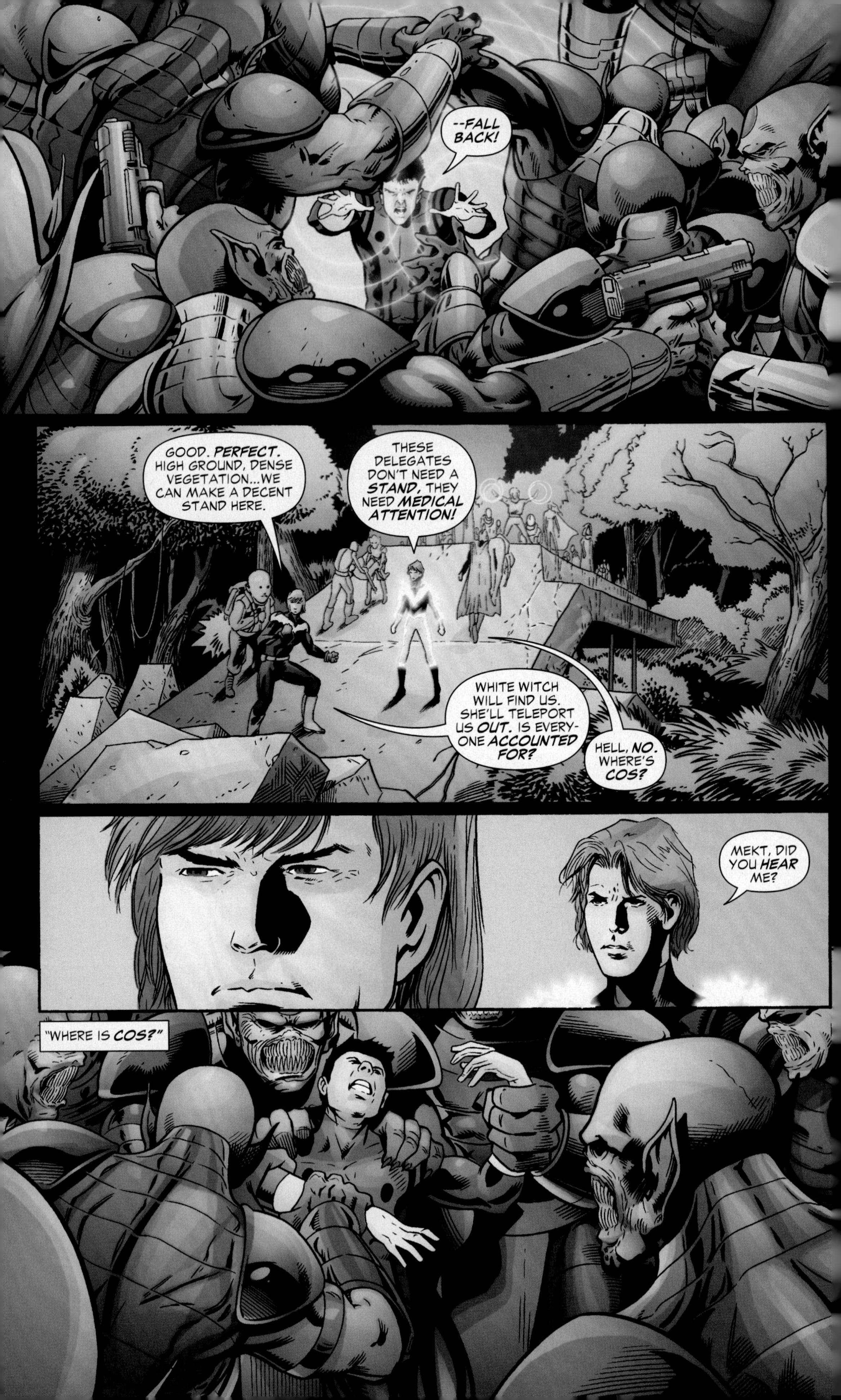
--FALL BACK!
GOOD. PERFECT. HIGH GROUND, DENSE VEGETATION...WE CAN MAKE A DECENT STAND HERE.
THESE DELEGATES DON'T NEED A STAND, THEY NEED MEDICAL ATTENTION!
WHITE WITCH WILL FIND US. SHE'LL TELEPORT US OUT. IS EVERY-ONE ACCOUNTED FOR?
HELL, NO. WHERE'S COS?
MEKT, DID YOU HEAR ME?
"WHERE IS COS?"

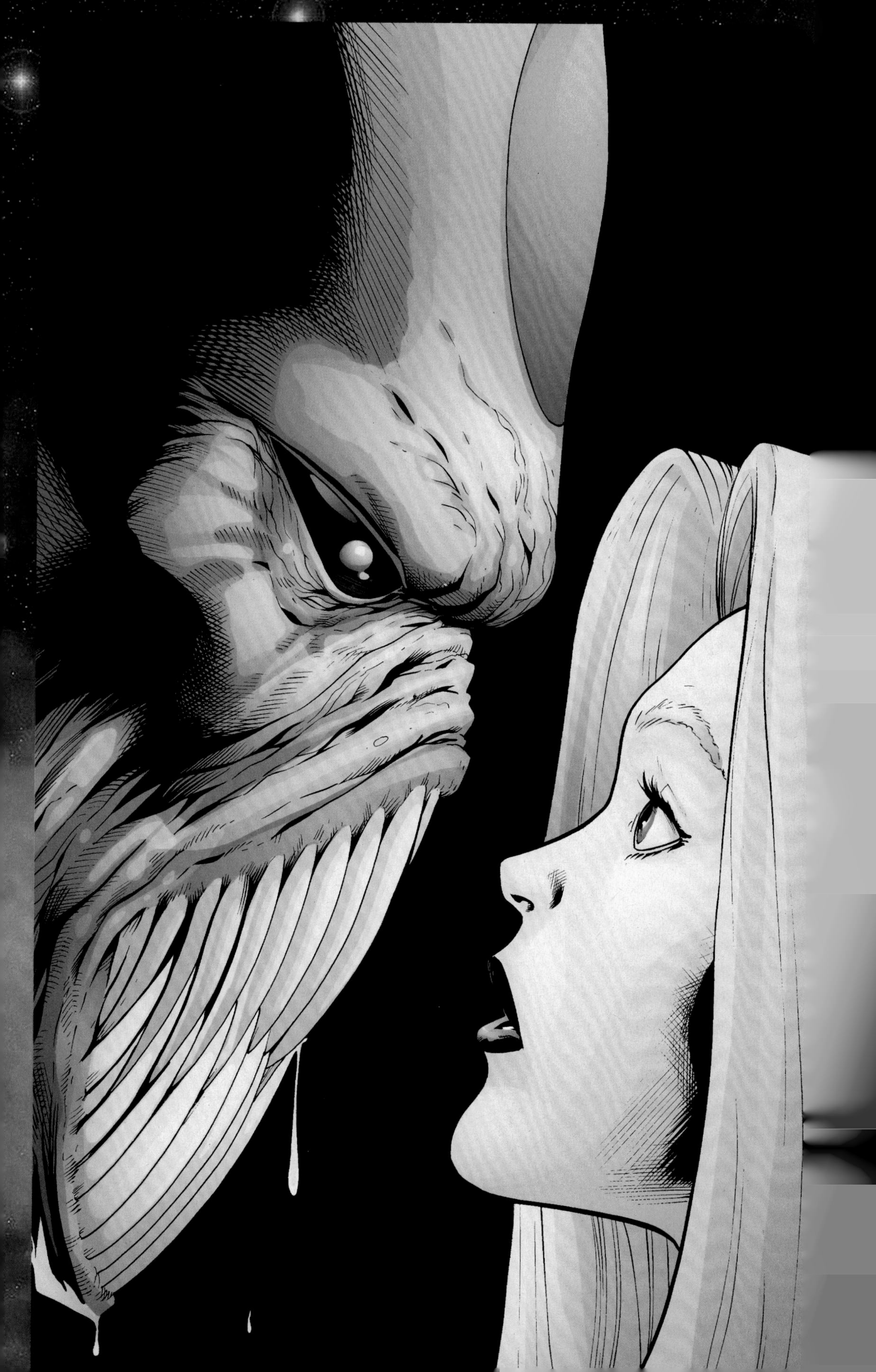

CHAPTER 3

Mark Waid Writer
Barry Kitson Penciller
Mick Gray & **Jimmy Palmiotti** Inkers
Barry Kitson & **Nathan Eyring** Cover

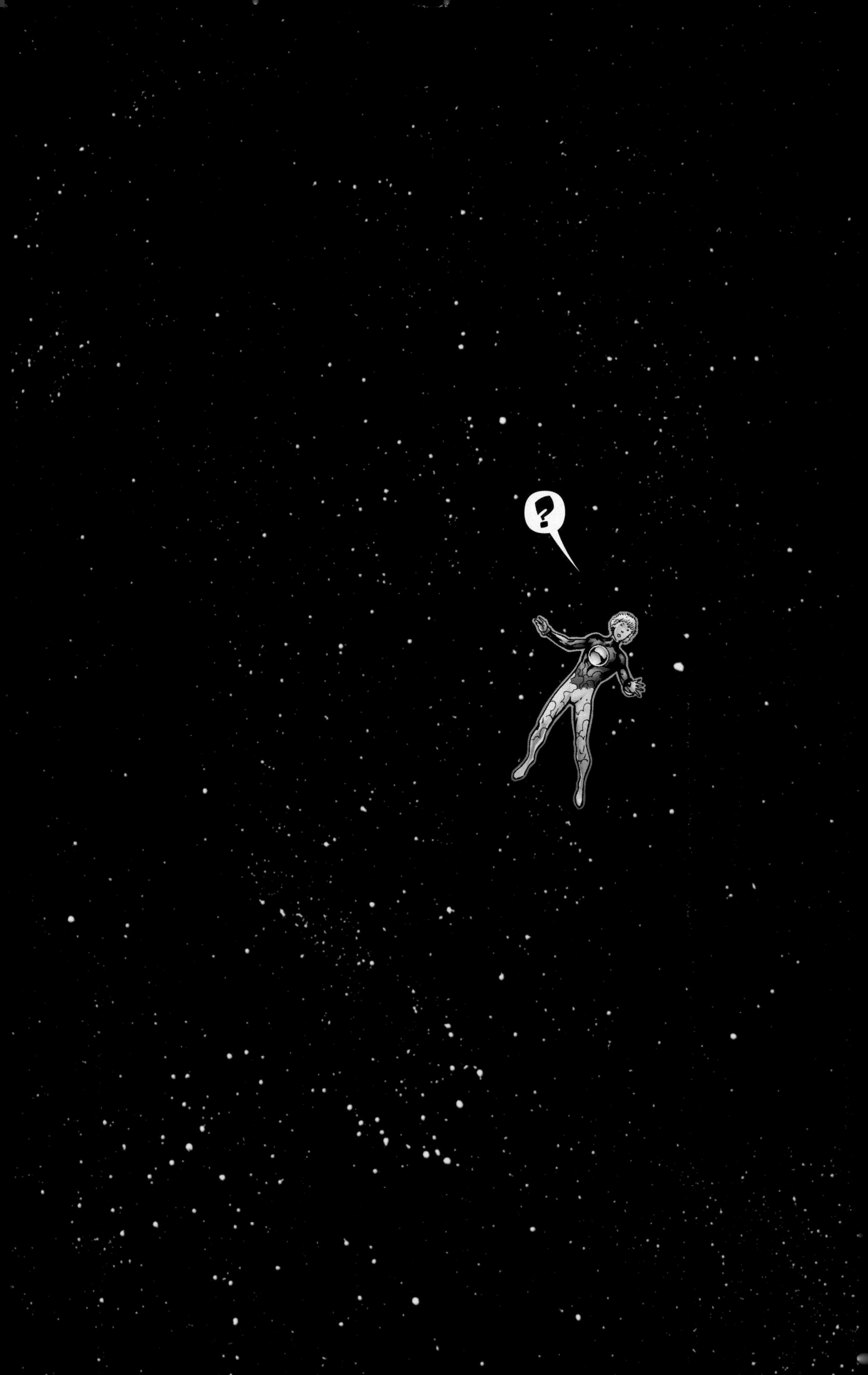
?

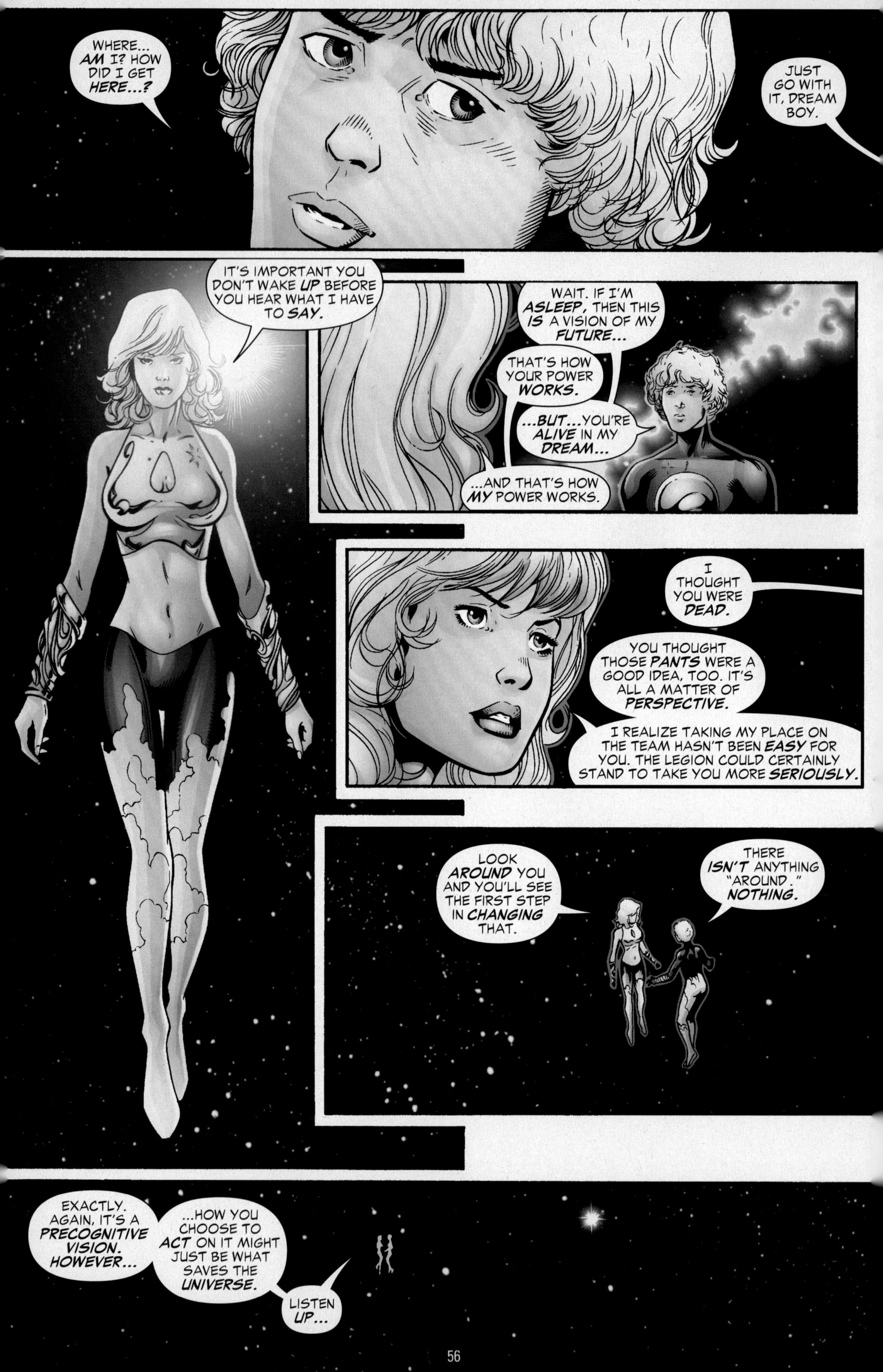
WHERE... AM I? HOW DID I GET HERE...?
JUST GO WITH IT, DREAM BOY.
IT'S IMPORTANT YOU DON'T WAKE UP BEFORE YOU HEAR WHAT I HAVE TO SAY.
WAIT. IF I'M ASLEEP, THEN THIS IS A VISION OF MY FUTURE...
THAT'S HOW YOUR POWER WORKS.
...BUT...YOU'RE ALIVE IN MY DREAM...
...AND THAT'S HOW MY POWER WORKS.
I THOUGHT YOU WERE DEAD.
YOU THOUGHT THOSE PANTS WERE A GOOD IDEA, TOO. IT'S ALL A MATTER OF PERSPECTIVE.
I REALIZE TAKING MY PLACE ON THE TEAM HASN'T BEEN EASY FOR YOU. THE LEGION COULD CERTAINLY STAND TO TAKE YOU MORE SERIOUSLY.
LOOK AROUND YOU AND YOU'LL SEE THE FIRST STEP IN CHANGING THAT.
THERE ISN'T ANYTHING "AROUND." NOTHING.
EXACTLY. AGAIN, IT'S A PRECOGNITIVE VISION. HOWEVER...
...HOW YOU CHOOSE TO ACT ON IT MIGHT JUST BE WHAT SAVES THE UNIVERSE.
LISTEN UP...

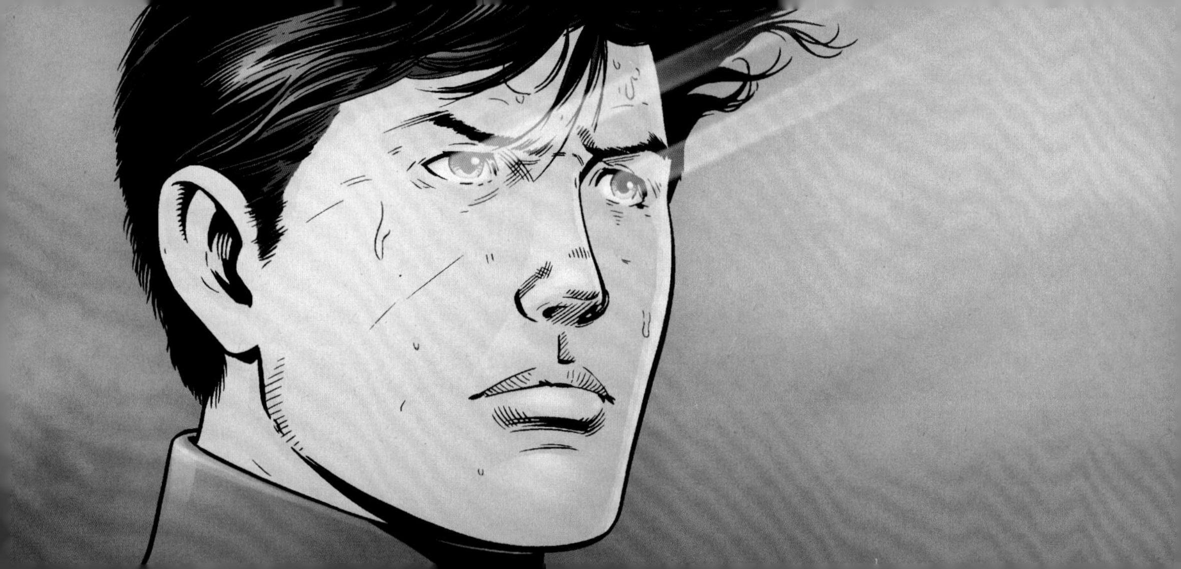

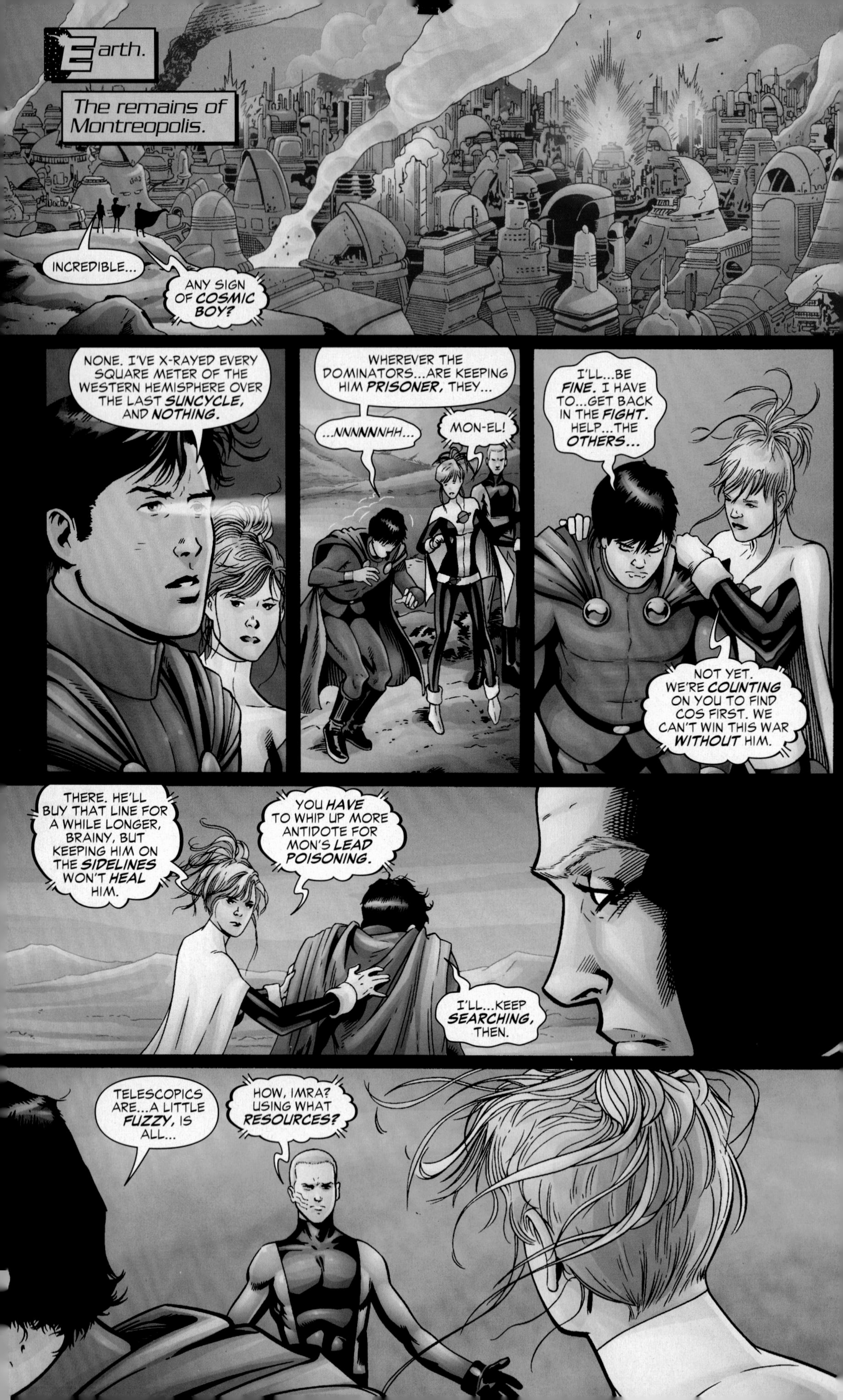
Earth.
The remains of Montreopolis.
INCREDIBLE...
ANY SIGN OF COSMIC BOY?
NONE. I'VE X-RAYED EVERY SQUARE METER OF THE WESTERN HEMISPHERE OVER THE LAST SUNCYCLE, AND NOTHING.
WHEREVER THE DOMINATORS...ARE KEEPING HIM PRISONER, THEY...
...NNNNNNHH...
MON-EL!
I'LL...BE FINE. I HAVE TO...GET BACK IN THE FIGHT. HELP...THE OTHERS...
NOT YET. WE'RE COUNTING ON YOU TO FIND COS FIRST. WE CAN'T WIN THIS WAR WITHOUT HIM.
THERE. HE'LL BUY THAT LINE FOR A WHILE LONGER, BRAINY, BUT KEEPING HIM ON THE SIDELINES WON'T HEAL HIM.
YOU HAVE TO WHIP UP MORE ANTIDOTE FOR MON'S LEAD POISONING.
I'LL...KEEP SEARCHING, THEN.
TELESCOPICS ARE...A LITTLE FUZZY, IS ALL...
HOW, IMRA? USING WHAT RESOURCES?

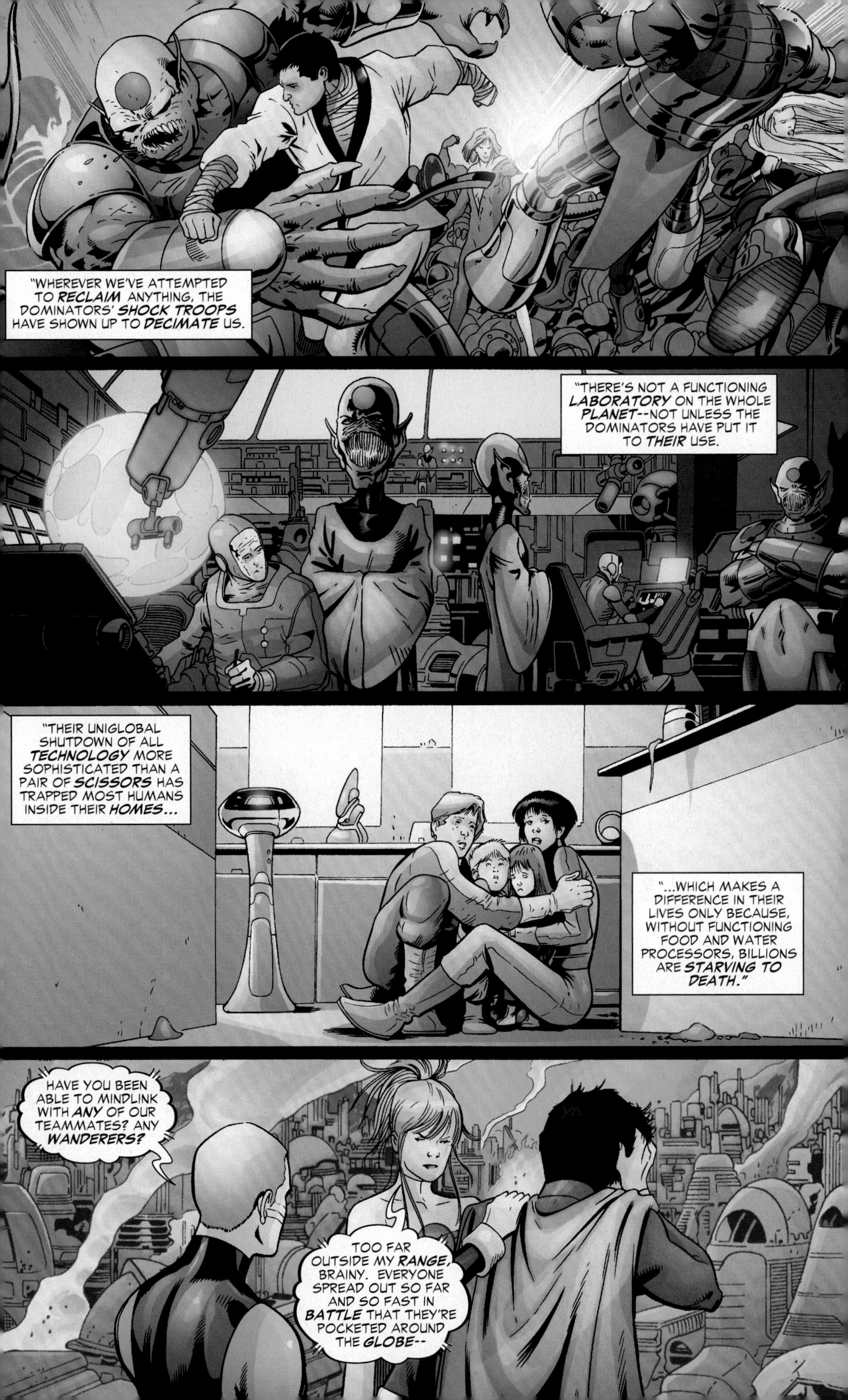
"WHEREVER WE'VE ATTEMPTED TO RECLAIM ANYTHING, THE DOMINATORS' SHOCK TROOPS HAVE SHOWN UP TO DECIMATE US.
"THERE'S NOT A FUNCTIONING LABORATORY ON THE WHOLE PLANET--NOT UNLESS THE DOMINATORS HAVE PUT IT TO THEIR USE.
"THEIR UNIGLOBAL SHUTDOWN OF ALL TECHNOLOGY MORE SOPHISTICATED THAN A PAIR OF SCISSORS HAS TRAPPED MOST HUMANS INSIDE THEIR HOMES...
"...WHICH MAKES A DIFFERENCE IN THEIR LIVES ONLY BECAUSE, WITHOUT FUNCTIONING FOOD AND WATER PROCESSORS, BILLIONS ARE STARVING TO DEATH."
HAVE YOU BEEN ABLE TO MINDLINK WITH ANY OF OUR TEAMMATES? ANY WANDERERS?
TOO FAR OUTSIDE MY RANGE, BRAINY. EVERYONE SPREAD OUT SO FAR AND SO FAST IN BATTLE THAT THEY'RE POCKETED AROUND THE GLOBE--

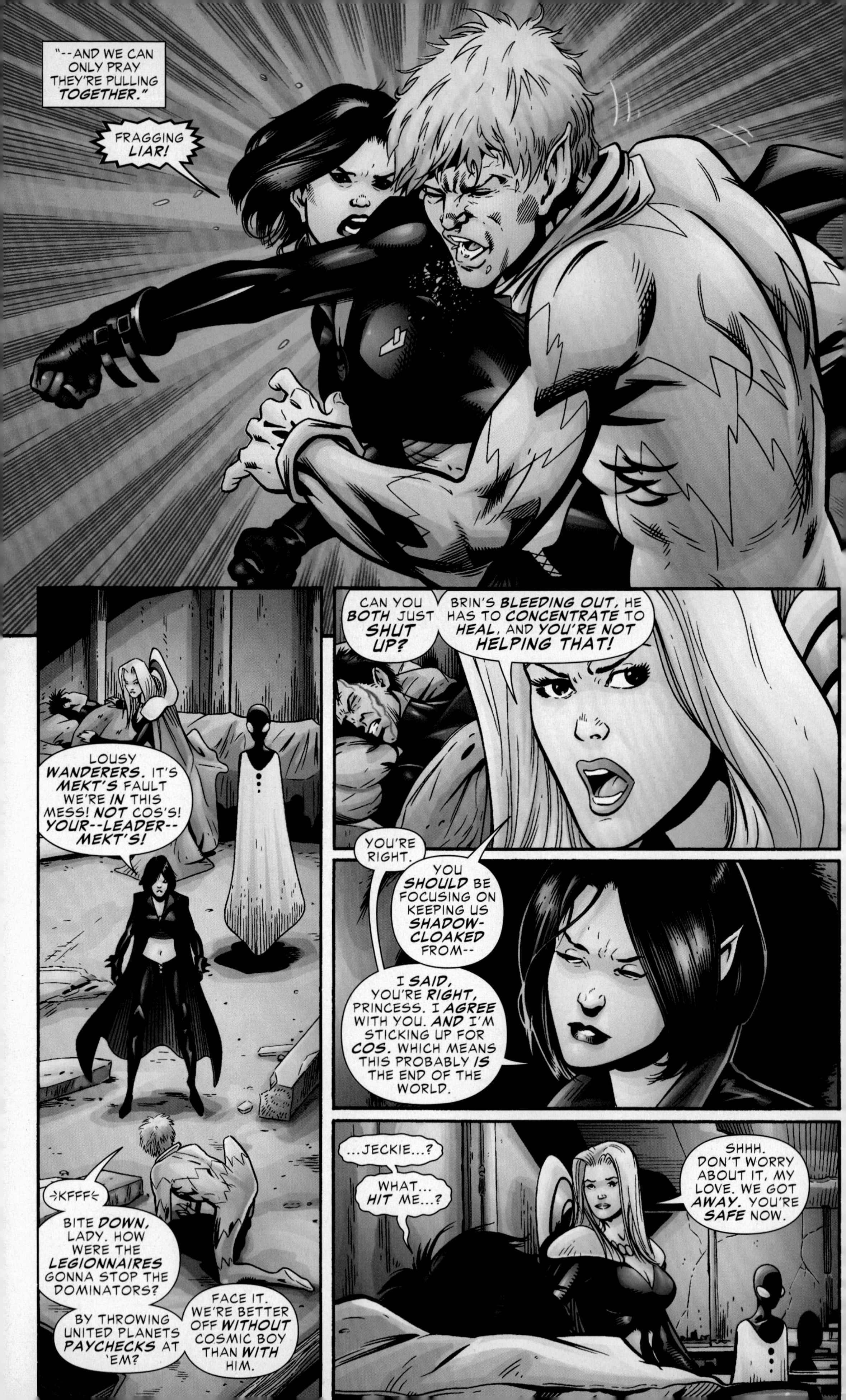
"--AND WE CAN ONLY PRAY THEY'RE PULLING TOGETHER."
FRAGGING LIAR!
LOUSY WANDERERS. IT'S MEKT'S FAULT WE'RE IN THIS MESS! NOT COS'S! YOUR--LEADER--MEKT'S!
>KFFF<
BITE DOWN, LADY. HOW WERE THE LEGIONNAIRES GONNA STOP THE DOMINATORS?
BY THROWING UNITED PLANETS PAYCHECKS AT 'EM?
FACE IT. WE'RE BETTER OFF WITHOUT COSMIC BOY THAN WITH HIM.
CAN YOU BOTH JUST SHUT UP?
BRIN'S BLEEDING OUT, HE HAS TO CONCENTRATE TO HEAL, AND YOU'RE NOT HELPING THAT!
YOU'RE RIGHT.
YOU SHOULD BE FOCUSING ON KEEPING US SHADOW-CLOAKED FROM--
I SAID, YOU'RE RIGHT, PRINCESS. I AGREE WITH YOU. AND I'M STICKING UP FOR COS. WHICH MEANS THIS PROBABLY IS THE END OF THE WORLD.
...JECKIE...?
WHAT... HIT ME...?
SHHH. DON'T WORRY ABOUT IT, MY LOVE. WE GOT AWAY. YOU'RE SAFE NOW.

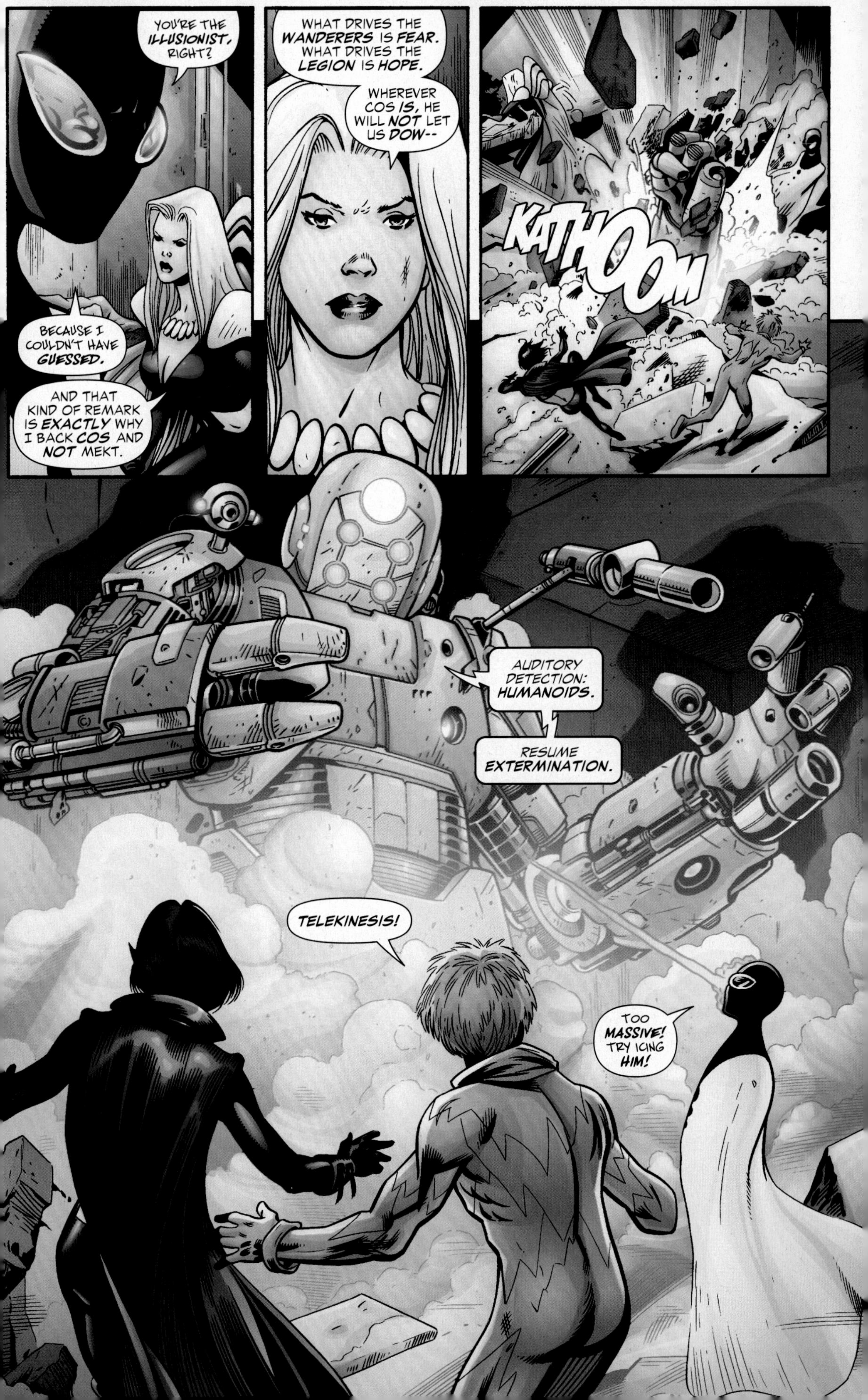
YOU'RE THE ILLUSIONIST, RIGHT?
BECAUSE I COULDN'T HAVE GUESSED.
AND THAT KIND OF REMARK IS EXACTLY WHY I BACK COS AND NOT MEKT.
WHAT DRIVES THE WANDERERS IS FEAR. WHAT DRIVES THE LEGION IS HOPE.
WHEREVER COS IS, HE WILL NOT LET US DOW--
KATHOOM
AUDITORY DETECTION: HUMANOIDS.
RESUME EXTERMINATION.
TELEKINESIS!
TOO MASSIVE! TRY ICING HIM!

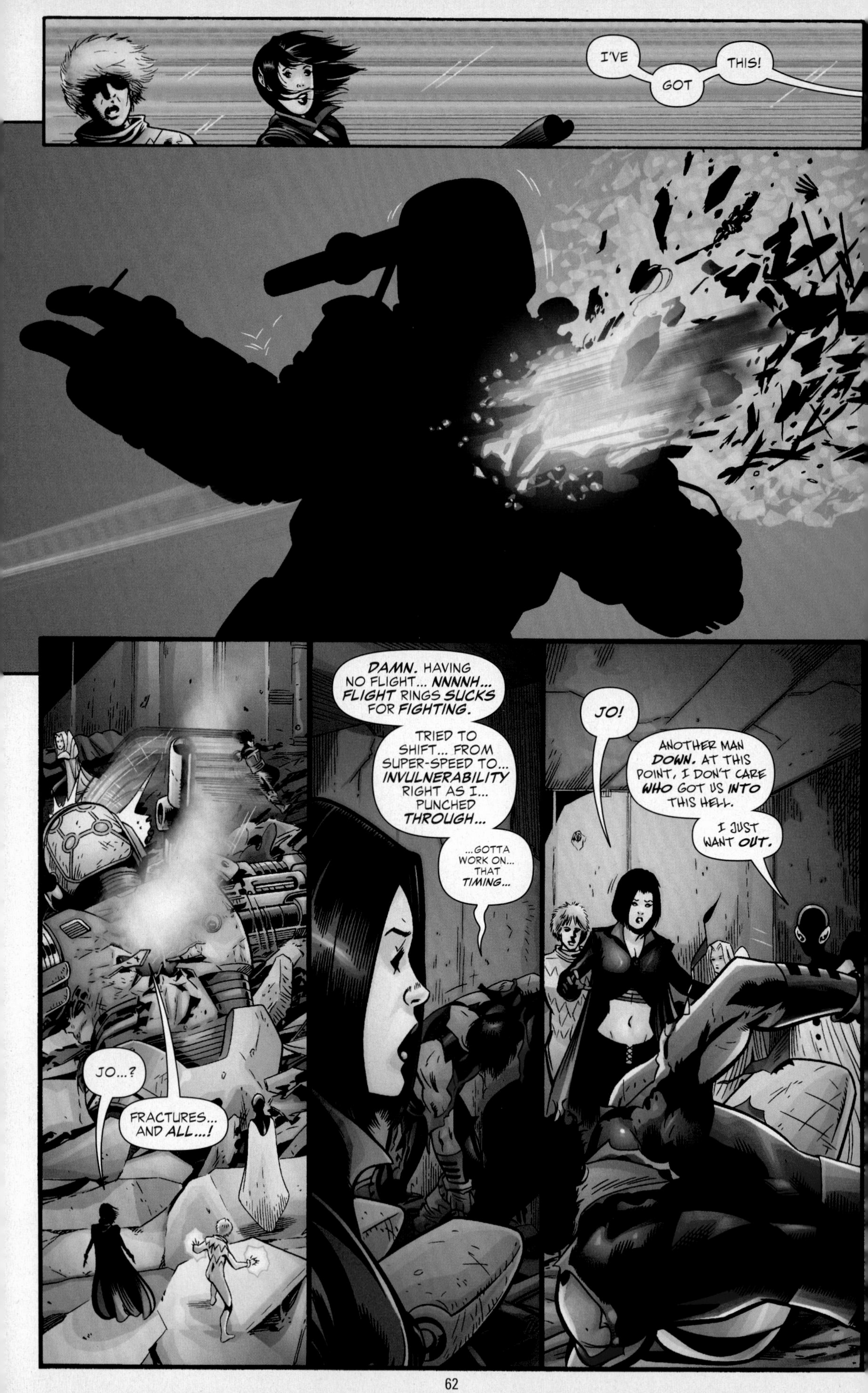

I'VE
GOT
THIS!
JO...?
FRACTURES... AND ALL...!
DAMN. HAVING NO FLIGHT... NNNNH... FLIGHT RINGS SUCKS FOR FIGHTING.
TRIED TO SHIFT... FROM SUPER-SPEED TO... INVULNERABILITY RIGHT AS I... PUNCHED THROUGH...
...GOTTA WORK ON... THAT TIMING...
JO!
ANOTHER MAN DOWN. AT THIS POINT, I DON'T CARE WHO GOT US INTO THIS HELL.
I JUST WANT OUT.

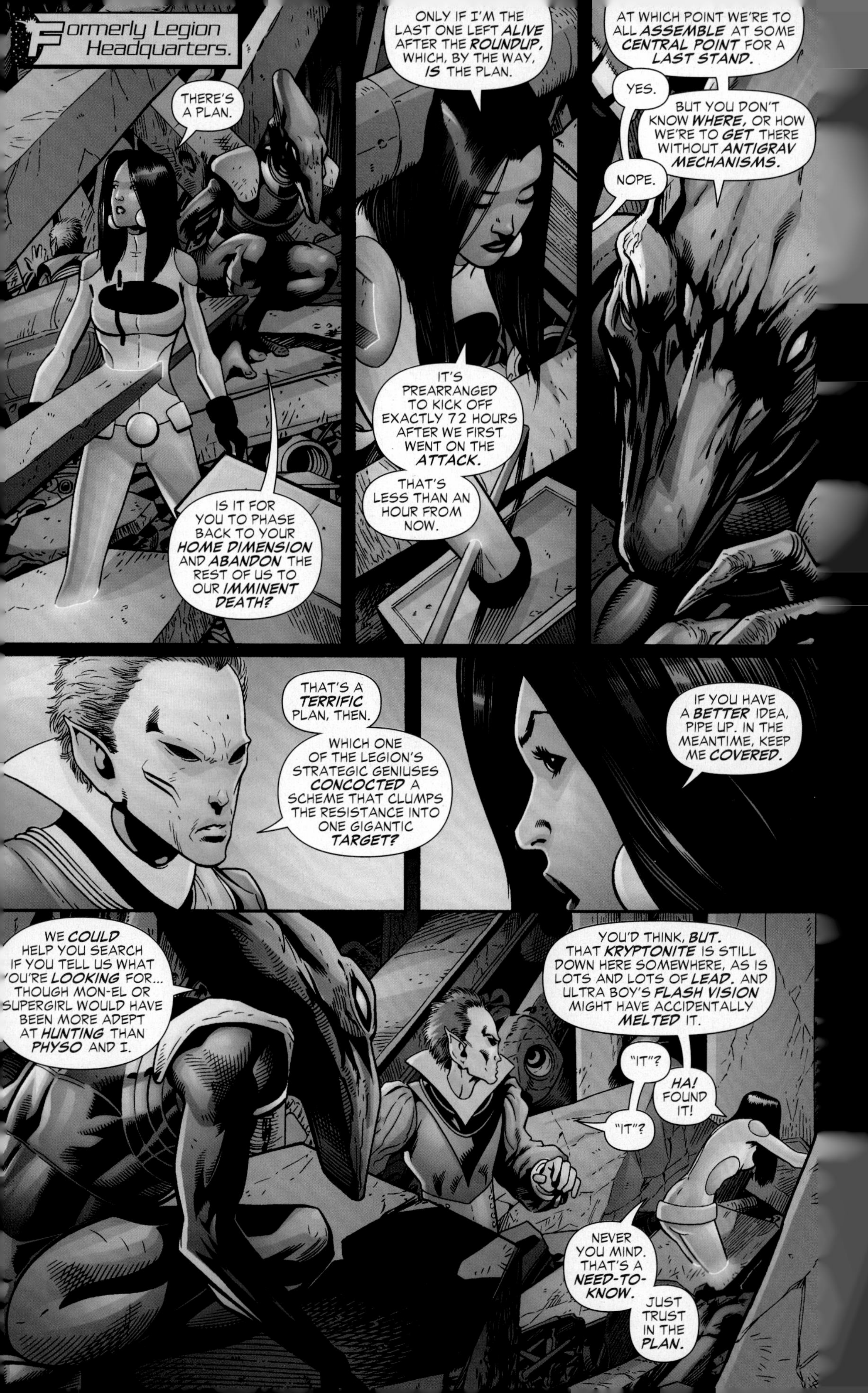
Formerly Legion Headquarters.
THERE'S A PLAN.
IS IT FOR YOU TO PHASE BACK TO YOUR HOME DIMENSION AND ABANDON THE REST OF US TO OUR IMMINENT DEATH?
ONLY IF I'M THE LAST ONE LEFT ALIVE AFTER THE ROUNDUP, WHICH, BY THE WAY, IS THE PLAN.
IT'S PREARRANGED TO KICK OFF EXACTLY 72 HOURS AFTER WE FIRST WENT ON THE ATTACK.
THAT'S LESS THAN AN HOUR FROM NOW.
AT WHICH POINT WE'RE TO ALL ASSEMBLE AT SOME CENTRAL POINT FOR A LAST STAND.
YES.
BUT YOU DON'T KNOW WHERE, OR HOW WE'RE TO GET THERE WITHOUT ANTIGRAV MECHANISMS.
NOPE.
THAT'S A TERRIFIC PLAN, THEN.
WHICH ONE OF THE LEGION'S STRATEGIC GENIUSES CONCOCTED A SCHEME THAT CLUMPS THE RESISTANCE INTO ONE GIGANTIC TARGET?
IF YOU HAVE A BETTER IDEA, PIPE UP. IN THE MEANTIME, KEEP ME COVERED.
WE COULD HELP YOU SEARCH IF YOU TELL US WHAT YOU'RE LOOKING FOR... THOUGH MON-EL OR SUPERGIRL WOULD HAVE BEEN MORE ADEPT AT HUNTING THAN PHYSO AND I.
YOU'D THINK, BUT. THAT KRYPTONITE IS STILL DOWN HERE SOMEWHERE, AS IS LOTS AND LOTS OF LEAD. AND ULTRA BOY'S FLASH VISION MIGHT HAVE ACCIDENTALLY MELTED IT.
"IT"?
"IT"?
HA! FOUND IT!
NEVER YOU MIND. THAT'S A NEED-TO-KNOW.
JUST TRUST IN THE PLAN.

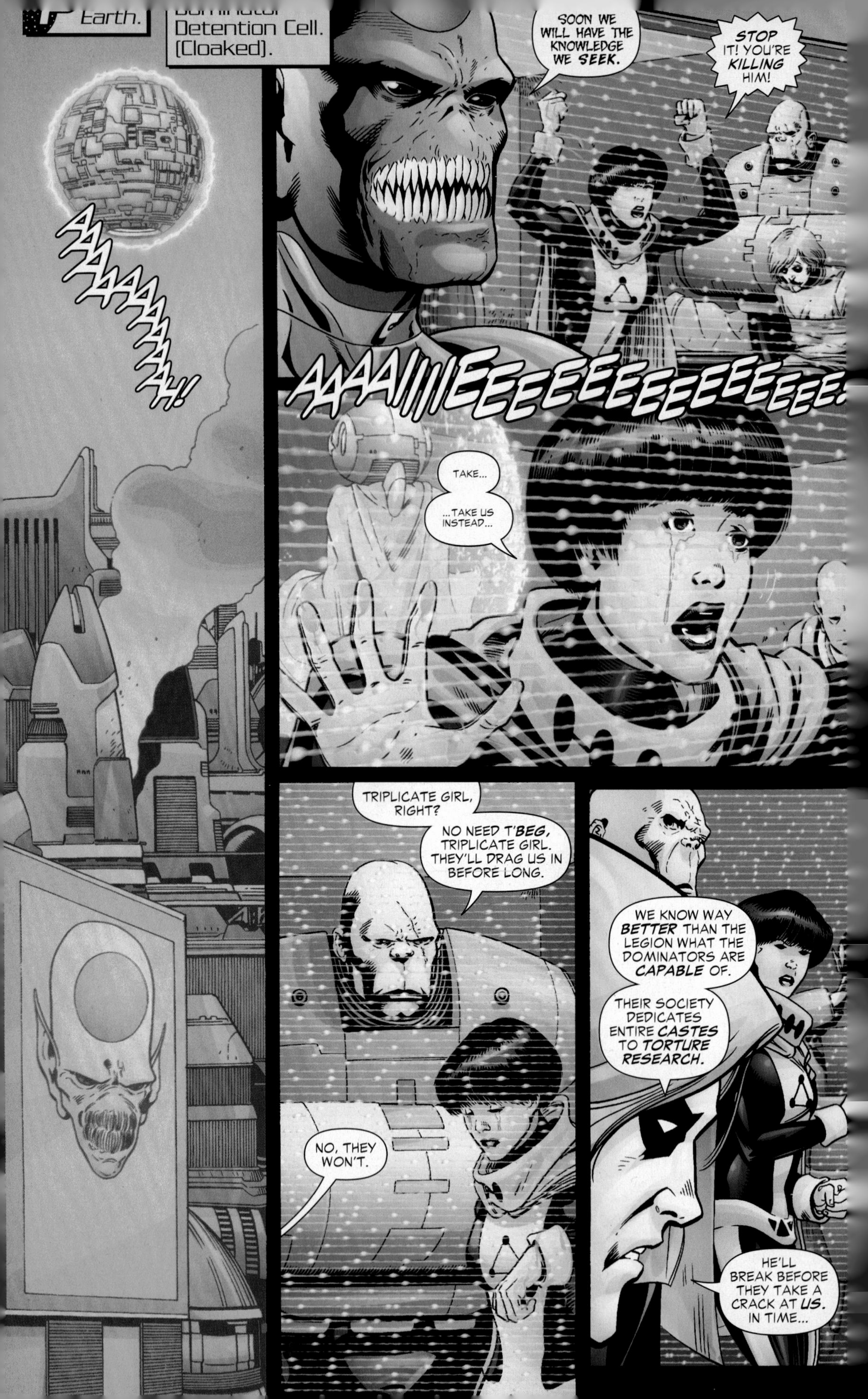
Earth.
Dominator Detention Cell. (Cloaked).
AAAAAAAAAAAAH!
SOON WE WILL HAVE THE KNOWLEDGE WE SEEK.
STOP IT! YOU'RE KILLING HIM!
AAAAIIIIIEEEEEEEEEEEEEEEE...
TAKE...
...TAKE US INSTEAD...
TRIPLICATE GIRL, RIGHT?
NO NEED T'BEG, TRIPLICATE GIRL. THEY'LL DRAG US IN BEFORE LONG.
NO, THEY WON'T.
WE KNOW WAY BETTER THAN THE LEGION WHAT THE DOMINATORS ARE CAPABLE OF.
THEIR SOCIETY DEDICATES ENTIRE CASTES TO TORTURE RESEARCH.
HE'LL BREAK BEFORE THEY TAKE A CRACK AT US. IN TIME...

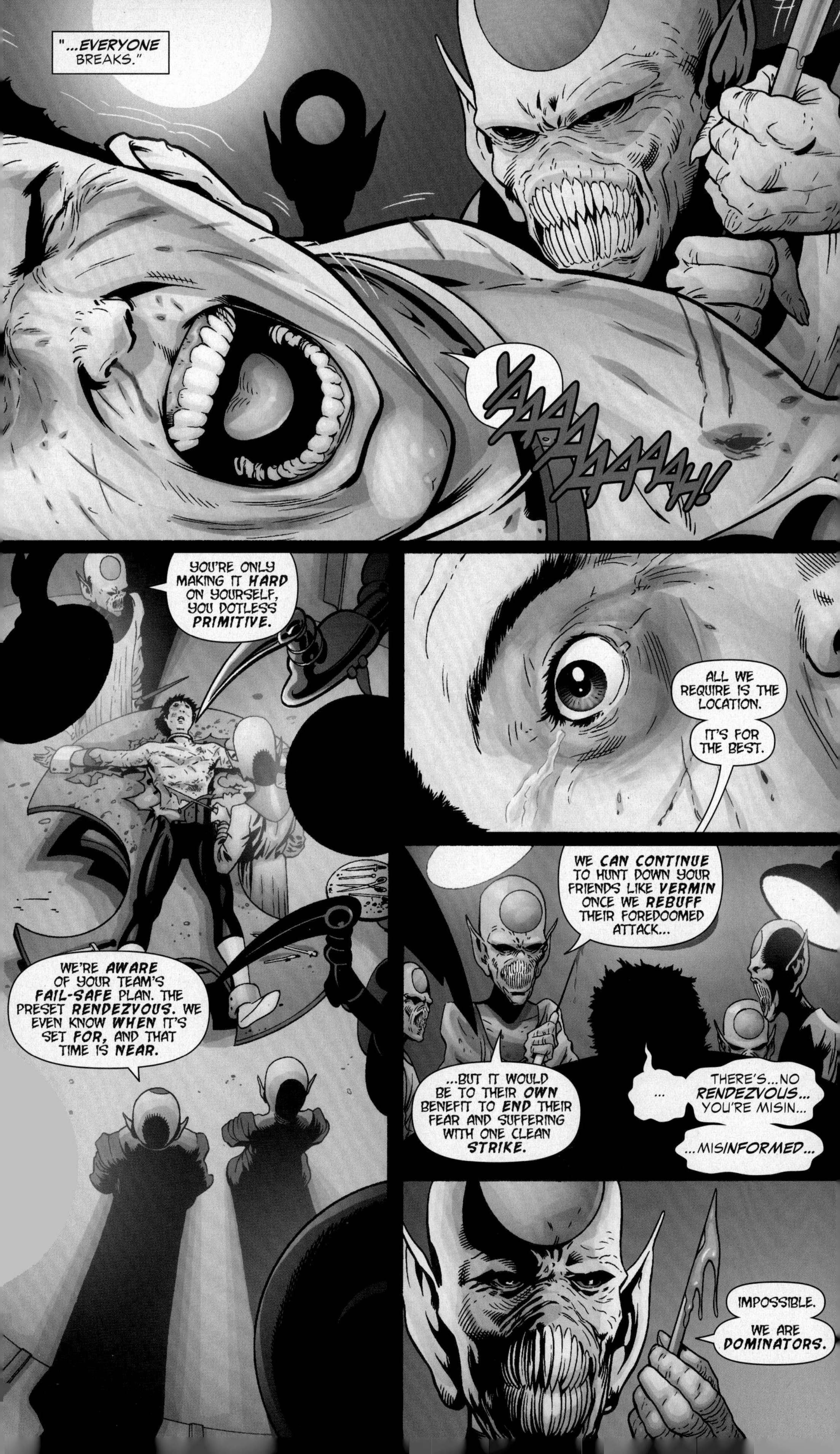
"...EVERYONE BREAKS."
YAAAAAAAAAAH!
YOU'RE ONLY MAKING IT HARD ON YOURSELF, YOU DOTLESS PRIMITIVE.
WE'RE AWARE OF YOUR TEAM'S FAIL-SAFE PLAN. THE PRESET RENDEZVOUS. WE EVEN KNOW WHEN IT'S SET FOR, AND THAT TIME IS NEAR.
ALL WE REQUIRE IS THE LOCATION.
IT'S FOR THE BEST.
WE CAN CONTINUE TO HUNT DOWN YOUR FRIENDS LIKE VERMIN ONCE WE REBUFF THEIR FOREDOOMED ATTACK...
...BUT IT WOULD BE TO THEIR OWN BENEFIT TO END THEIR FEAR AND SUFFERING WITH ONE CLEAN STRIKE.
...
THERE'S...NO RENDEZVOUS... YOU'RE MISIN...
...MISINFORMED...
IMPOSSIBLE.
WE ARE DOMINATORS.

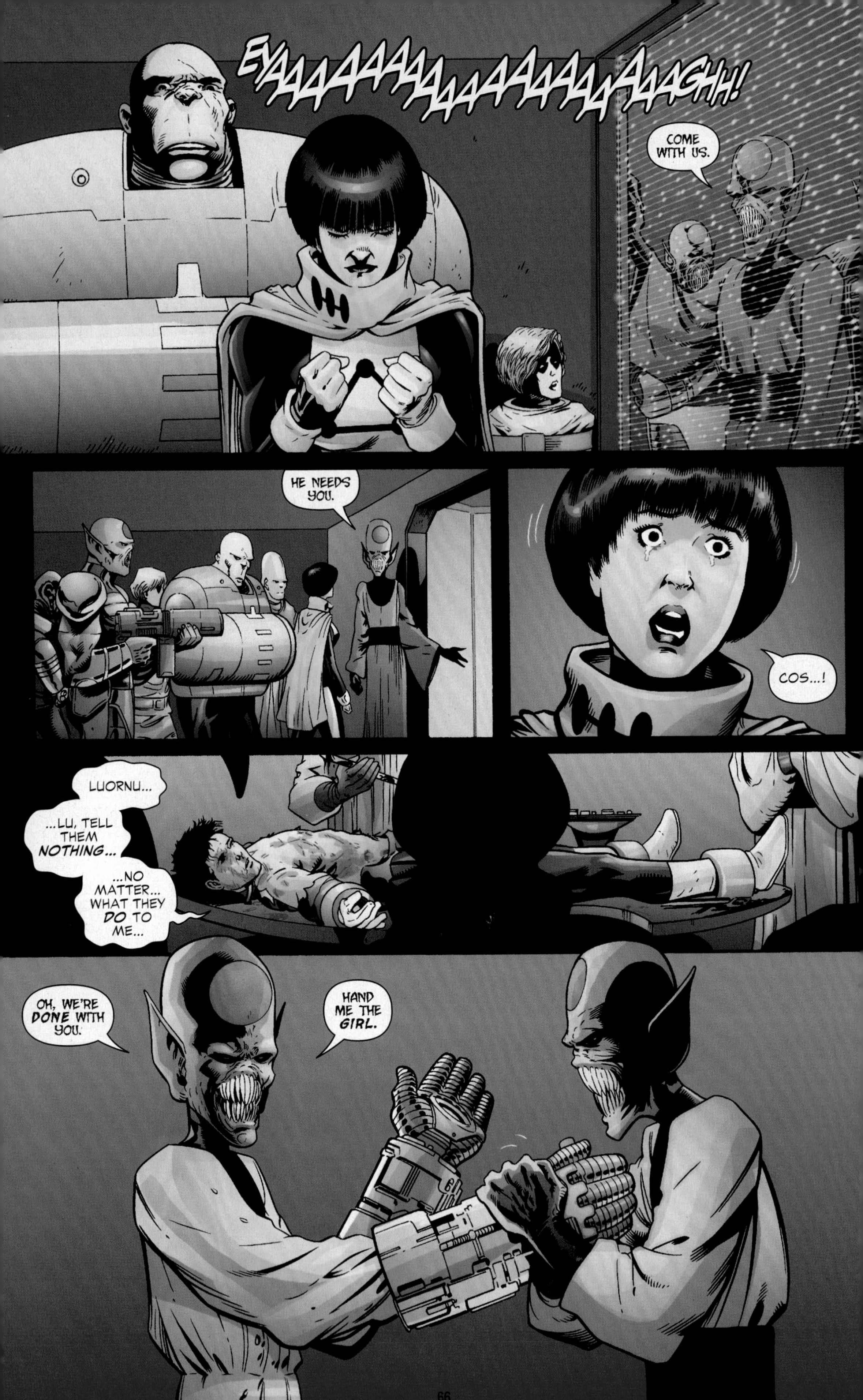
EYAAAAAAAAAAAAAAAAAAAGHH!
COME WITH US.
HE NEEDS YOU.
COS...!
LUORNU...
...LU, TELL THEM NOTHING...
...NO MATTER... WHAT THEY DO TO ME...
OH, WE'RE DONE WITH YOU.
HAND ME THE GIRL.

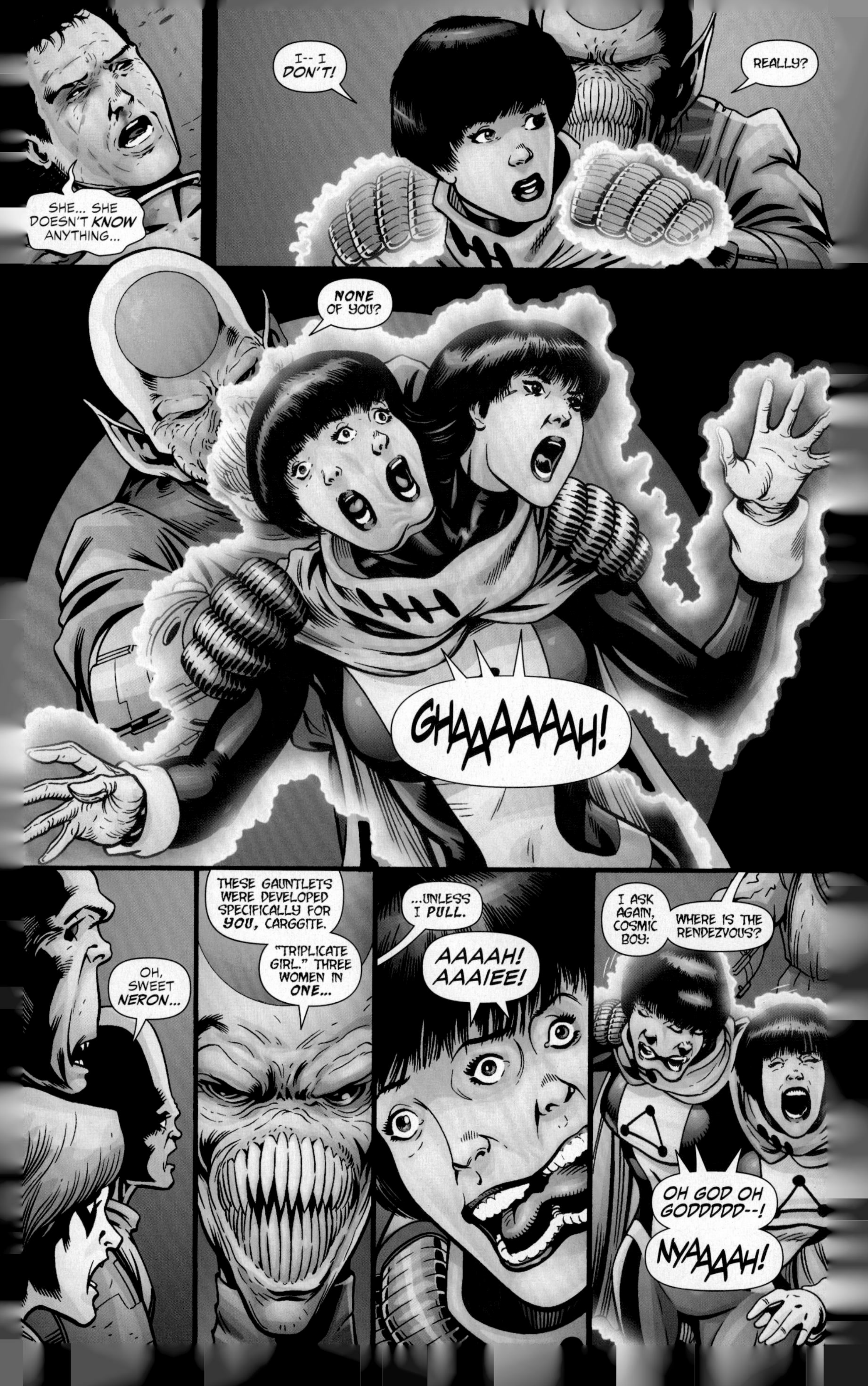
SHE... SHE DOESN'T KNOW ANYTHING...
I-- I DON'T!
REALLY?
NONE OF YOU?
GHAAAAAAH!
OH, SWEET NERON...
THESE GAUNTLETS WERE DEVELOPED SPECIFICALLY FOR YOU, CARGGITE.
"TRIPLICATE GIRL." THREE WOMEN IN ONE...
...UNLESS I PULL.
AAAAH! AAAIEE!
I ASK AGAIN, COSMIC BOY:
WHERE IS THE RENDEZVOUS?
OH GOD OH GODDDDD--!
NYAAAAH!

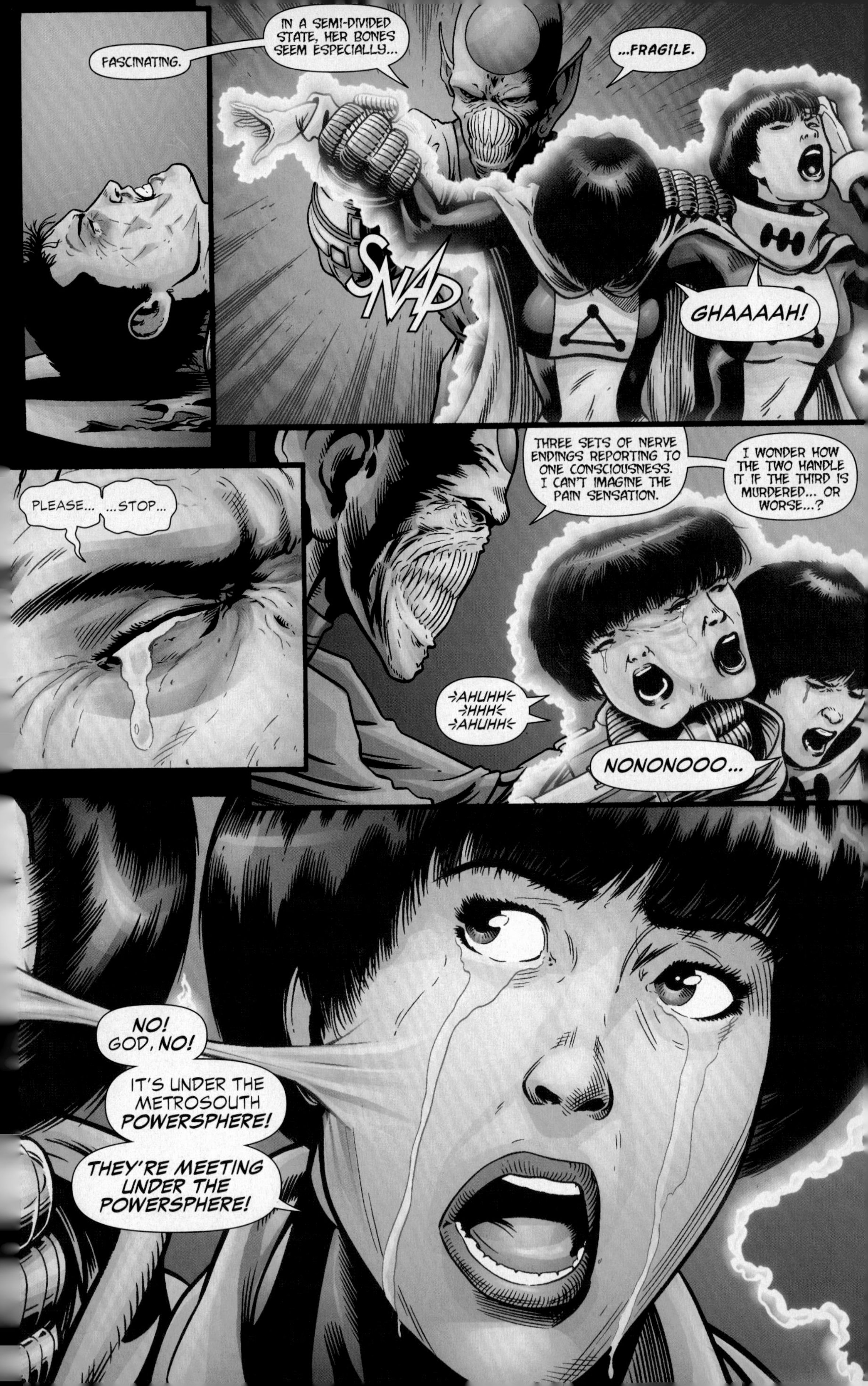
FASCINATING.
IN A SEMI-DIVIDED STATE, HER BONES SEEM ESPECIALLY...
...FRAGILE.
SNAP
GHAAAAH!
PLEASE...
...STOP...
THREE SETS OF NERVE ENDINGS REPORTING TO ONE CONSCIOUSNESS. I CAN'T IMAGINE THE PAIN SENSATION.
I WONDER HOW THE TWO HANDLE IT IF THE THIRD IS MURDERED... OR WORSE...?
AHUHH HHH AHUHH
NONONOOO...
NO! GOD, NO!
IT'S UNDER THE METROSOUTH POWERSPHERE!
THEY'RE MEETING UNDER THE POWERSPHERE!

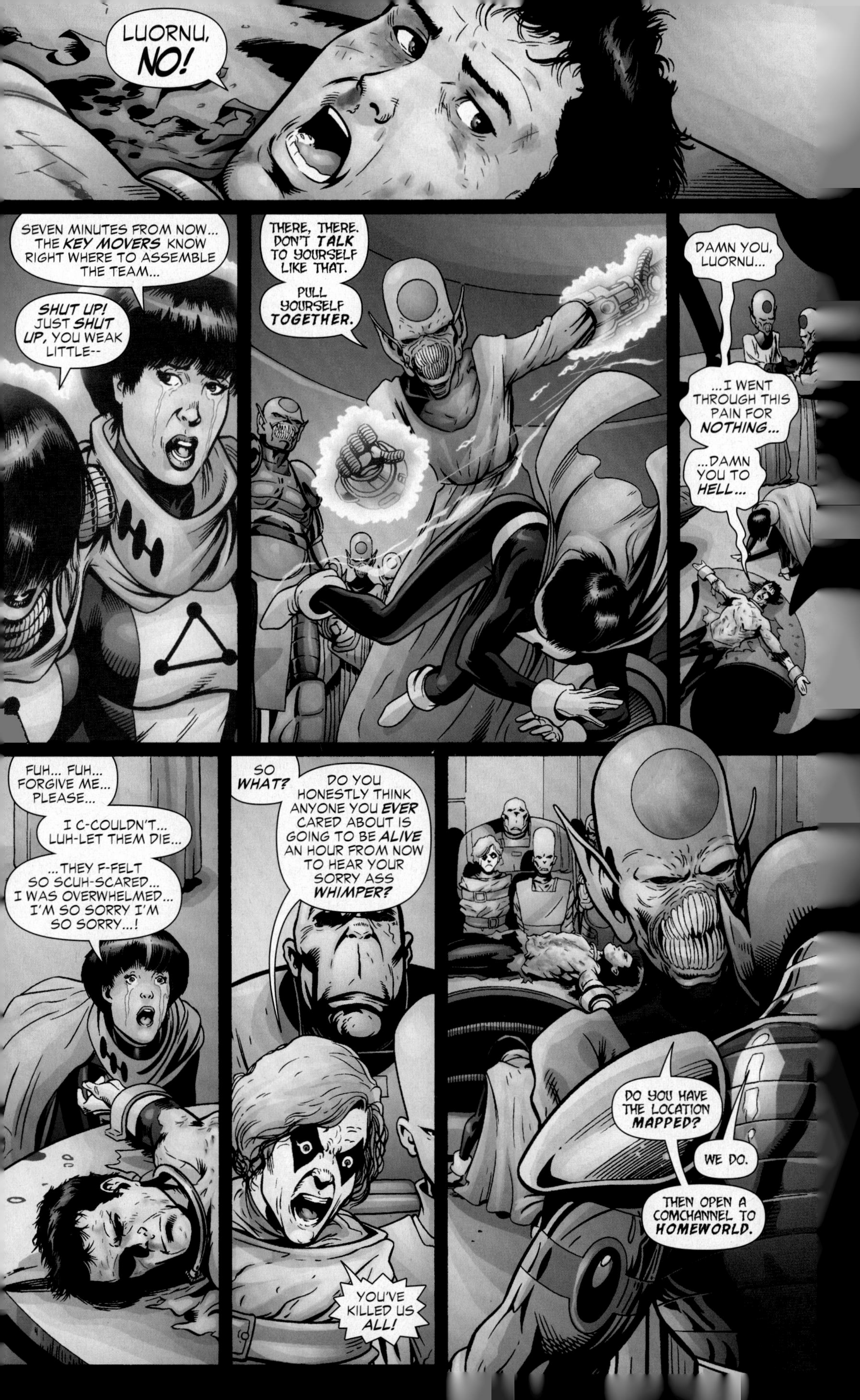
LUORNU, NO!
SEVEN MINUTES FROM NOW... THE KEY MOVERS KNOW RIGHT WHERE TO ASSEMBLE THE TEAM...
SHUT UP! JUST SHUT UP, YOU WEAK LITTLE--
THERE, THERE. DON'T TALK TO YOURSELF LIKE THAT.
PULL YOURSELF TOGETHER.
DAMN YOU, LUORNU...
...I WENT THROUGH THIS PAIN FOR NOTHING...
...DAMN YOU TO HELL...
FUH... FUH... FORGIVE ME... PLEASE...
I C-COULDN'T... LUH-LET THEM DIE...
...THEY F-FELT SO SCUH-SCARED... I WAS OVERWHELMED... I'M SO SORRY I'M SO SORRY...!
SO WHAT?
DO YOU HONESTLY THINK ANYONE YOU EVER CARED ABOUT IS GOING TO BE ALIVE AN HOUR FROM NOW TO HEAR YOUR SORRY ASS WHIMPER?
YOU'VE KILLED US ALL!
DO YOU HAVE THE LOCATION MAPPED?
WE DO.
THEN OPEN A COMCHANNEL TO HOMEWORLD.

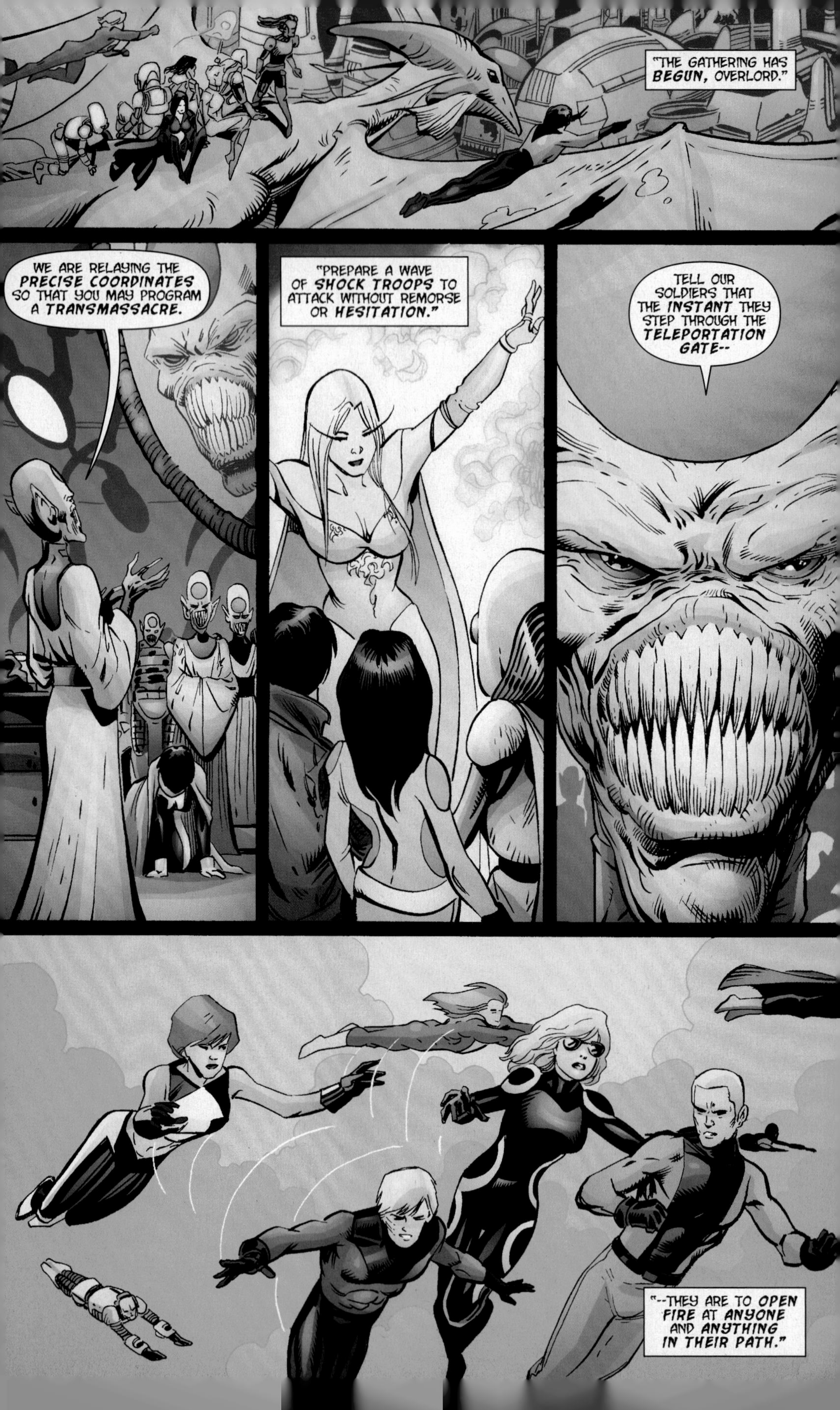
"THE GATHERING HAS BEGUN, OVERLORD."
WE ARE RELAYING THE PRECISE COORDINATES SO THAT YOU MAY PROGRAM A TRANSMASSACRE.
"PREPARE A WAVE OF SHOCK TROOPS TO ATTACK WITHOUT REMORSE OR HESITATION."
TELL OUR SOLDIERS THAT THE INSTANT THEY STEP THROUGH THE TELEPORTATION GATE--
"--THEY ARE TO OPEN FIRE AT ANYONE AND ANYTHING IN THEIR PATH."

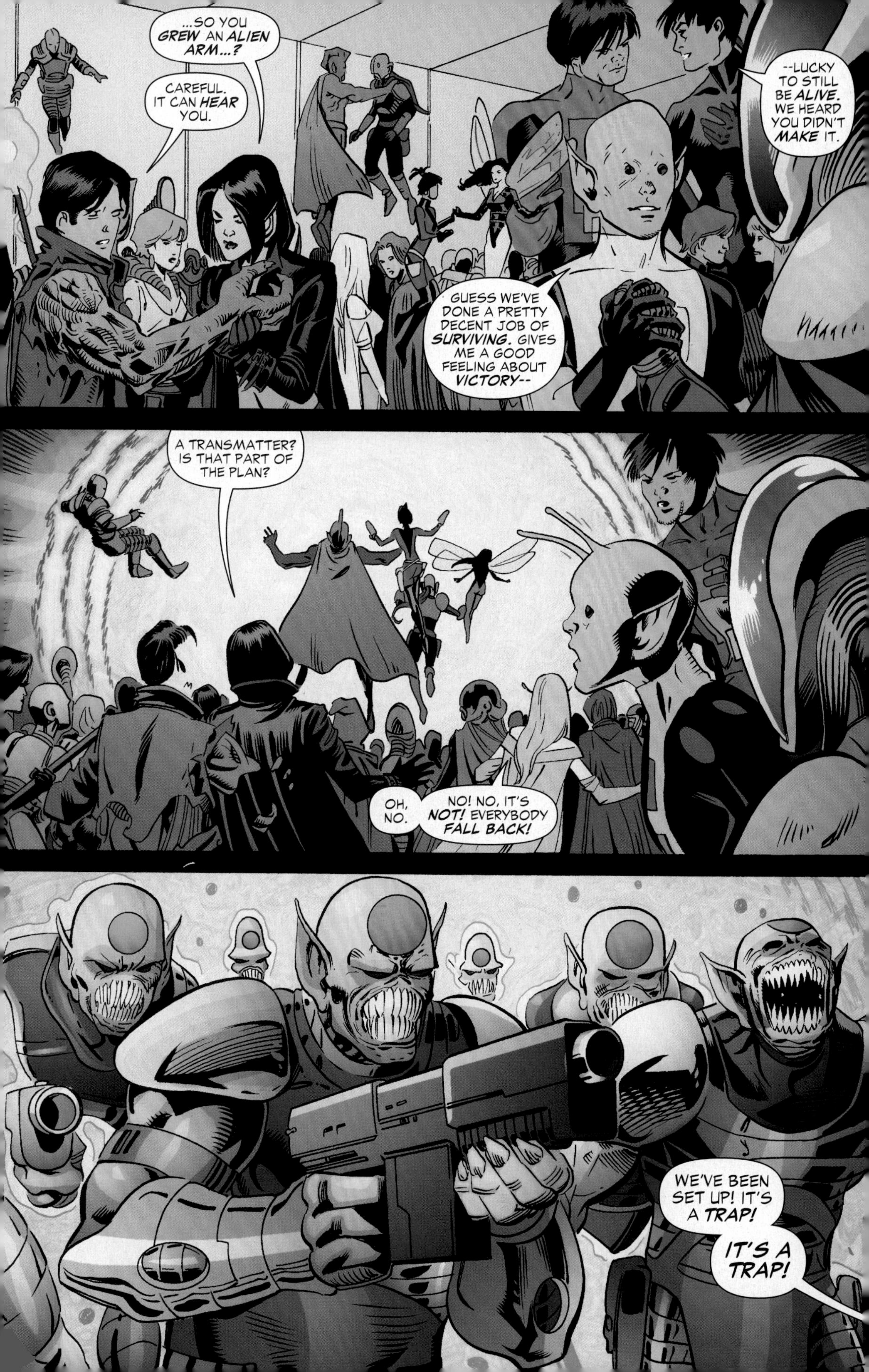
...SO YOU GREW AN ALIEN ARM...?
CAREFUL. IT CAN HEAR YOU.
--LUCKY TO STILL BE ALIVE. WE HEARD YOU DIDN'T MAKE IT.
GUESS WE'VE DONE A PRETTY DECENT JOB OF SURVIVING. GIVES ME A GOOD FEELING ABOUT VICTORY--
A TRANSMATTER? IS THAT PART OF THE PLAN?
OH, NO.
NO! NO, IT'S NOT! EVERYBODY FALL BACK!
WE'VE BEEN SET UP! IT'S A TRAP!
IT'S A TRAP!

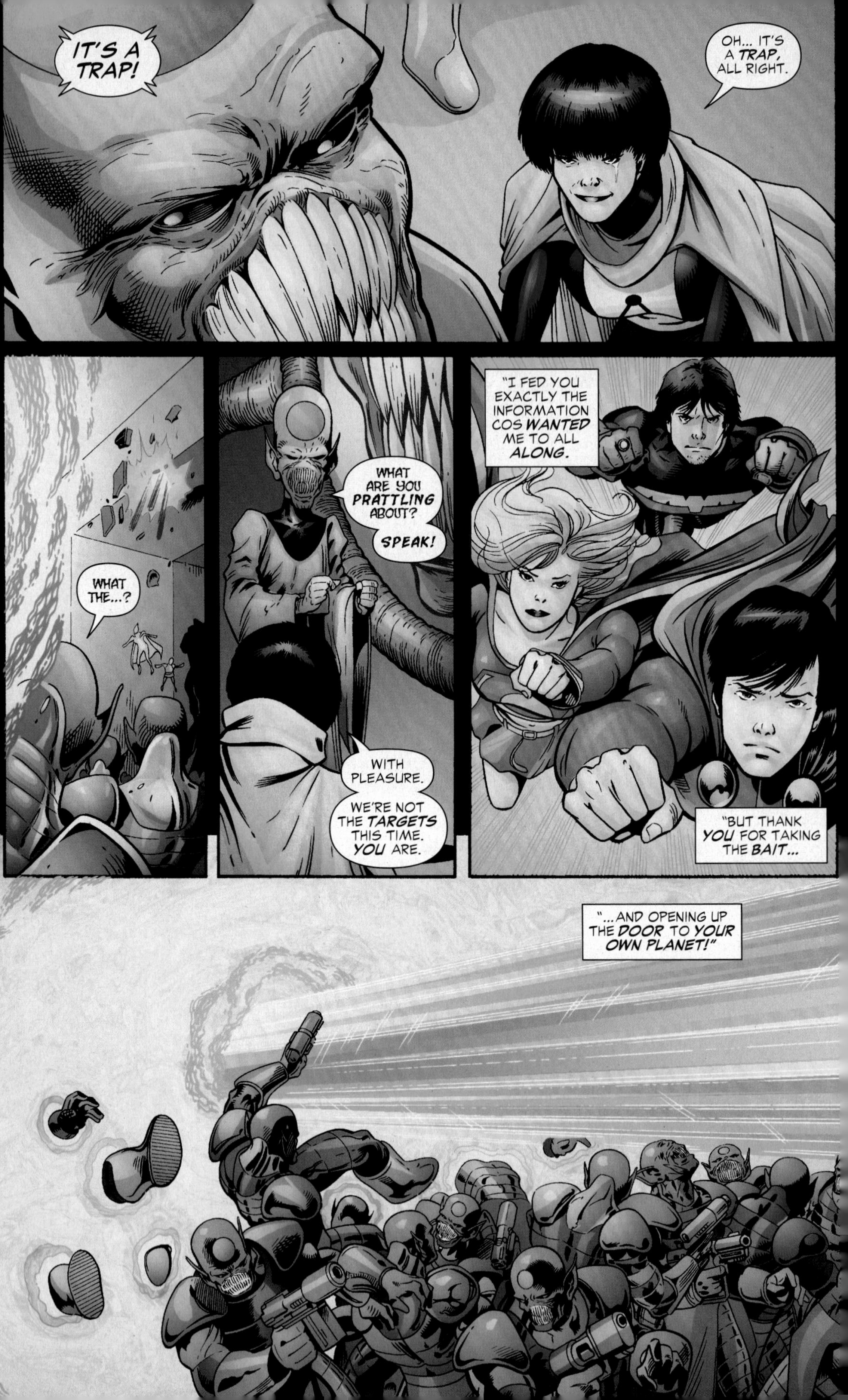
IT'S A TRAP!
OH... IT'S A TRAP, ALL RIGHT.
WHAT THE...?
WHAT ARE YOU PRATTLING ABOUT?
SPEAK!
WITH PLEASURE.
WE'RE NOT THE TARGETS THIS TIME. YOU ARE.
"I FED YOU EXACTLY THE INFORMATION COS WANTED ME TO ALL ALONG.
"BUT THANK YOU FOR TAKING THE BAIT...
"...AND OPENING UP THE DOOR TO YOUR OWN PLANET!"

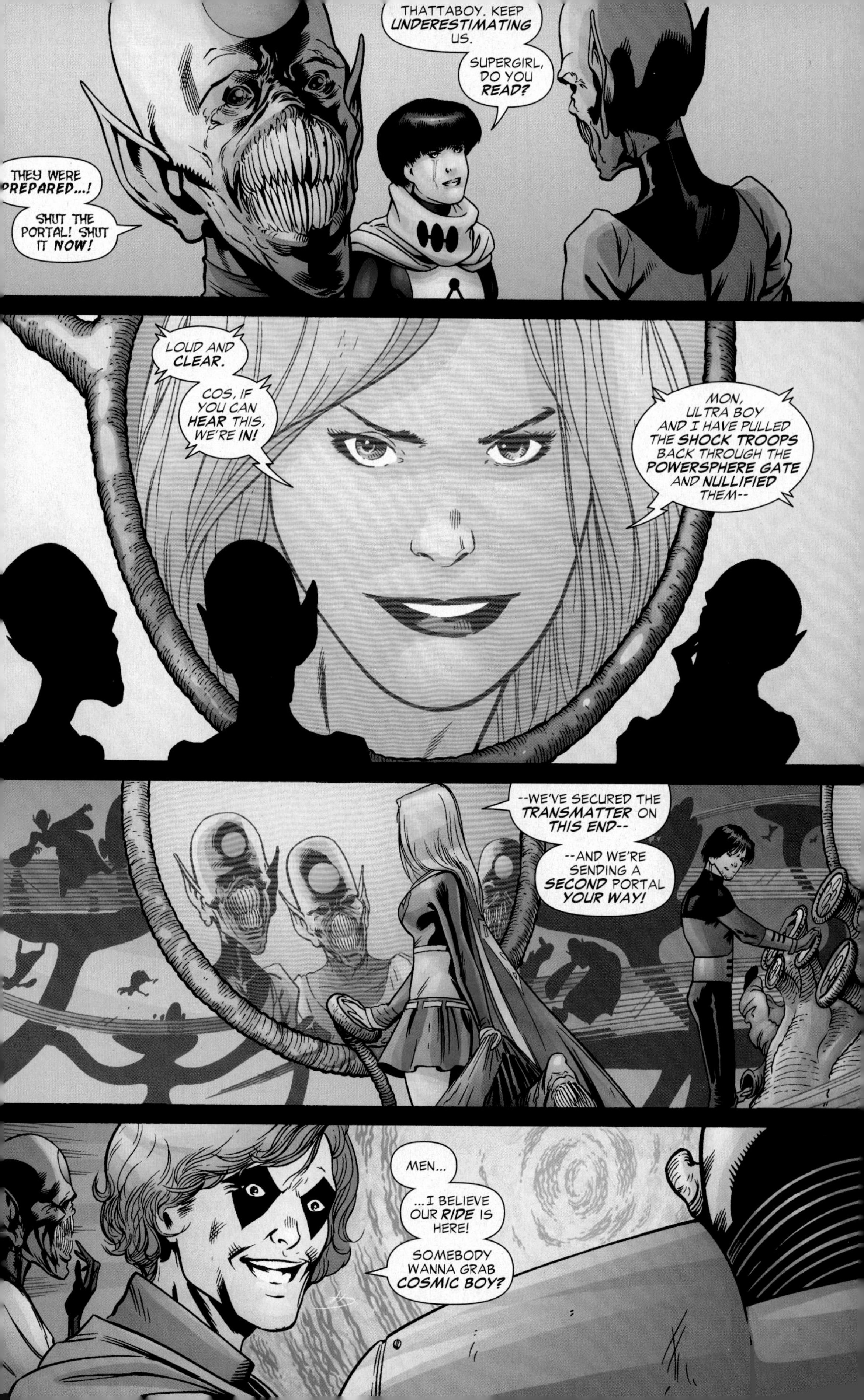
THATTABOY. KEEP UNDERESTIMATING US.
SUPERGIRL, DO YOU READ?
THEY WERE PREPARED...!
SHUT THE PORTAL! SHUT IT NOW!
LOUD AND CLEAR.
COS, IF YOU CAN HEAR THIS, WE'RE IN!
MON, ULTRA BOY AND I HAVE PULLED THE SHOCK TROOPS BACK THROUGH THE POWERSPHERE GATE AND NULLIFIED THEM--
--WE'VE SECURED THE TRANSMATTER ON THIS END--
--AND WE'RE SENDING A SECOND PORTAL YOUR WAY!
MEN...
...I BELIEVE OUR RIDE IS HERE!
SOMEBODY WANNA GRAB COSMIC BOY?

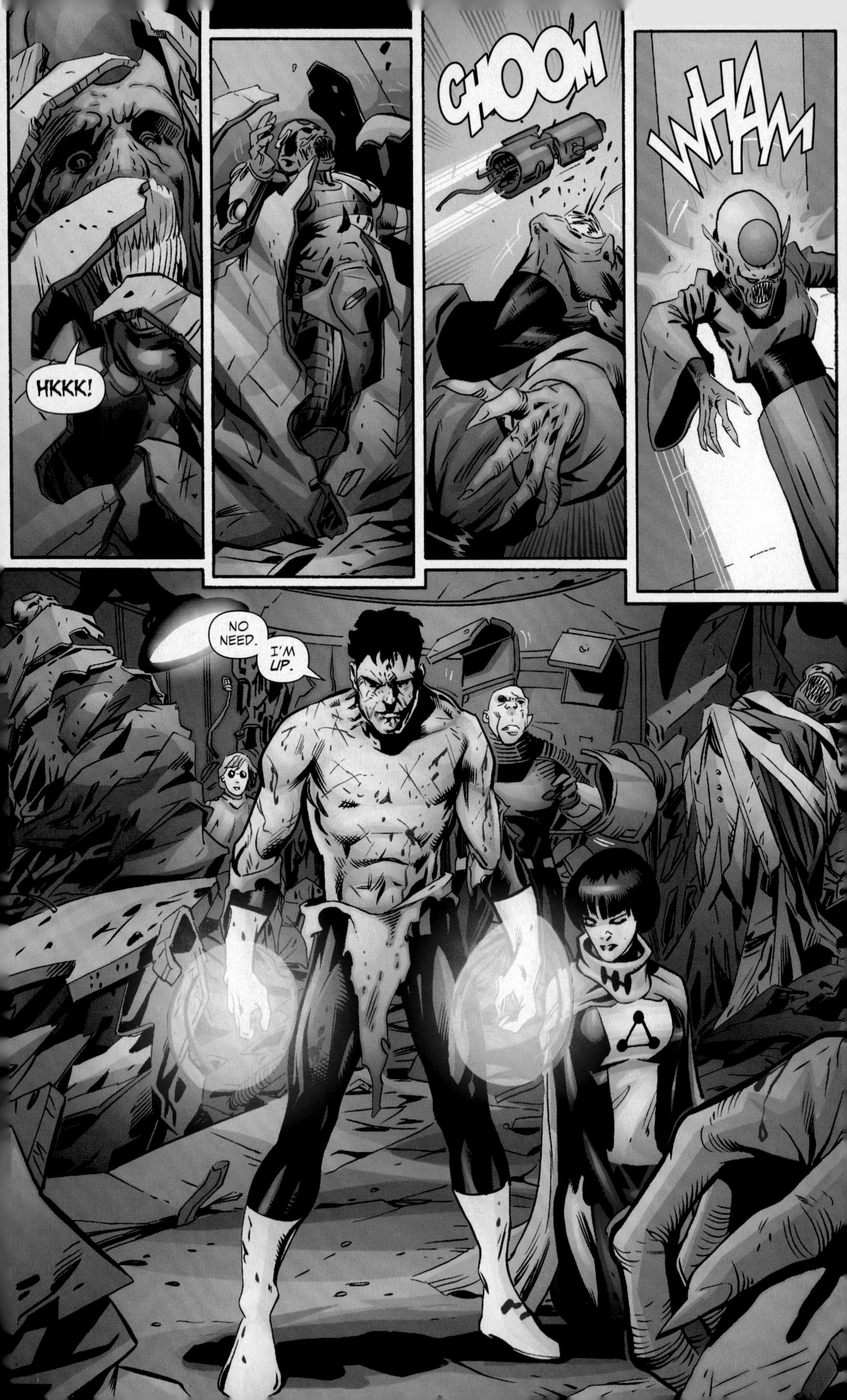
HKKK!
CHOOM
WHAM
NO NEED.
I'M UP.

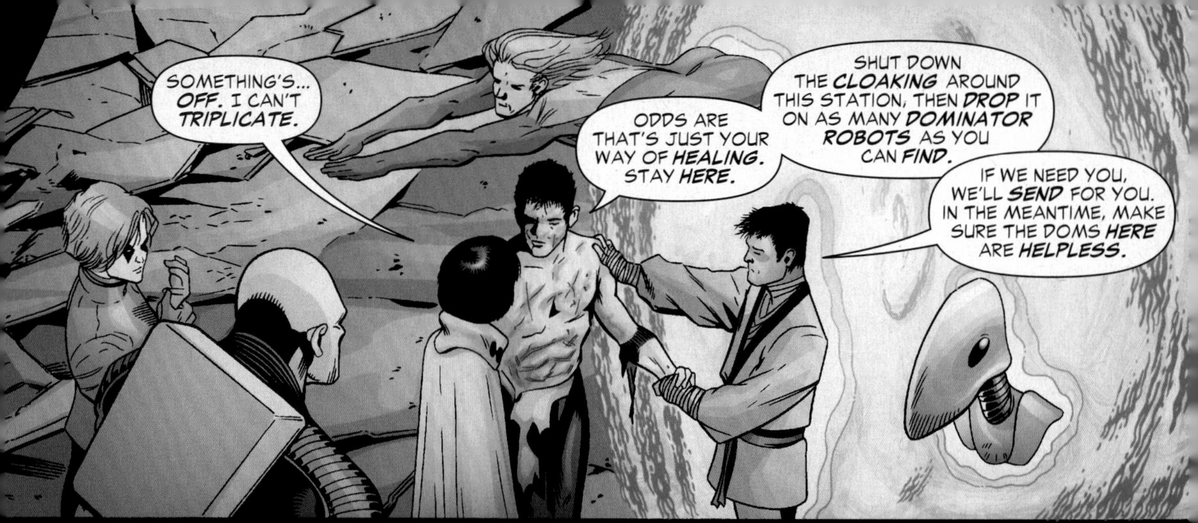
SOMETHING'S... OFF. I CAN'T TRIPLICATE.
SHUT DOWN THE CLOAKING AROUND THIS STATION, THEN DROP IT ON AS MANY DOMINATOR ROBOTS AS YOU CAN FIND.
ODDS ARE THAT'S JUST YOUR WAY OF HEALING. STAY HERE.
IF WE NEED YOU, WE'LL SEND FOR YOU. IN THE MEANTIME, MAKE SURE THE DOMS HERE ARE HELPLESS.

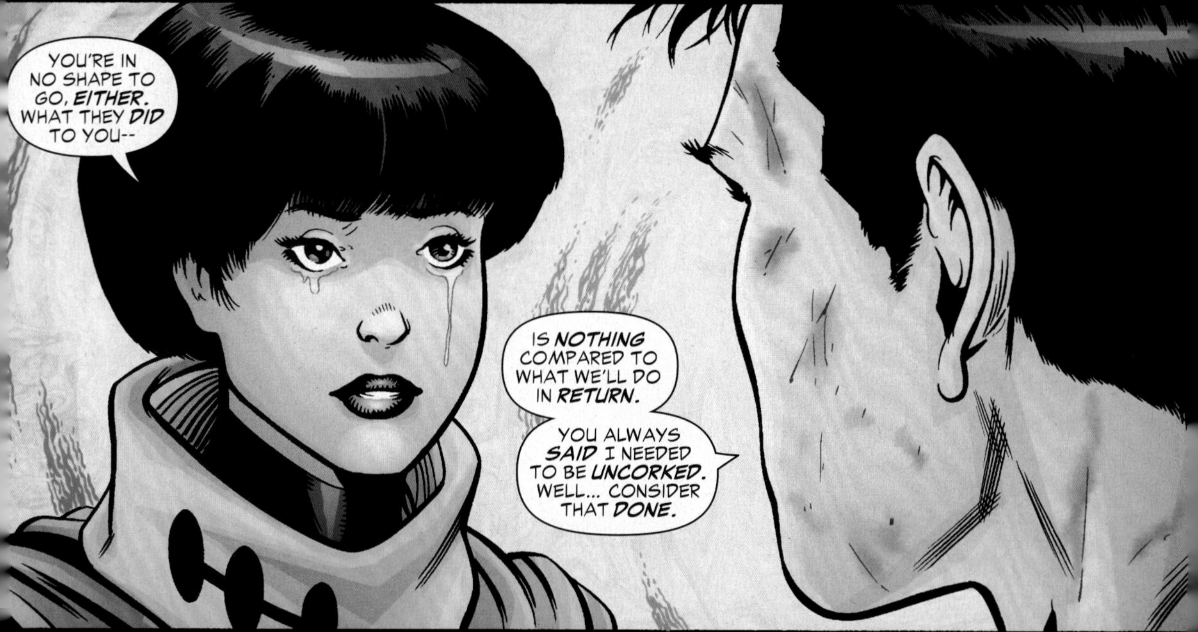
YOU'RE IN NO SHAPE TO GO, EITHER. WHAT THEY DID TO YOU--
IS NOTHING COMPARED TO WHAT WE'LL DO IN RETURN.
YOU ALWAYS SAID I NEEDED TO BE UNCORKED. WELL... CONSIDER THAT DONE.

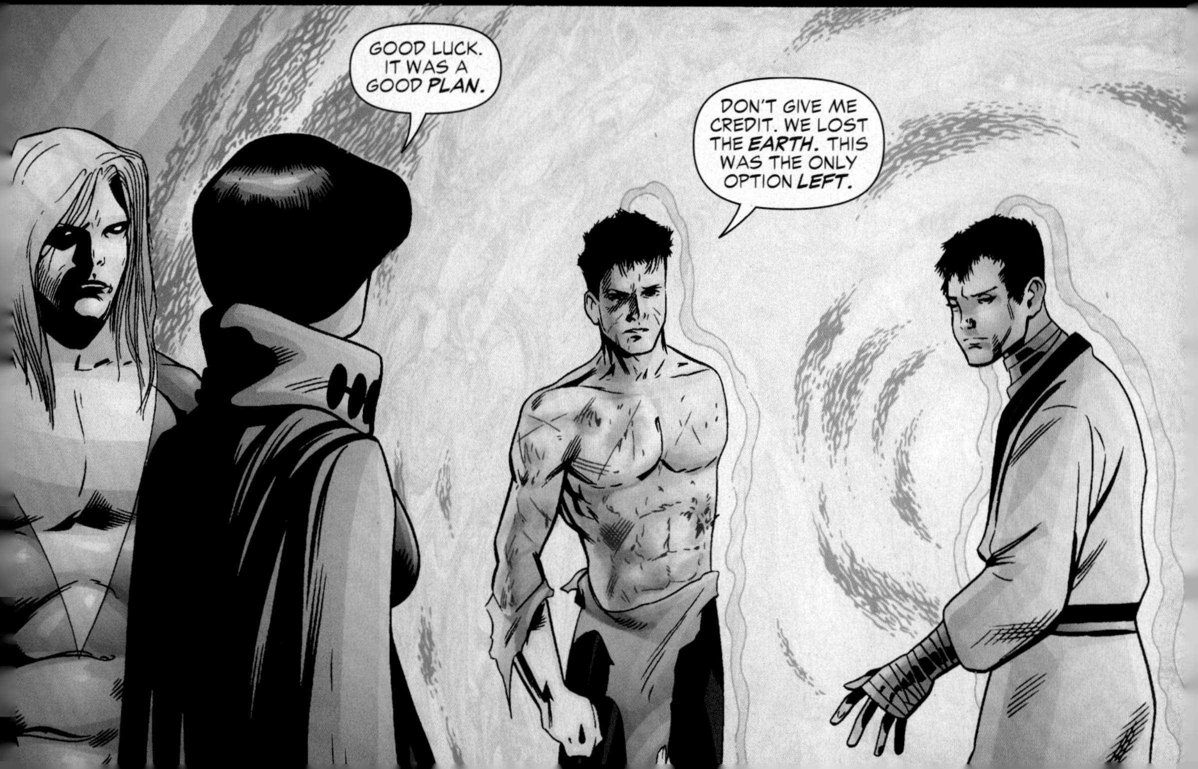
GOOD LUCK. IT WAS A GOOD PLAN.
DON'T GIVE ME CREDIT. WE LOST THE EARTH. THIS WAS THE ONLY OPTION LEFT.

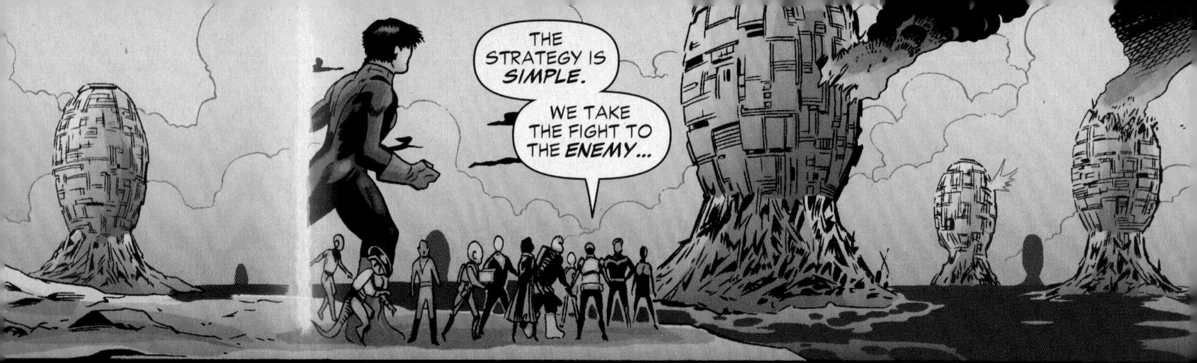
THE STRATEGY IS SIMPLE.
WE TAKE THE FIGHT TO THE ENEMY...

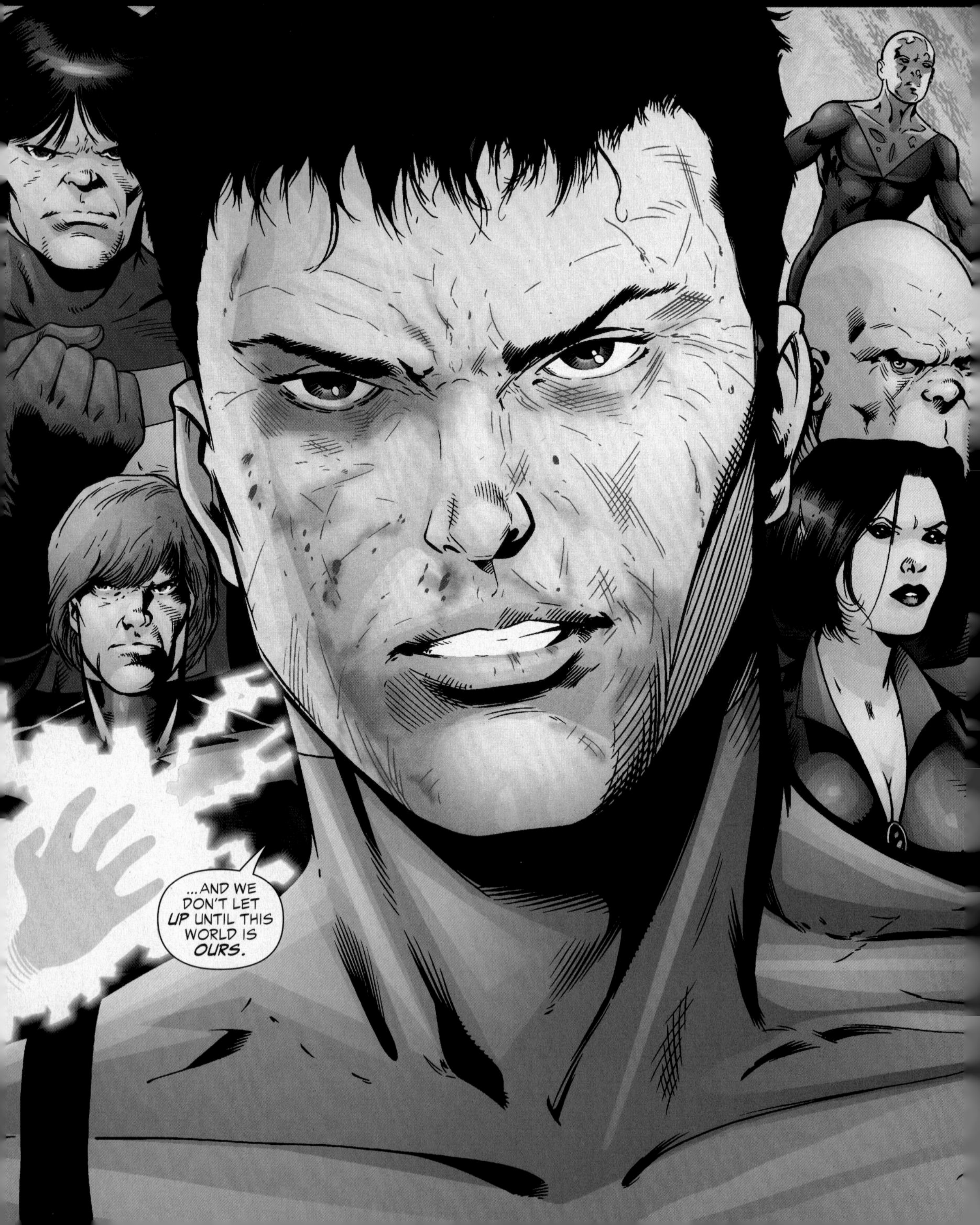
...AND WE DON'T LET UP UNTIL THIS WORLD IS OURS.

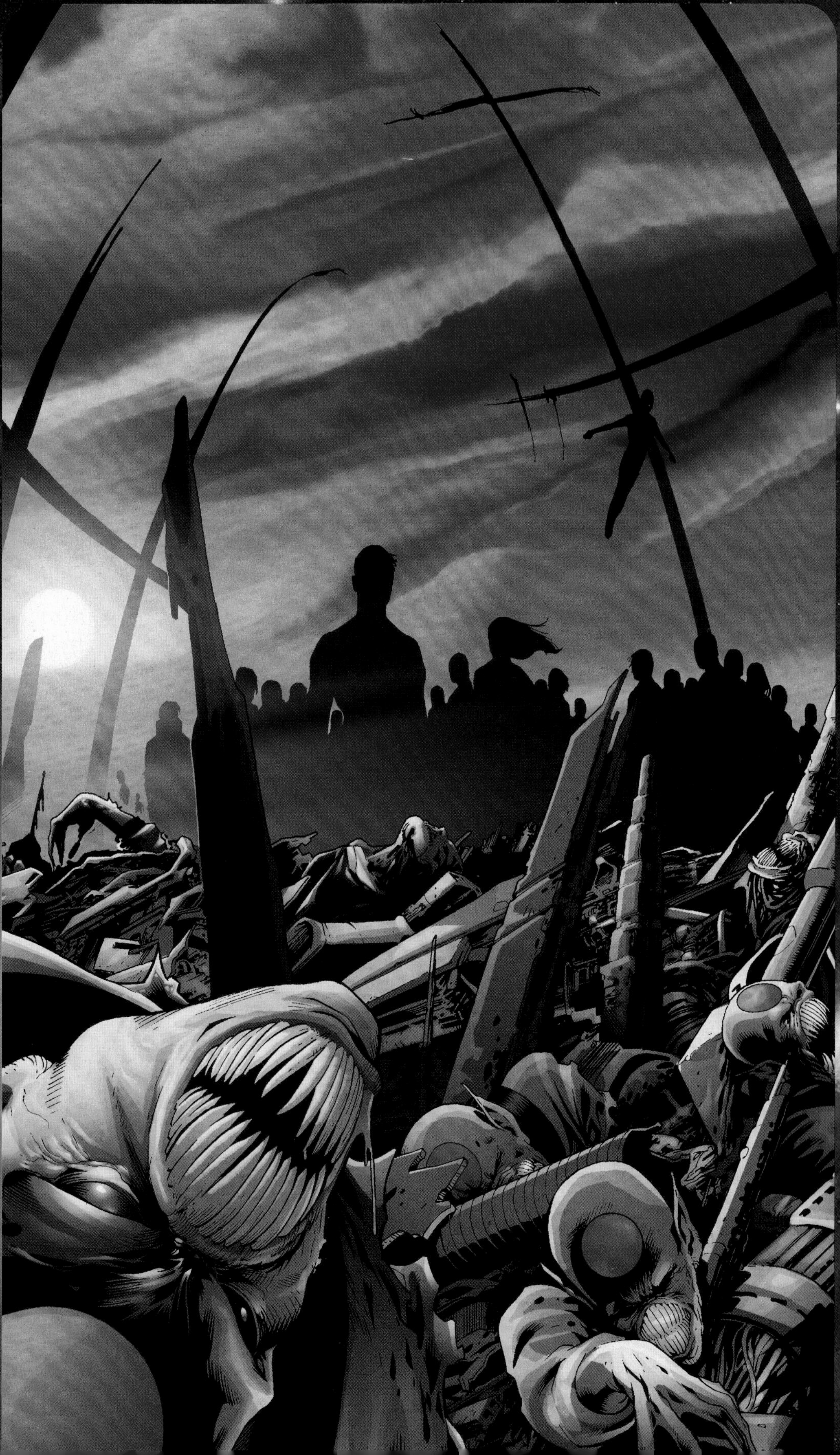

CHAPTER 4

Tony Bedard Writer
Kevin Sharpe Penciller
Mark McKenna & **Jack Purcell** Inkers
Barry Kitson & **Nathan Eyring** Cover

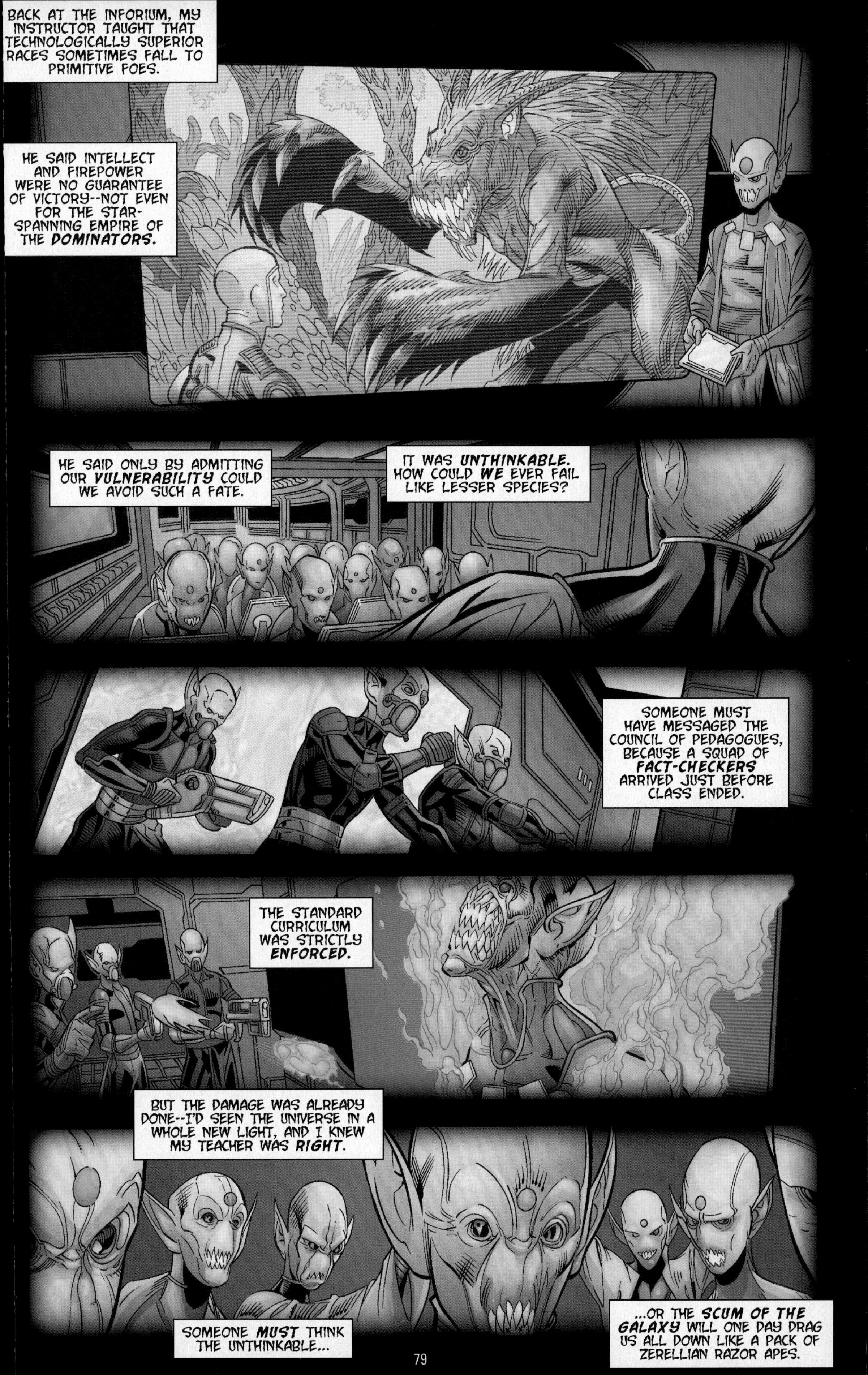
BACK AT THE INFORIUM, MY INSTRUCTOR TAUGHT THAT TECHNOLOGICALLY SUPERIOR RACES SOMETIMES FALL TO PRIMITIVE FOES.
HE SAID INTELLECT AND FIREPOWER WERE NO GUARANTEE OF VICTORY--NOT EVEN FOR THE STAR-SPANNING EMPIRE OF THE *DOMINATORS*.
HE SAID ONLY BY ADMITTING OUR *VULNERABILITY* COULD WE AVOID SUCH A FATE.
IT WAS *UNTHINKABLE*. HOW COULD *WE* EVER FAIL LIKE LESSER SPECIES?
SOMEONE MUST HAVE MESSAGED THE COUNCIL OF PEDAGOGUES, BECAUSE A SQUAD OF *FACT-CHECKERS* ARRIVED JUST BEFORE CLASS ENDED.
THE STANDARD CURRICULUM WAS STRICTLY *ENFORCED*.
BUT THE DAMAGE WAS ALREADY DONE--I'D SEEN THE UNIVERSE IN A WHOLE NEW LIGHT, AND I KNEW MY TEACHER WAS *RIGHT*.
SOMEONE *MUST* THINK THE UNTHINKABLE...
...OR THE *SCUM OF THE GALAXY* WILL ONE DAY DRAG US ALL DOWN LIKE A PACK OF ZERELLIAN RAZOR APES.

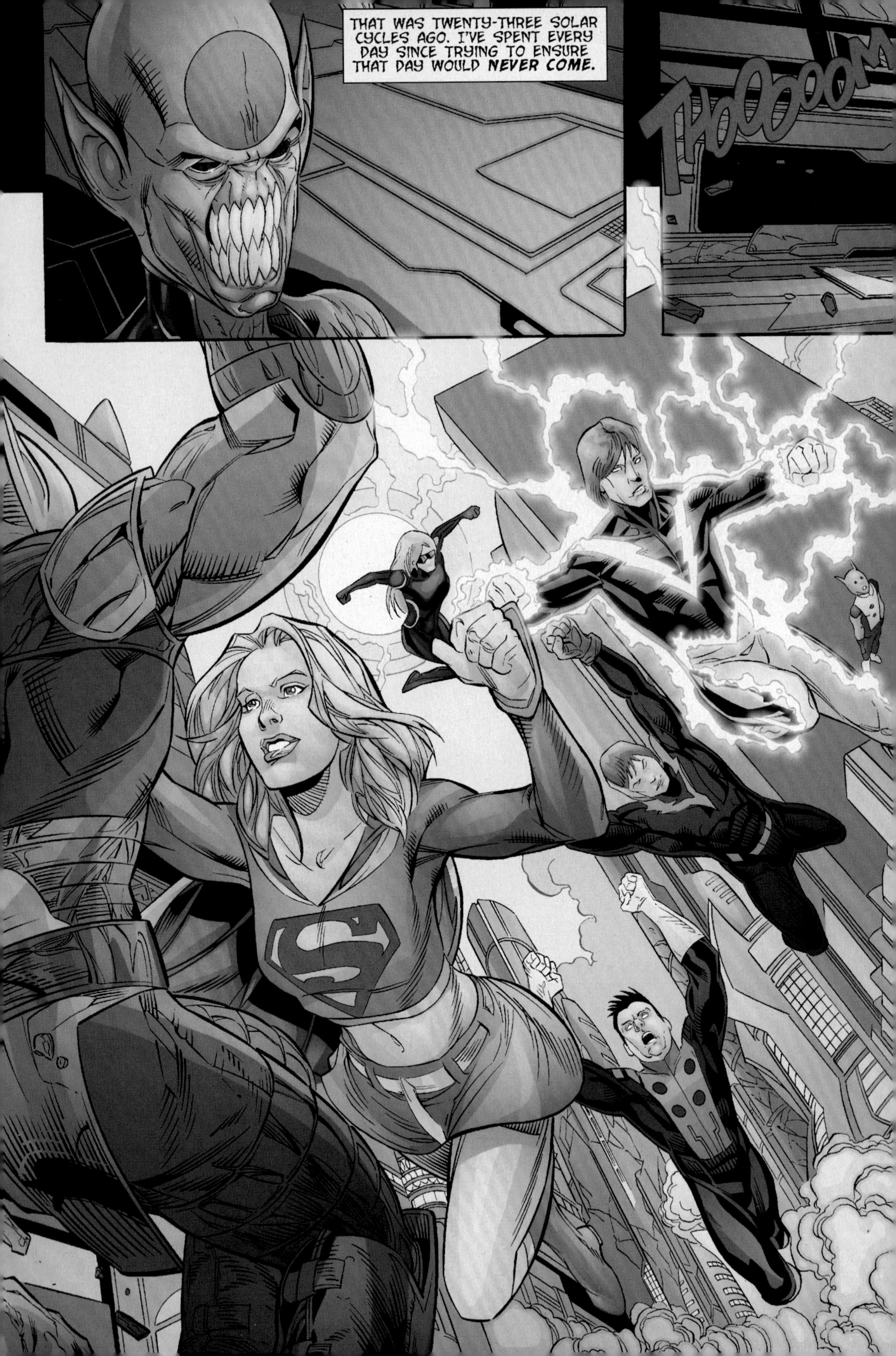

THAT WAS TWENTY-THREE SOLAR CYCLES AGO. I'VE SPENT EVERY DAY SINCE TRYING TO ENSURE THAT DAY WOULD NEVER COME.

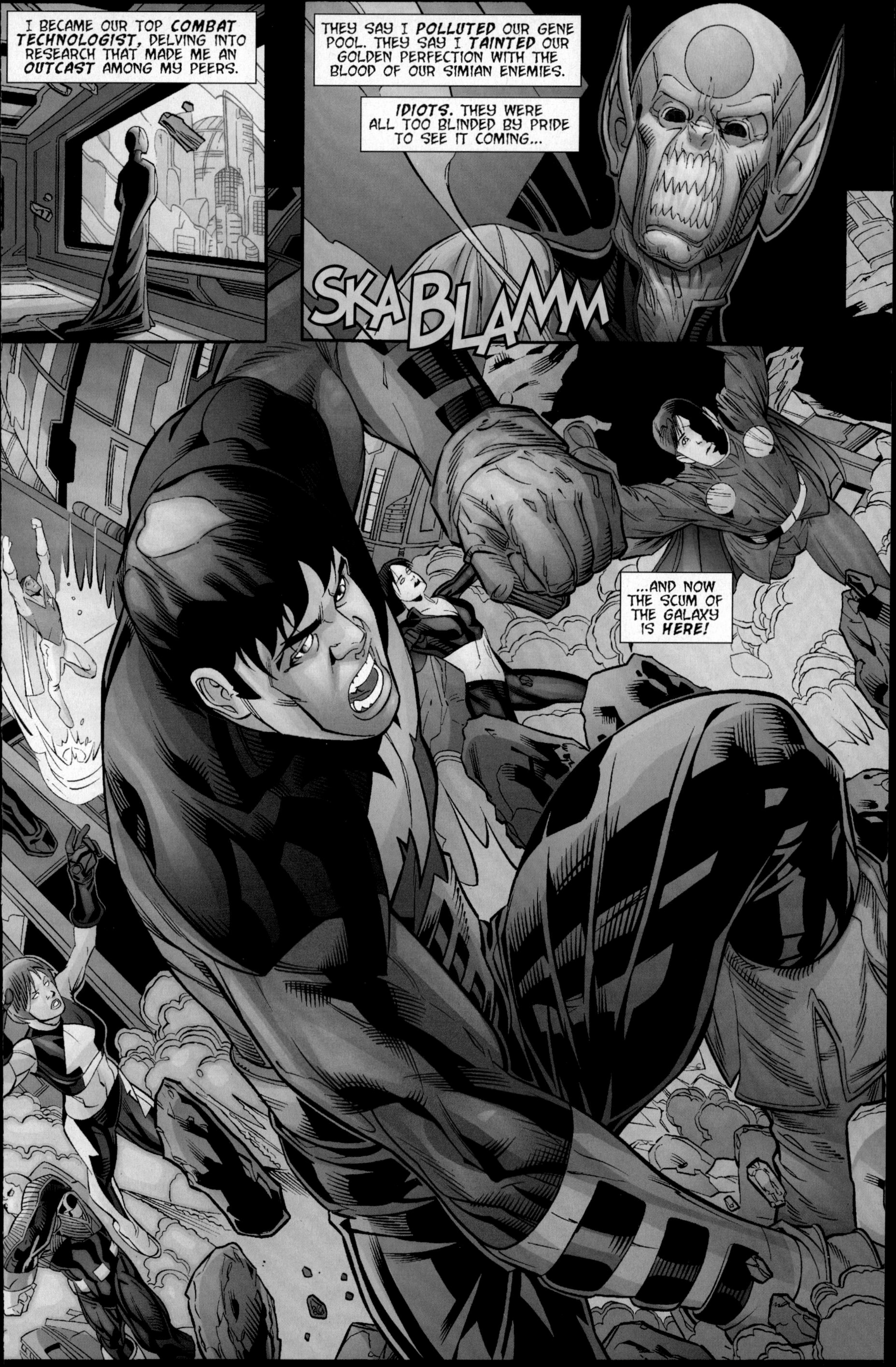
I BECAME OUR TOP COMBAT TECHNOLOGIST, DELVING INTO RESEARCH THAT MADE ME AN OUTCAST AMONG MY PEERS.
THEY SAY I POLLUTED OUR GENE POOL. THEY SAY I TAINTED OUR GOLDEN PERFECTION WITH THE BLOOD OF OUR SIMIAN ENEMIES.
IDIOTS. THEY WERE ALL TOO BLINDED BY PRIDE TO SEE IT COMING...
SKABLAMM
...AND NOW THE SCUM OF THE GALAXY IS HERE!

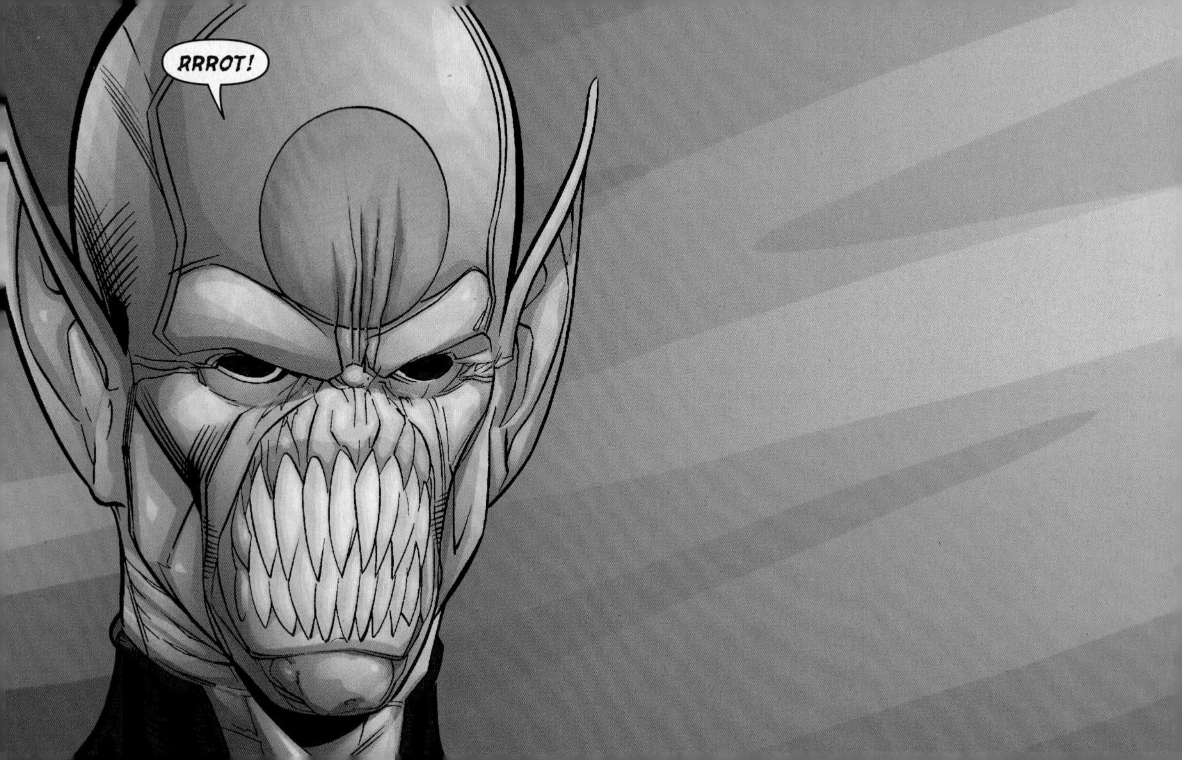
RRROT!

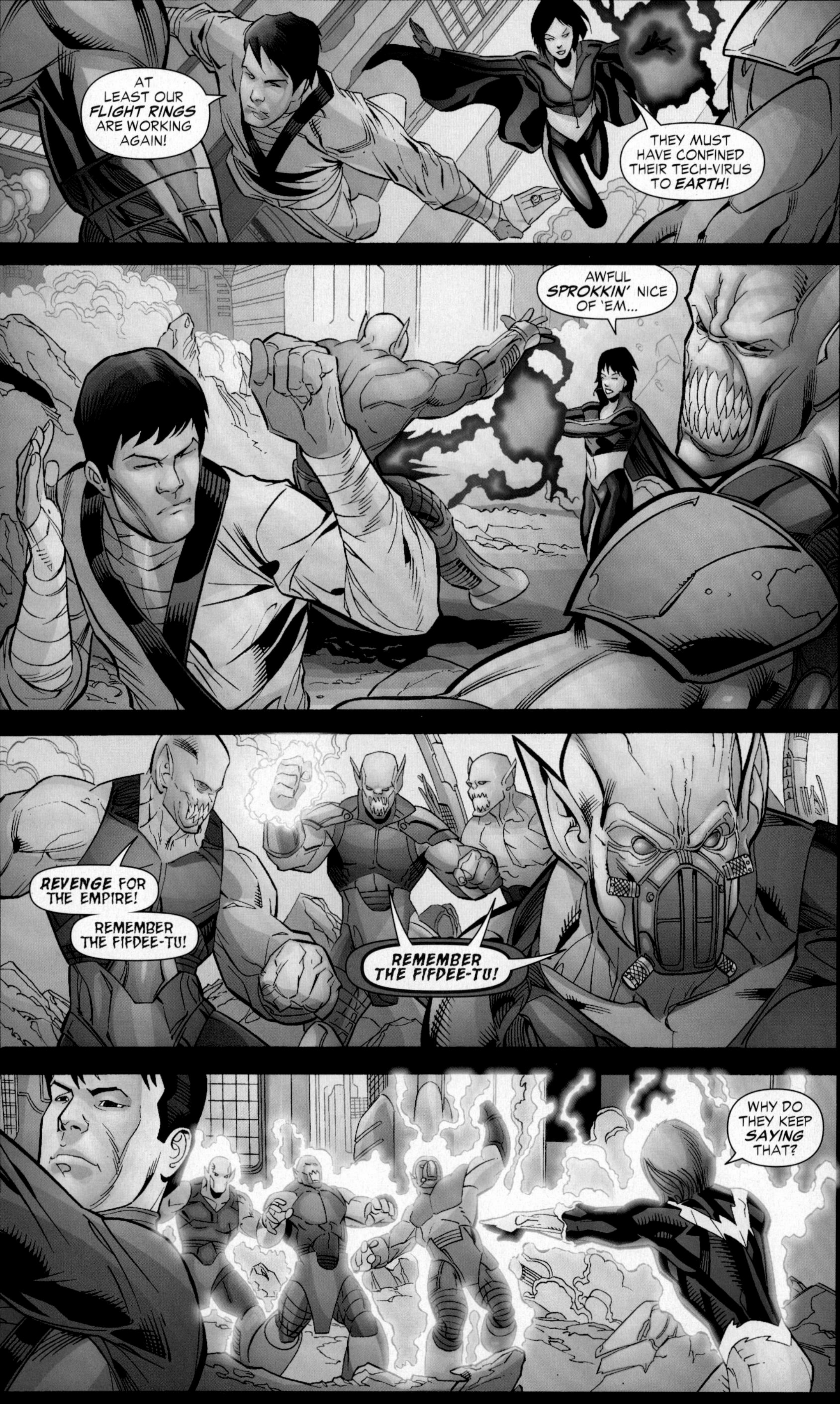

AT LEAST OUR FLIGHT RINGS ARE WORKING AGAIN!
THEY MUST HAVE CONFINED THEIR TECH-VIRUS TO EARTH!
AWFUL SPROKKIN' NICE OF 'EM...
REVENGE FOR THE EMPIRE!
REMEMBER THE FIFDEE-TU!
REMEMBER THE FIFDEE-TU!
WHY DO THEY KEEP SAYING THAT?

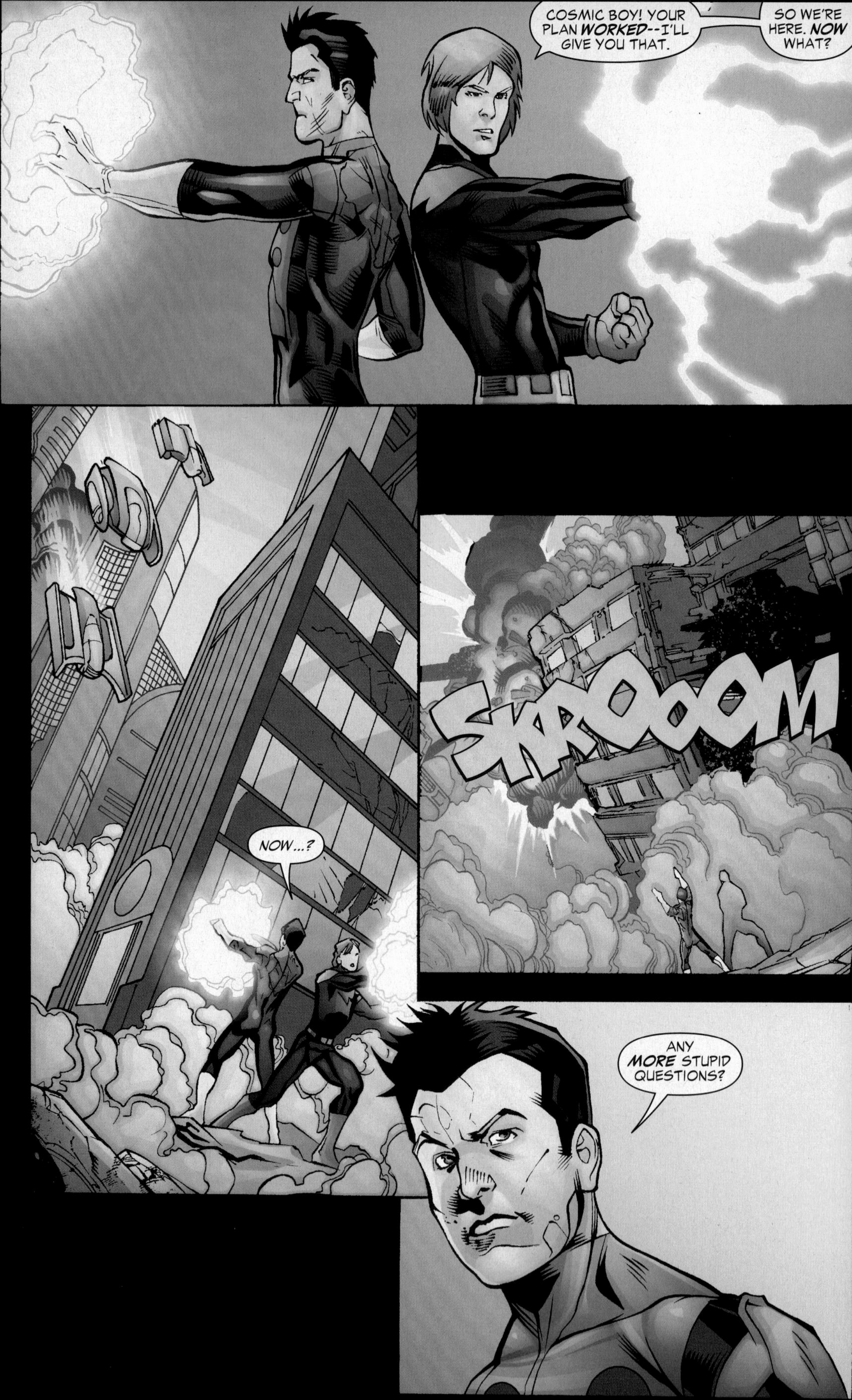
COSMIC BOY! YOUR PLAN WORKED--I'LL GIVE YOU THAT.
SO WE'RE HERE. NOW WHAT?
NOW...?
SKROOOM
ANY MORE STUPID QUESTIONS?

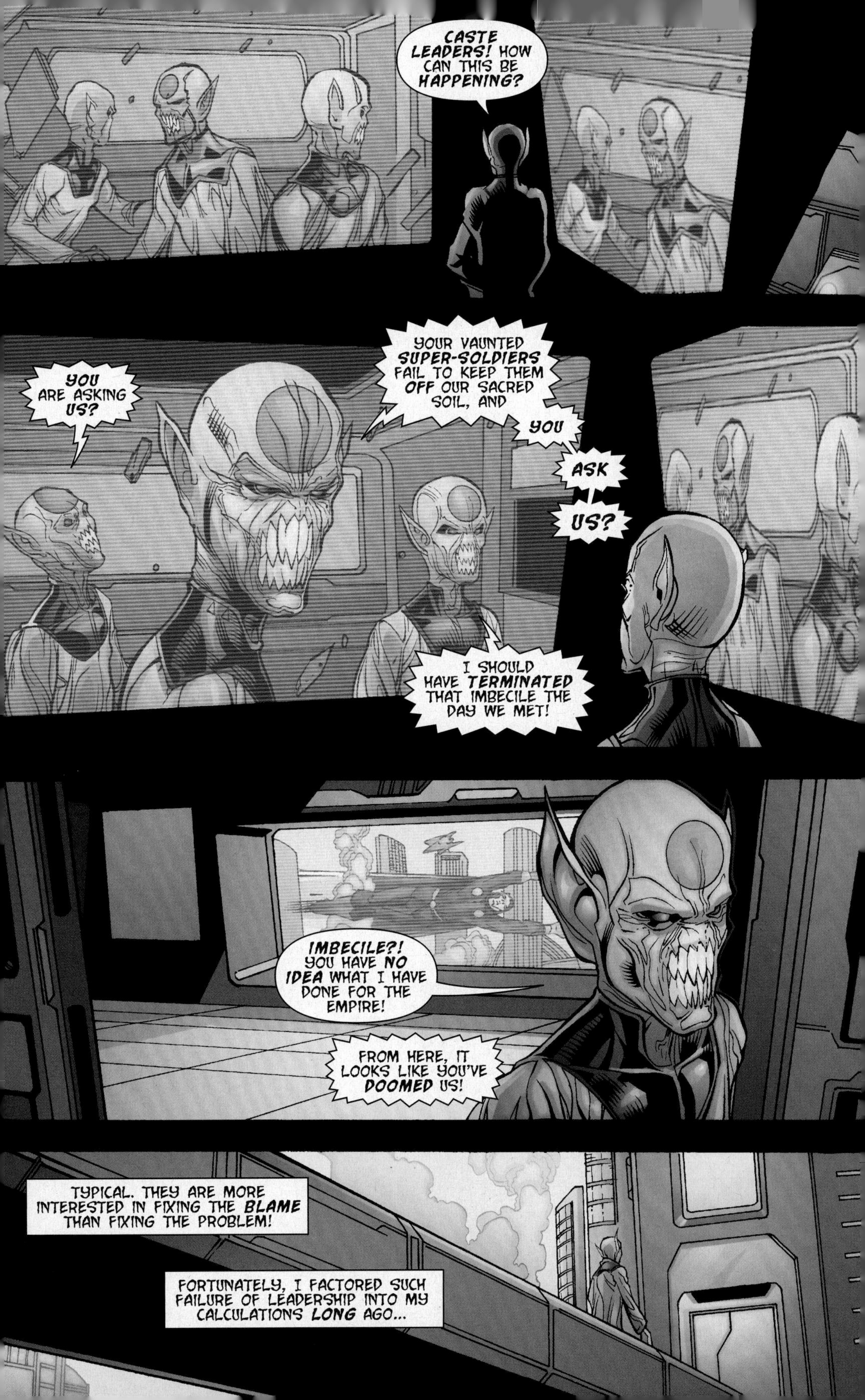
CASTE LEADERS! HOW CAN THIS BE HAPPENING?
YOU ARE ASKING US?
YOUR VAUNTED SUPER-SOLDIERS FAIL TO KEEP THEM OFF OUR SACRED SOIL, AND
YOU
ASK
US?
I SHOULD HAVE TERMINATED THAT IMBECILE THE DAY WE MET!
IMBECILE?! YOU HAVE NO IDEA WHAT I HAVE DONE FOR THE EMPIRE!
FROM HERE, IT LOOKS LIKE YOU'VE DOOMED US!
TYPICAL. THEY ARE MORE INTERESTED IN FIXING THE BLAME THAN FIXING THE PROBLEM!
FORTUNATELY, I FACTORED SUCH FAILURE OF LEADERSHIP INTO MY CALCULATIONS LONG AGO...

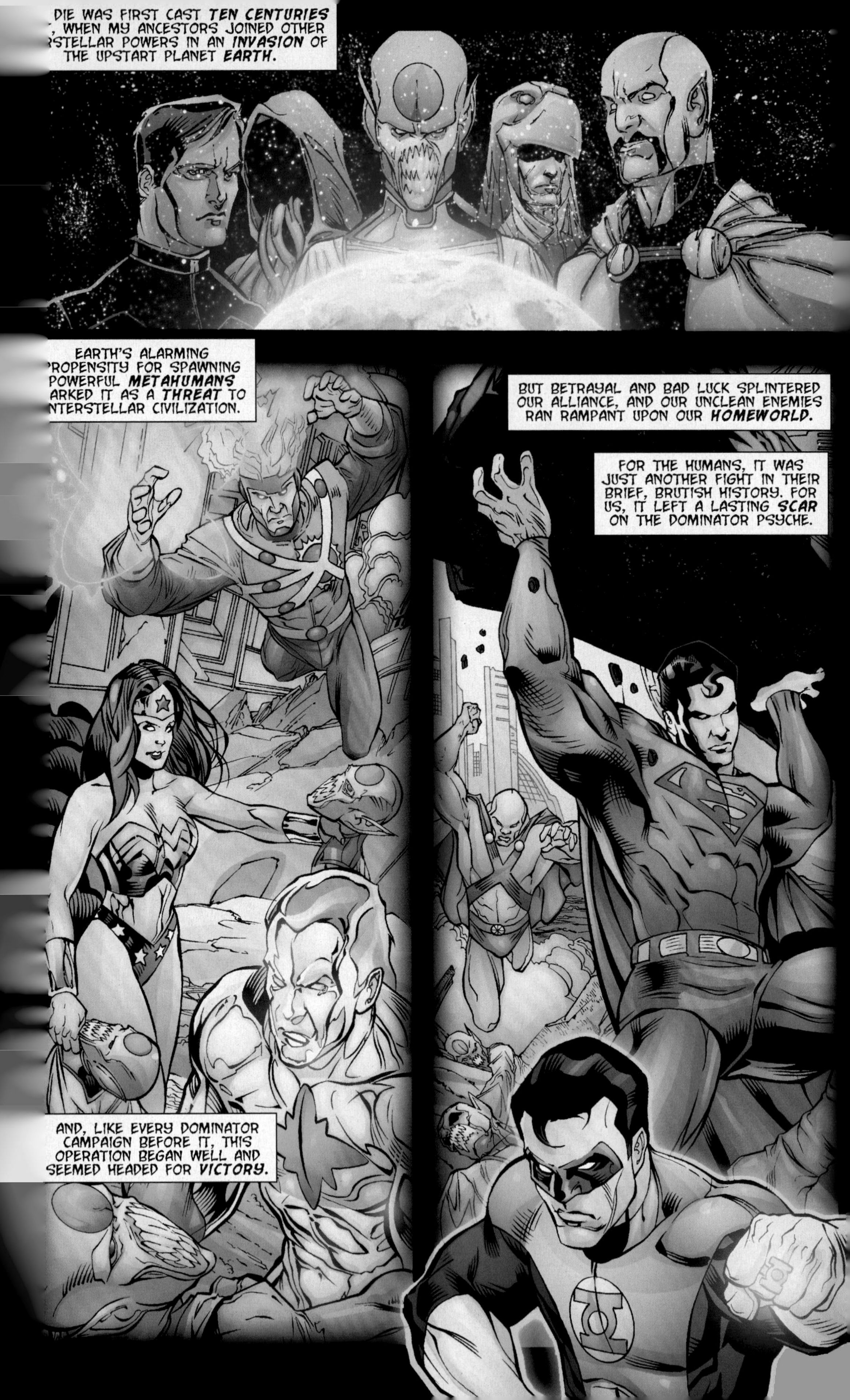
DIE WAS FIRST CAST TEN CENTURIES
, WHEN MY ANCESTORS JOINED OTHER
RSTELLAR POWERS IN AN INVASION OF
THE UPSTART PLANET EARTH.
EARTH'S ALARMING PROPENSITY FOR SPAWNING POWERFUL METAHUMANS ARKED IT AS A THREAT TO NTERSTELLAR CIVILIZATION.
AND, LIKE EVERY DOMINATOR CAMPAIGN BEFORE IT, THIS OPERATION BEGAN WELL AND SEEMED HEADED FOR VICTORY.
BUT BETRAYAL AND BAD LUCK SPLINTERED OUR ALLIANCE, AND OUR UNCLEAN ENEMIES RAN RAMPANT UPON OUR HOMEWORLD.
FOR THE HUMANS, IT WAS JUST ANOTHER FIGHT IN THEIR BRIEF, BRUTISH HISTORY. FOR US, IT LEFT A LASTING SCAR ON THE DOMINATOR PSYCHE.

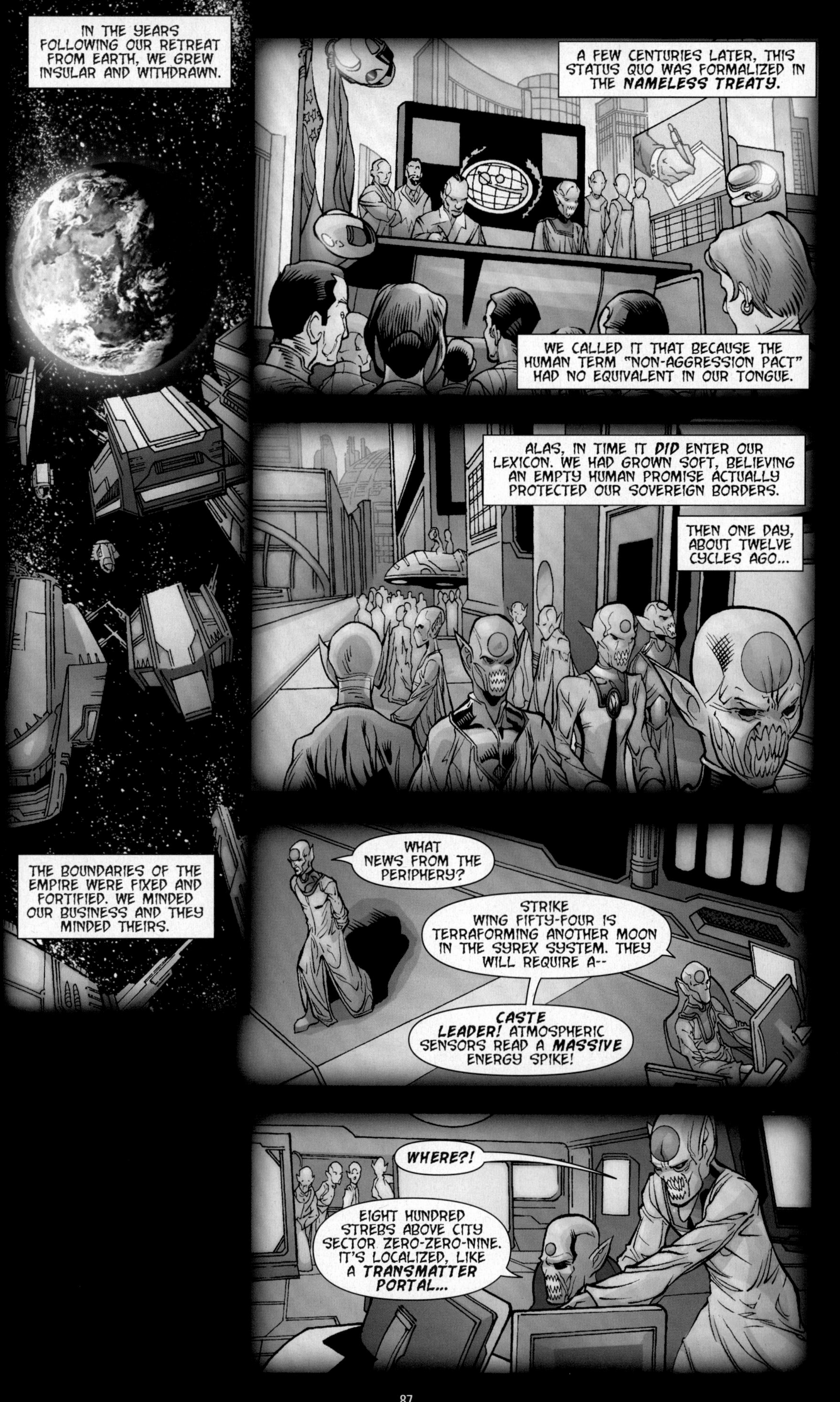

IN THE YEARS FOLLOWING OUR RETREAT FROM EARTH, WE GREW INSULAR AND WITHDRAWN.
A FEW CENTURIES LATER, THIS STATUS QUO WAS FORMALIZED IN THE NAMELESS TREATY.
WE CALLED IT THAT BECAUSE THE HUMAN TERM "NON-AGGRESSION PACT" HAD NO EQUIVALENT IN OUR TONGUE.
THE BOUNDARIES OF THE EMPIRE WERE FIXED AND FORTIFIED. WE MINDED OUR BUSINESS AND THEY MINDED THEIRS.
ALAS, IN TIME IT DID ENTER OUR LEXICON. WE HAD GROWN SOFT, BELIEVING AN EMPTY HUMAN PROMISE ACTUALLY PROTECTED OUR SOVEREIGN BORDERS.
THEN ONE DAY, ABOUT TWELVE CYCLES AGO...
WHAT NEWS FROM THE PERIPHERY?
STRIKE WING FIFTY-FOUR IS TERRAFORMING ANOTHER MOON IN THE SYREX SYSTEM. THEY WILL REQUIRE A--
CASTE LEADER! ATMOSPHERIC SENSORS READ A MASSIVE ENERGY SPIKE!
WHERE?!
EIGHT HUNDRED STREBS ABOVE CITY SECTOR ZERO-ZERO-NINE. IT'S LOCALIZED, LIKE A TRANSMATTER PORTAL...

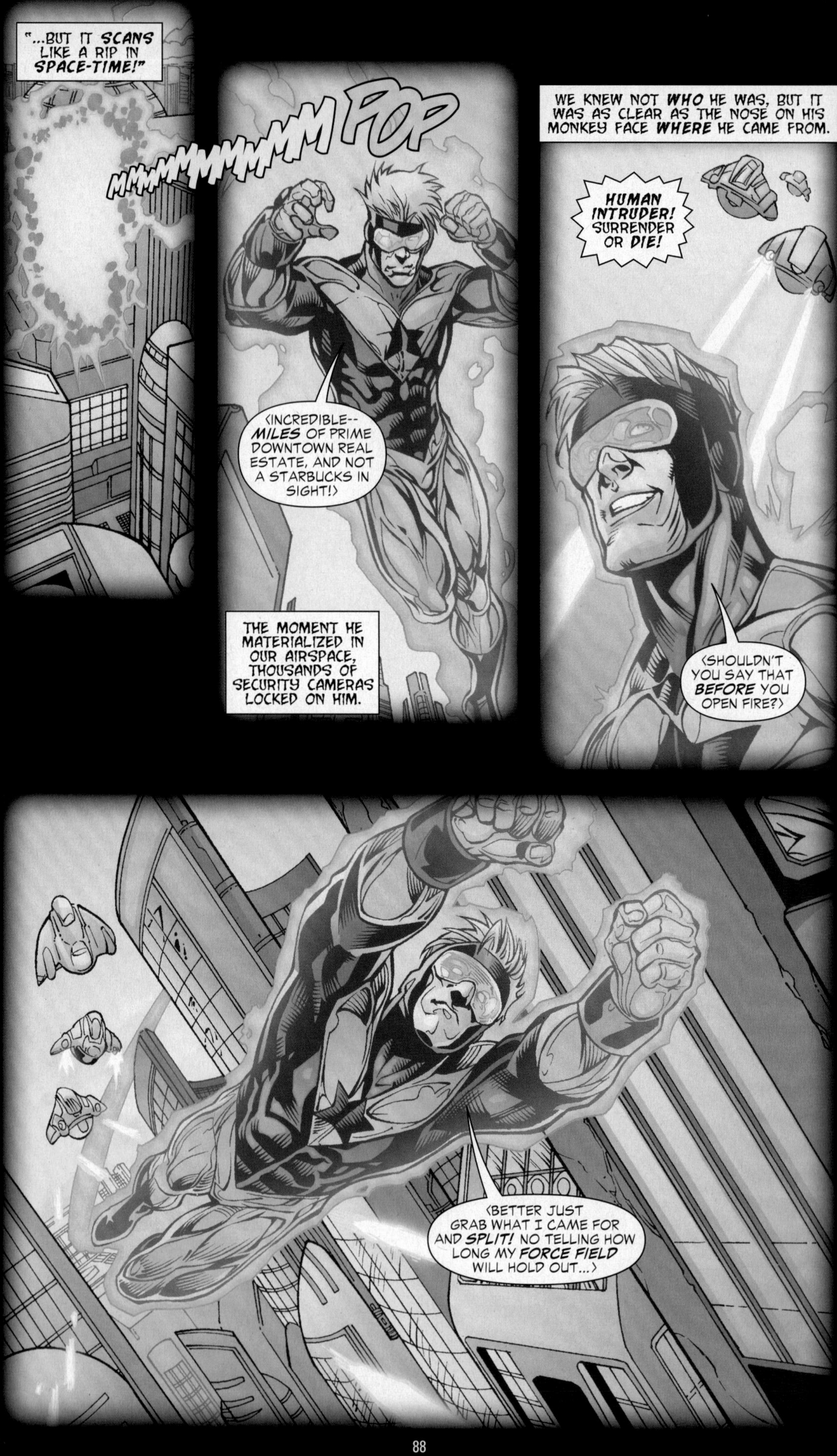
"...BUT IT SCANS LIKE A RIP IN SPACE-TIME!"
MMMMMMMMMMM POP
‹INCREDIBLE-- MILES OF PRIME DOWNTOWN REAL ESTATE, AND NOT A STARBUCKS IN SIGHT!›
THE MOMENT HE MATERIALIZED IN OUR AIRSPACE, THOUSANDS OF SECURITY CAMERAS LOCKED ON HIM.
WE KNEW NOT WHO HE WAS, BUT IT WAS AS CLEAR AS THE NOSE ON HIS MONKEY FACE WHERE HE CAME FROM.
HUMAN INTRUDER! SURRENDER OR DIE!
‹SHOULDN'T YOU SAY THAT BEFORE YOU OPEN FIRE?›
‹BETTER JUST GRAB WHAT I CAME FOR AND SPLIT! NO TELLING HOW LONG MY FORCE FIELD WILL HOLD OUT...›

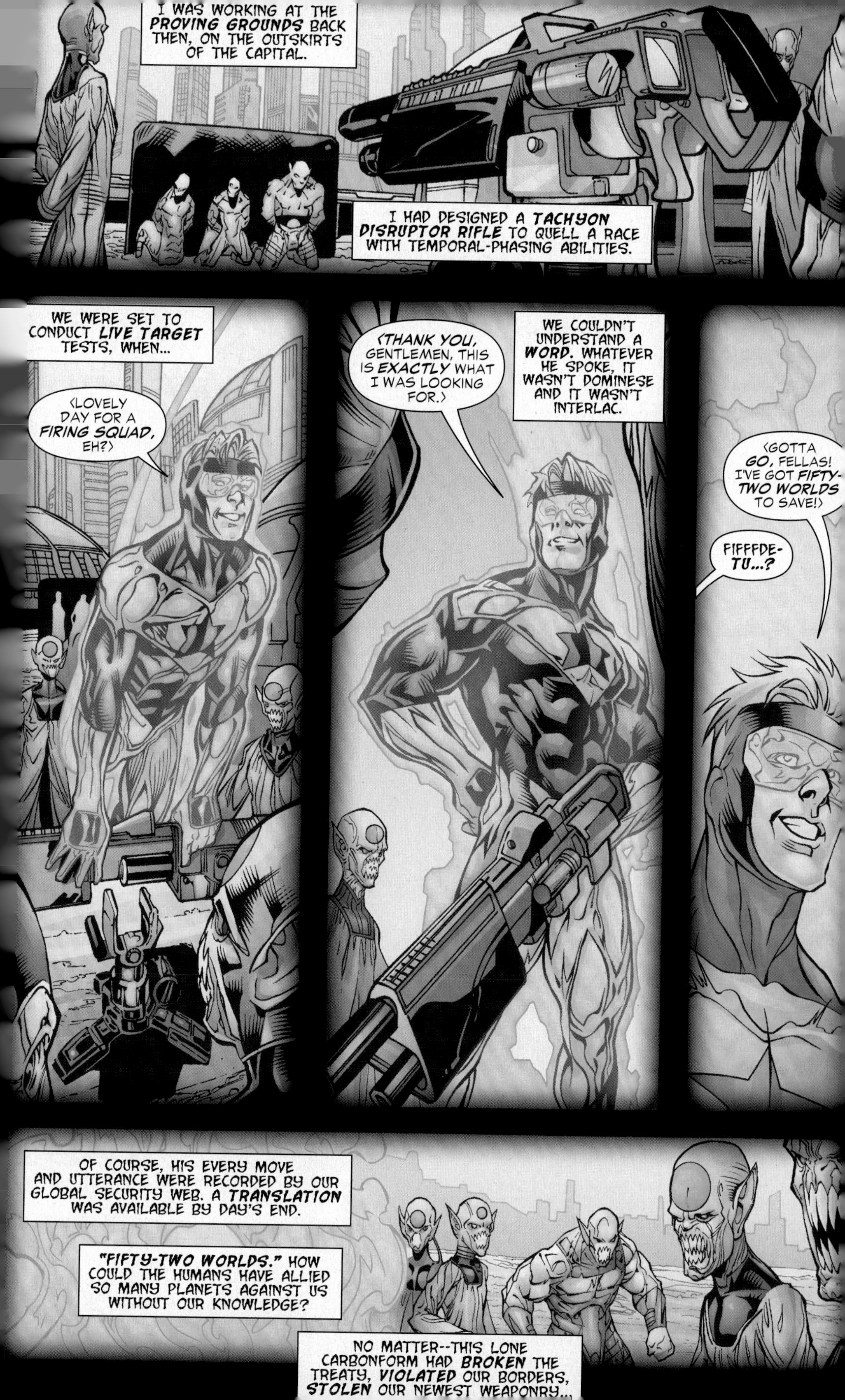
I WAS WORKING AT THE PROVING GROUNDS BACK THEN, ON THE OUTSKIRTS OF THE CAPITAL.
I HAD DESIGNED A TACHYON DISRUPTOR RIFLE TO QUELL A RACE WITH TEMPORAL-PHASING ABILITIES.
WE WERE SET TO CONDUCT LIVE TARGET TESTS, WHEN...
‹LOVELY DAY FOR A FIRING SQUAD, EH?›
‹THANK YOU, GENTLEMEN, THIS IS EXACTLY WHAT I WAS LOOKING FOR.›
WE COULDN'T UNDERSTAND A WORD. WHATEVER HE SPOKE, IT WASN'T DOMINESE AND IT WASN'T INTERLAC.
‹GOTTA GO, FELLAS! I'VE GOT FIFTY-TWO WORLDS TO SAVE!›
FIFFFDE-TU...?
OF COURSE, HIS EVERY MOVE AND UTTERANCE WERE RECORDED BY OUR GLOBAL SECURITY WEB. A TRANSLATION WAS AVAILABLE BY DAY'S END.
"FIFTY-TWO WORLDS." HOW COULD THE HUMANS HAVE ALLIED SO MANY PLANETS AGAINST US WITHOUT OUR KNOWLEDGE?
NO MATTER--THIS LONE CARBONFORM HAD BROKEN THE TREATY, VIOLATED OUR BORDERS, STOLEN OUR NEWEST WEAPONRY...

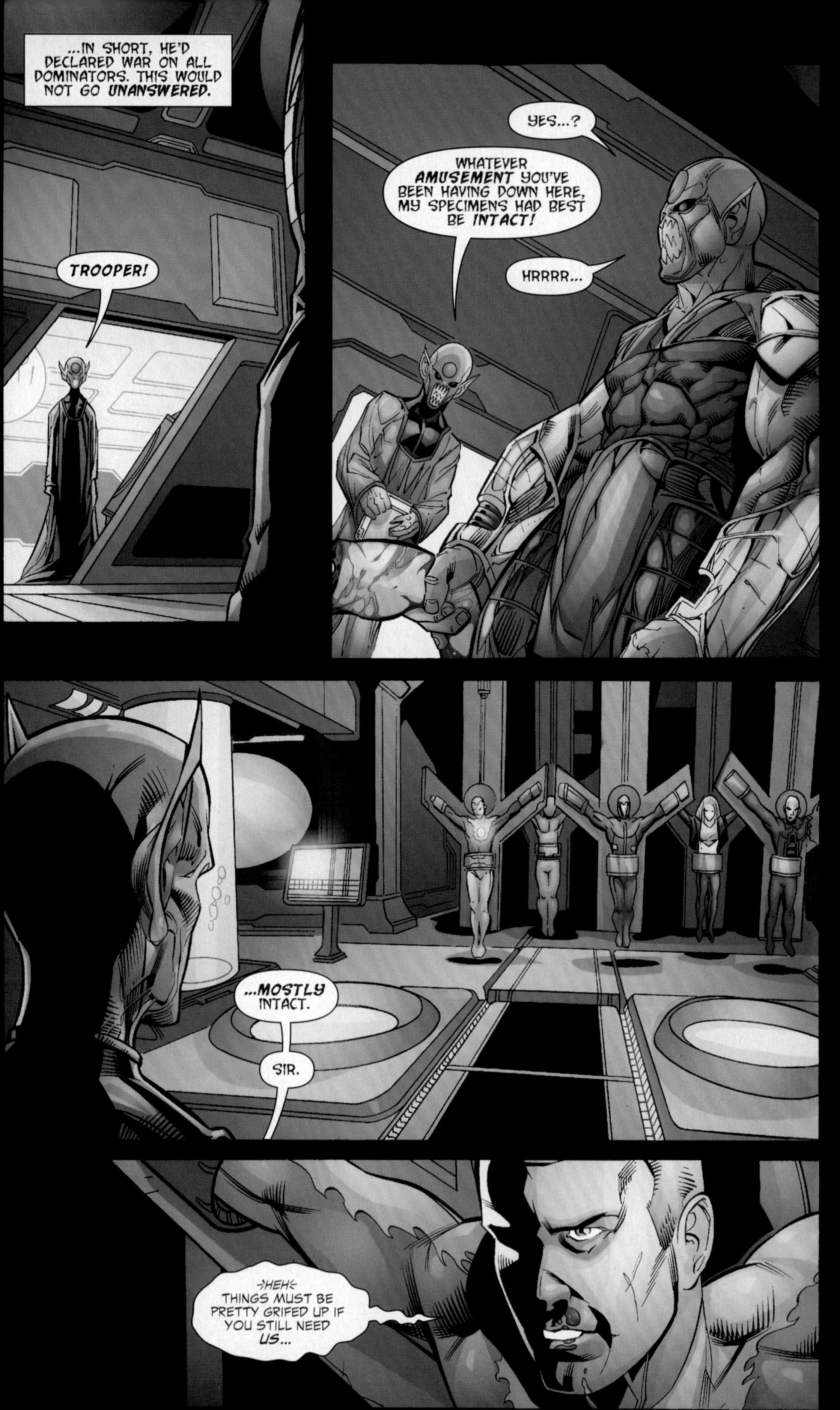
...IN SHORT, HE'D DECLARED WAR ON ALL DOMINATORS. THIS WOULD NOT GO UNANSWERED.
TROOPER!
YES...?
WHATEVER AMUSEMENT YOU'VE BEEN HAVING DOWN HERE, MY SPECIMENS HAD BEST BE INTACT!
HRRRR...
...MOSTLY INTACT.
SIR.
HEH
THINGS MUST BE PRETTY GRIFED UP IF YOU STILL NEED US...

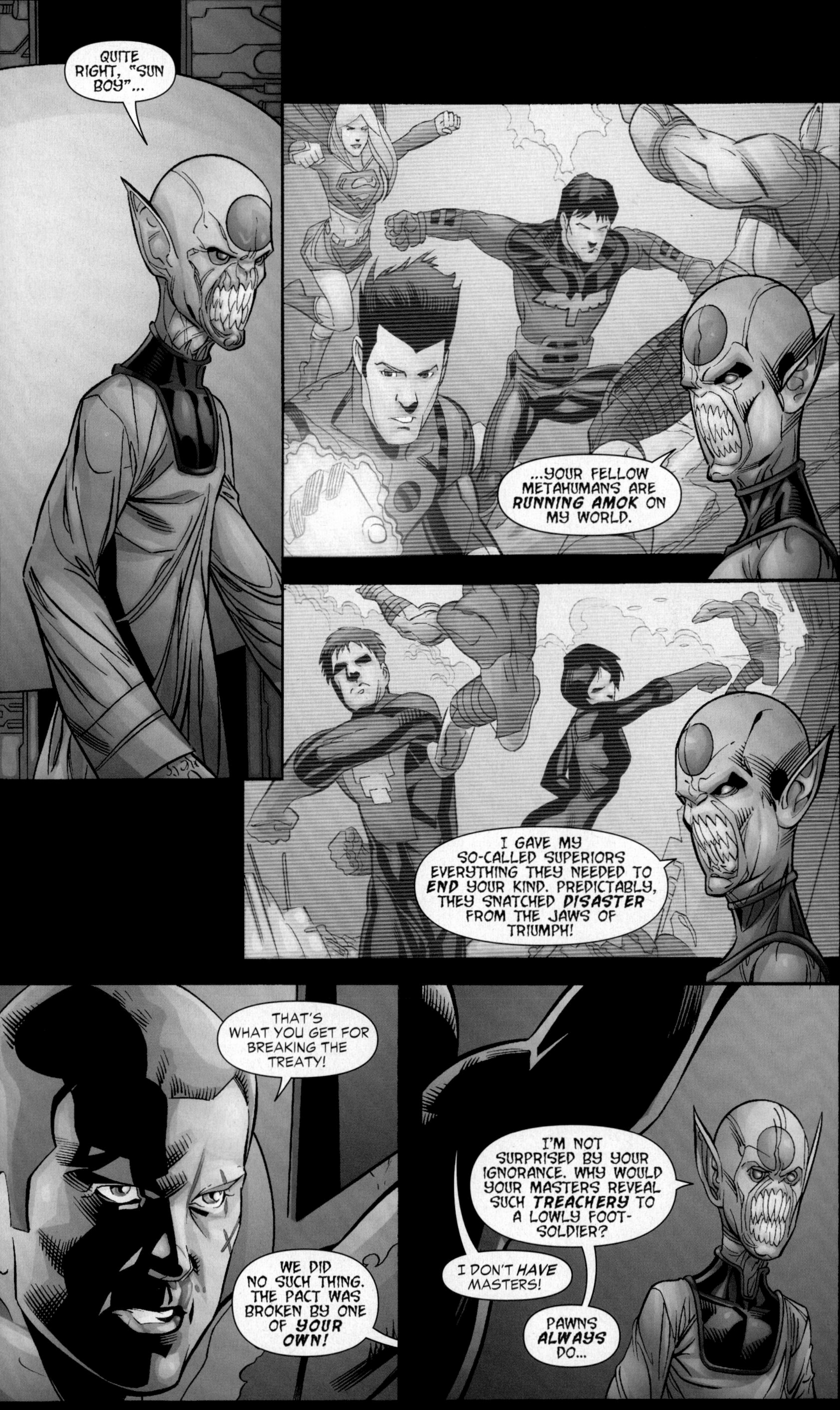
QUITE RIGHT, "SUN BOY"...
...YOUR FELLOW METAHUMANS ARE RUNNING AMOK ON MY WORLD.
I GAVE MY SO-CALLED SUPERIORS EVERYTHING THEY NEEDED TO END YOUR KIND. PREDICTABLY, THEY SNATCHED DISASTER FROM THE JAWS OF TRIUMPH!
THAT'S WHAT YOU GET FOR BREAKING THE TREATY!
WE DID NO SUCH THING. THE PACT WAS BROKEN BY ONE OF YOUR OWN!
I'M NOT SURPRISED BY YOUR IGNORANCE. WHY WOULD YOUR MASTERS REVEAL SUCH TREACHERY TO A LOWLY FOOT-SOLDIER?
I DON'T HAVE MASTERS!
PAWNS ALWAYS DO...

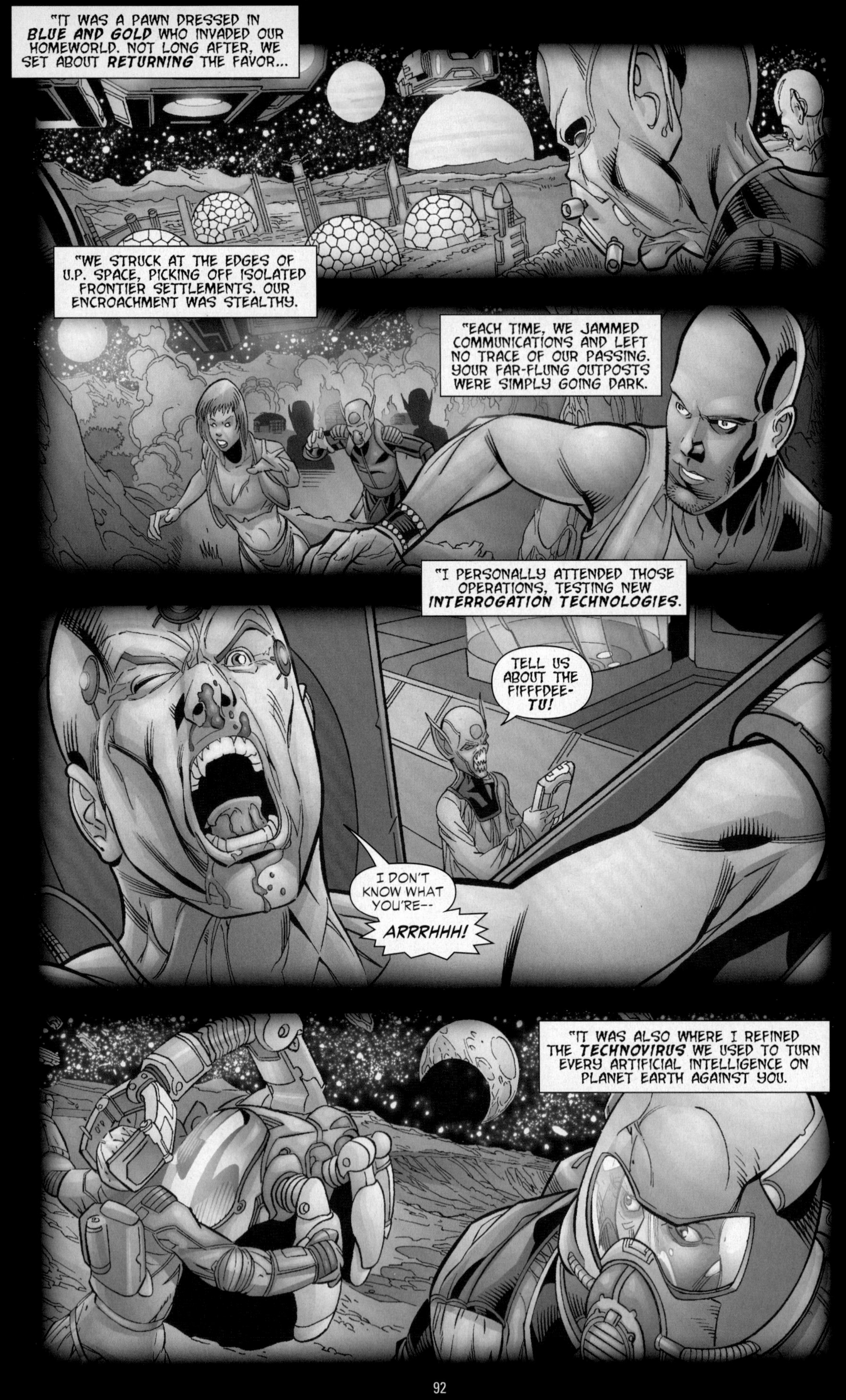
"IT WAS A PAWN DRESSED IN BLUE AND GOLD WHO INVADED OUR HOMEWORLD. NOT LONG AFTER, WE SET ABOUT RETURNING THE FAVOR...
"WE STRUCK AT THE EDGES OF U.P. SPACE, PICKING OFF ISOLATED FRONTIER SETTLEMENTS. OUR ENCROACHMENT WAS STEALTHY.
"EACH TIME, WE JAMMED COMMUNICATIONS AND LEFT NO TRACE OF OUR PASSING. YOUR FAR-FLUNG OUTPOSTS WERE SIMPLY GOING DARK.
"I PERSONALLY ATTENDED THOSE OPERATIONS, TESTING NEW INTERROGATION TECHNOLOGIES.
TELL US ABOUT THE FIFFFDEE-TU!
I DON'T KNOW WHAT YOU'RE-- ARRRHHH!
"IT WAS ALSO WHERE I REFINED THE TECHNOVIRUS WE USED TO TURN EVERY ARTIFICIAL INTELLIGENCE ON PLANET EARTH AGAINST YOU.

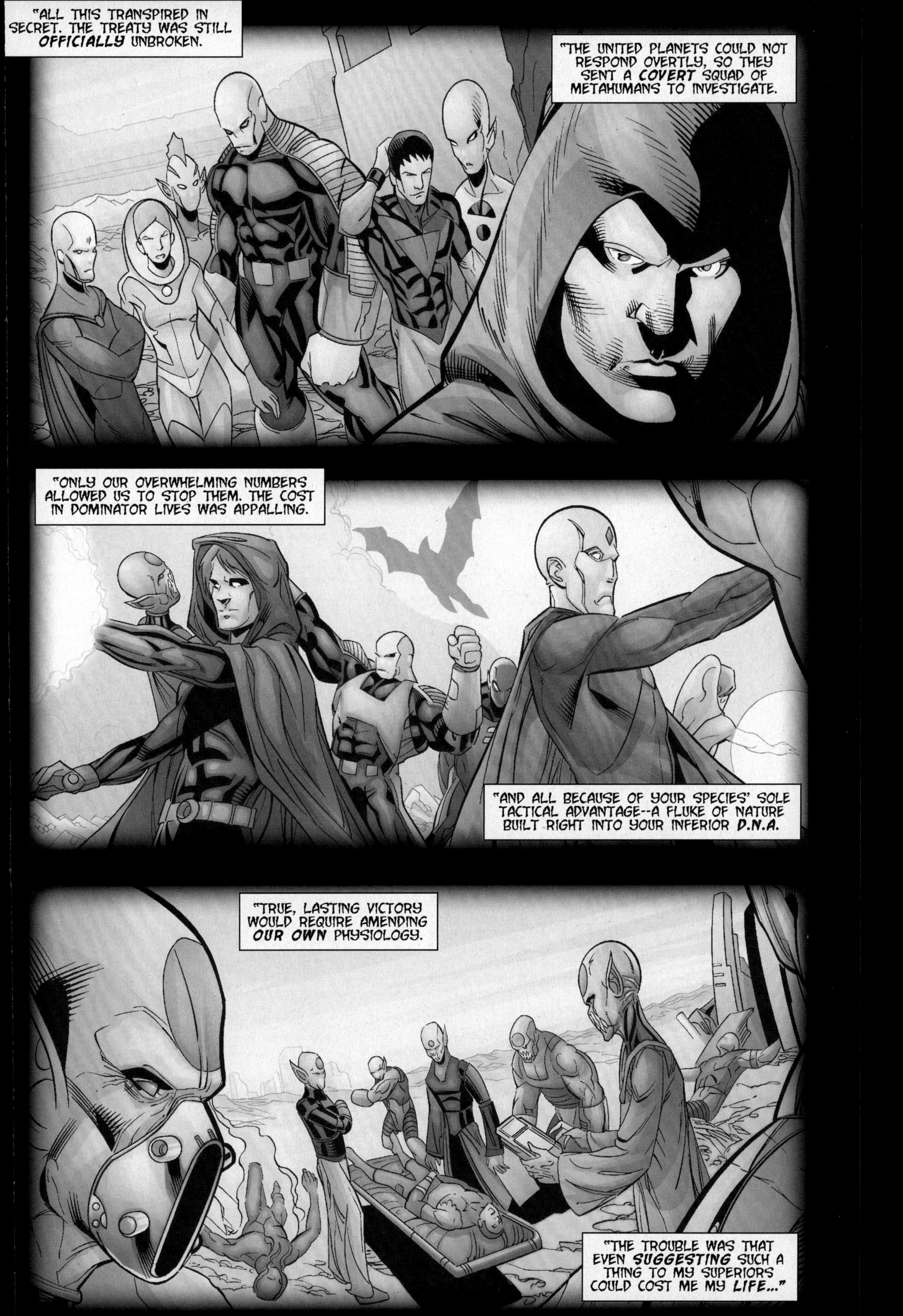
"ALL THIS TRANSPIRED IN SECRET. THE TREATY WAS STILL *OFFICIALLY* UNBROKEN.
"THE UNITED PLANETS COULD NOT RESPOND OVERTLY, SO THEY SENT A *COVERT* SQUAD OF METAHUMANS TO INVESTIGATE.
"ONLY OUR OVERWHELMING NUMBERS ALLOWED US TO STOP THEM. THE COST IN DOMINATOR LIVES WAS APPALLING.
"AND ALL BECAUSE OF YOUR SPECIES' SOLE TACTICAL ADVANTAGE--A FLUKE OF NATURE BUILT RIGHT INTO YOUR INFERIOR *D.N.A.*
"TRUE, LASTING VICTORY WOULD REQUIRE AMENDING *OUR OWN* PHYSIOLOGY.
"THE TROUBLE WAS THAT EVEN *SUGGESTING* SUCH A THING TO MY SUPERIORS COULD COST ME MY *LIFE*..."

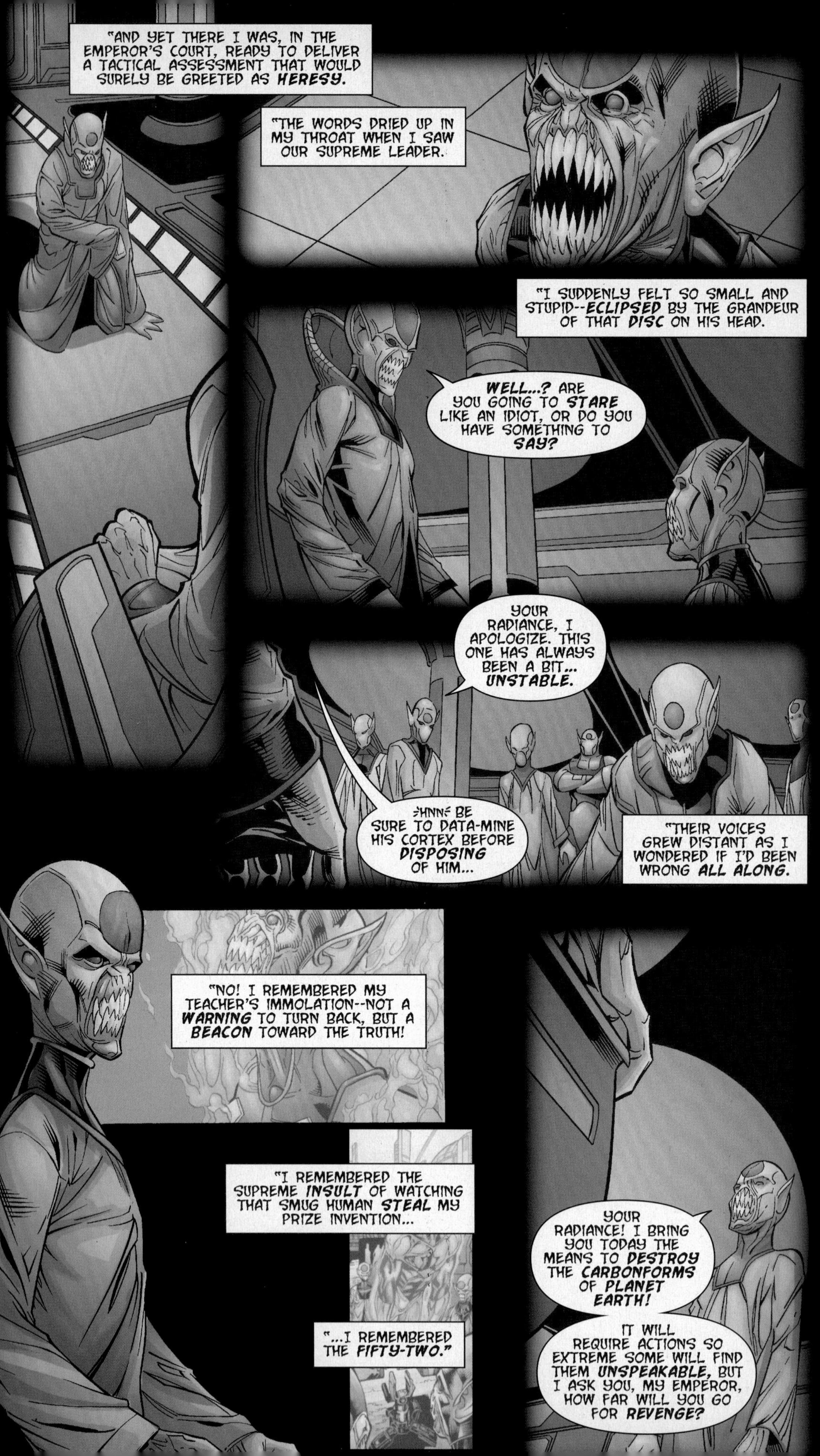
"AND YET THERE I WAS, IN THE EMPEROR'S COURT, READY TO DELIVER A TACTICAL ASSESSMENT THAT WOULD SURELY BE GREETED AS HERESY.
"THE WORDS DRIED UP IN MY THROAT WHEN I SAW OUR SUPREME LEADER.
"I SUDDENLY FELT SO SMALL AND STUPID--ECLIPSED BY THE GRANDEUR OF THAT DISC ON HIS HEAD.
WELL...? ARE YOU GOING TO STARE LIKE AN IDIOT, OR DO YOU HAVE SOMETHING TO SAY?
YOUR RADIANCE, I APOLOGIZE. THIS ONE HAS ALWAYS BEEN A BIT... UNSTABLE.
HNN BE SURE TO DATA-MINE HIS CORTEX BEFORE DISPOSING OF HIM...
"THEIR VOICES GREW DISTANT AS I WONDERED IF I'D BEEN WRONG ALL ALONG.
"NO! I REMEMBERED MY TEACHER'S IMMOLATION--NOT A WARNING TO TURN BACK, BUT A BEACON TOWARD THE TRUTH!
"I REMEMBERED THE SUPREME INSULT OF WATCHING THAT SMUG HUMAN STEAL MY PRIZE INVENTION...
"...I REMEMBERED THE FIFTY-TWO."
YOUR RADIANCE! I BRING YOU TODAY THE MEANS TO DESTROY THE CARBONFORMS OF PLANET EARTH!
IT WILL REQUIRE ACTIONS SO EXTREME SOME WILL FIND THEM UNSPEAKABLE, BUT I ASK YOU, MY EMPEROR, HOW FAR WILL YOU GO FOR REVENGE?

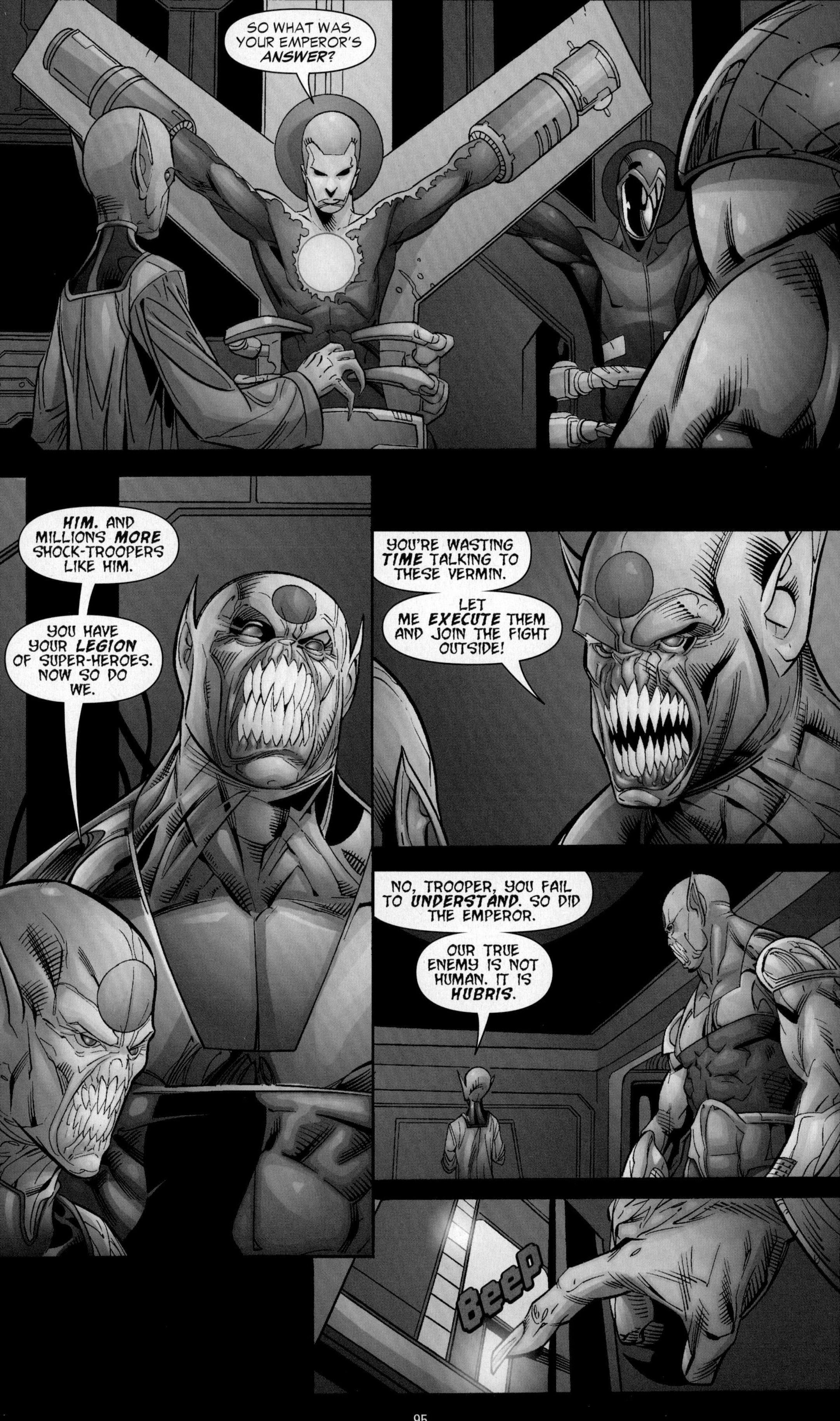

SO WHAT WAS YOUR EMPEROR'S ANSWER?
HIM. AND MILLIONS MORE SHOCK-TROOPERS LIKE HIM.
YOU HAVE YOUR LEGION OF SUPER-HEROES. NOW SO DO WE.
YOU'RE WASTING TIME TALKING TO THESE VERMIN.
LET ME EXECUTE THEM AND JOIN THE FIGHT OUTSIDE!
NO, TROOPER, YOU FAIL TO UNDERSTAND. SO DID THE EMPEROR.
OUR TRUE ENEMY IS NOT HUMAN. IT IS HUBRIS.
BEEP

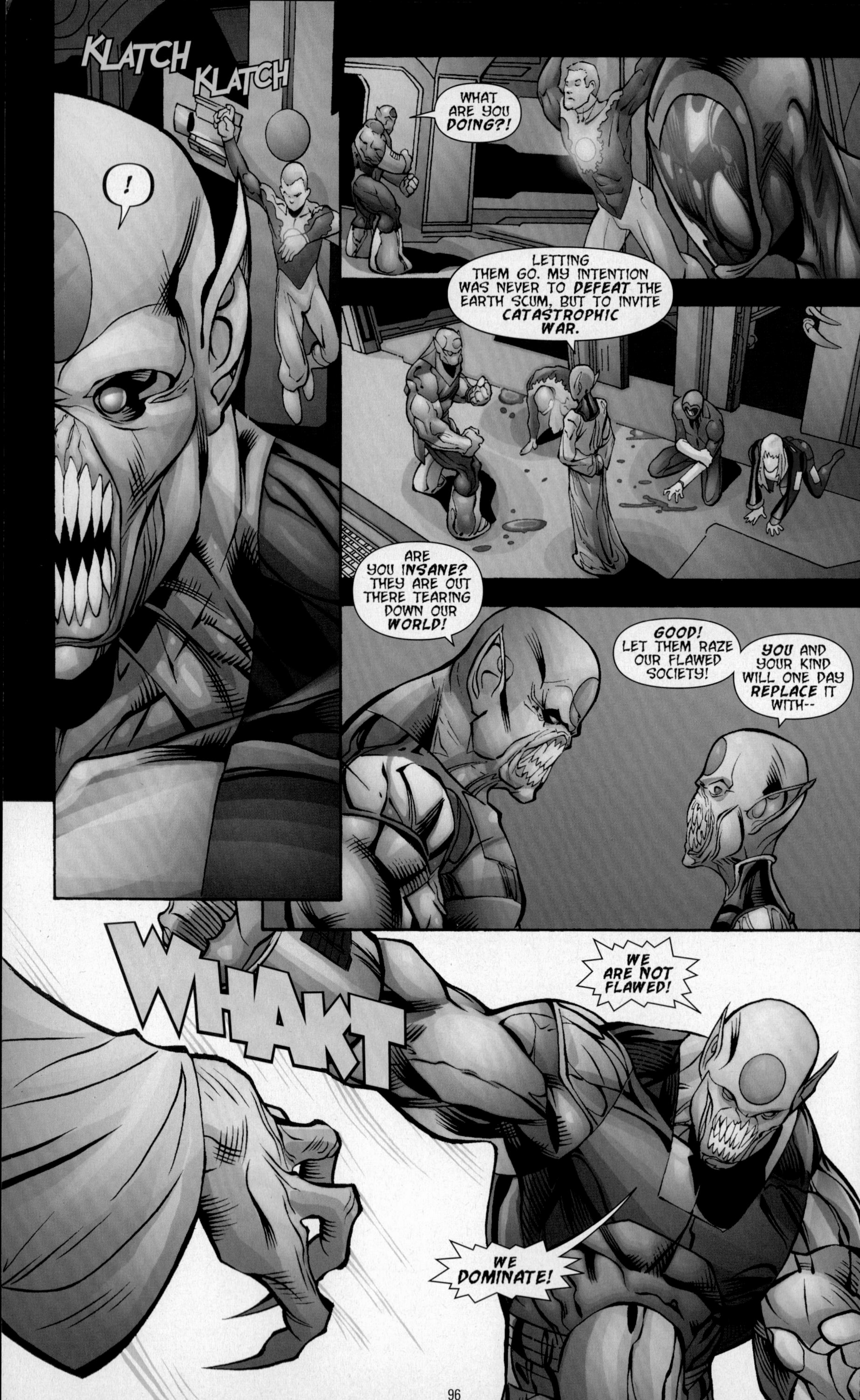
KLATCH KLATCH
!
WHAT ARE YOU DOING?!
LETTING THEM GO. MY INTENTION WAS NEVER TO DEFEAT THE EARTH SCUM, BUT TO INVITE CATASTROPHIC WAR.
ARE YOU INSANE? THEY ARE OUT THERE TEARING DOWN OUR WORLD!
GOOD! LET THEM RAZE OUR FLAWED SOCIETY!
YOU AND YOUR KIND WILL ONE DAY REPLACE IT WITH--
WHAKT
WE ARE NOT FLAWED!
WE DOMINATE!

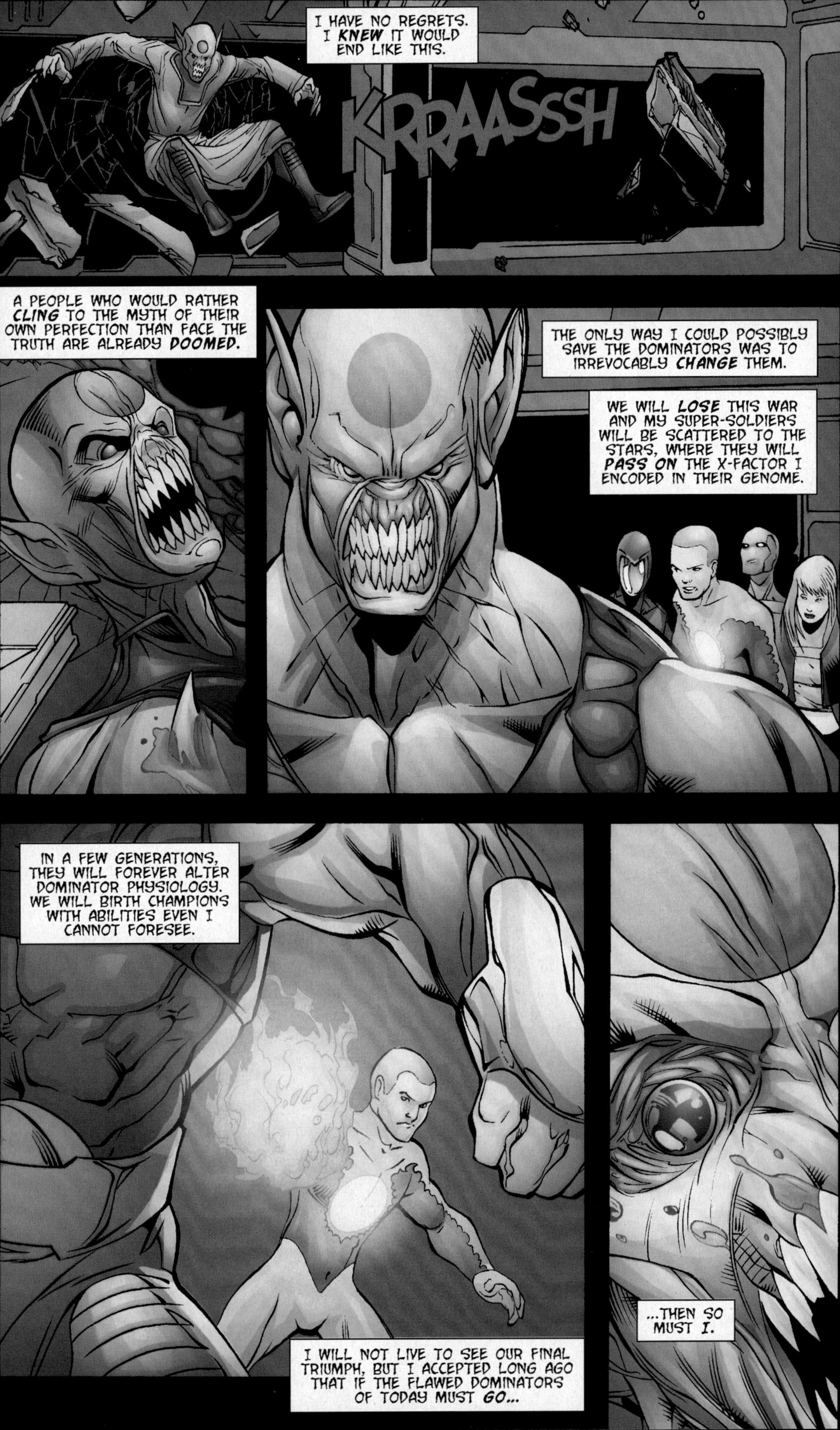
I HAVE NO REGRETS. I KNEW IT WOULD END LIKE THIS.
KRRAASSSH
A PEOPLE WHO WOULD RATHER CLING TO THE MYTH OF THEIR OWN PERFECTION THAN FACE THE TRUTH ARE ALREADY DOOMED.
THE ONLY WAY I COULD POSSIBLY SAVE THE DOMINATORS WAS TO IRREVOCABLY CHANGE THEM.
WE WILL LOSE THIS WAR AND MY SUPER-SOLDIERS WILL BE SCATTERED TO THE STARS, WHERE THEY WILL PASS ON THE X-FACTOR I ENCODED IN THEIR GENOME.
IN A FEW GENERATIONS, THEY WILL FOREVER ALTER DOMINATOR PHYSIOLOGY. WE WILL BIRTH CHAMPIONS WITH ABILITIES EVEN I CANNOT FORESEE.
I WILL NOT LIVE TO SEE OUR FINAL TRIUMPH, BUT I ACCEPTED LONG AGO THAT IF THE FLAWED DOMINATORS OF TODAY MUST GO...
...THEN SO MUST I.

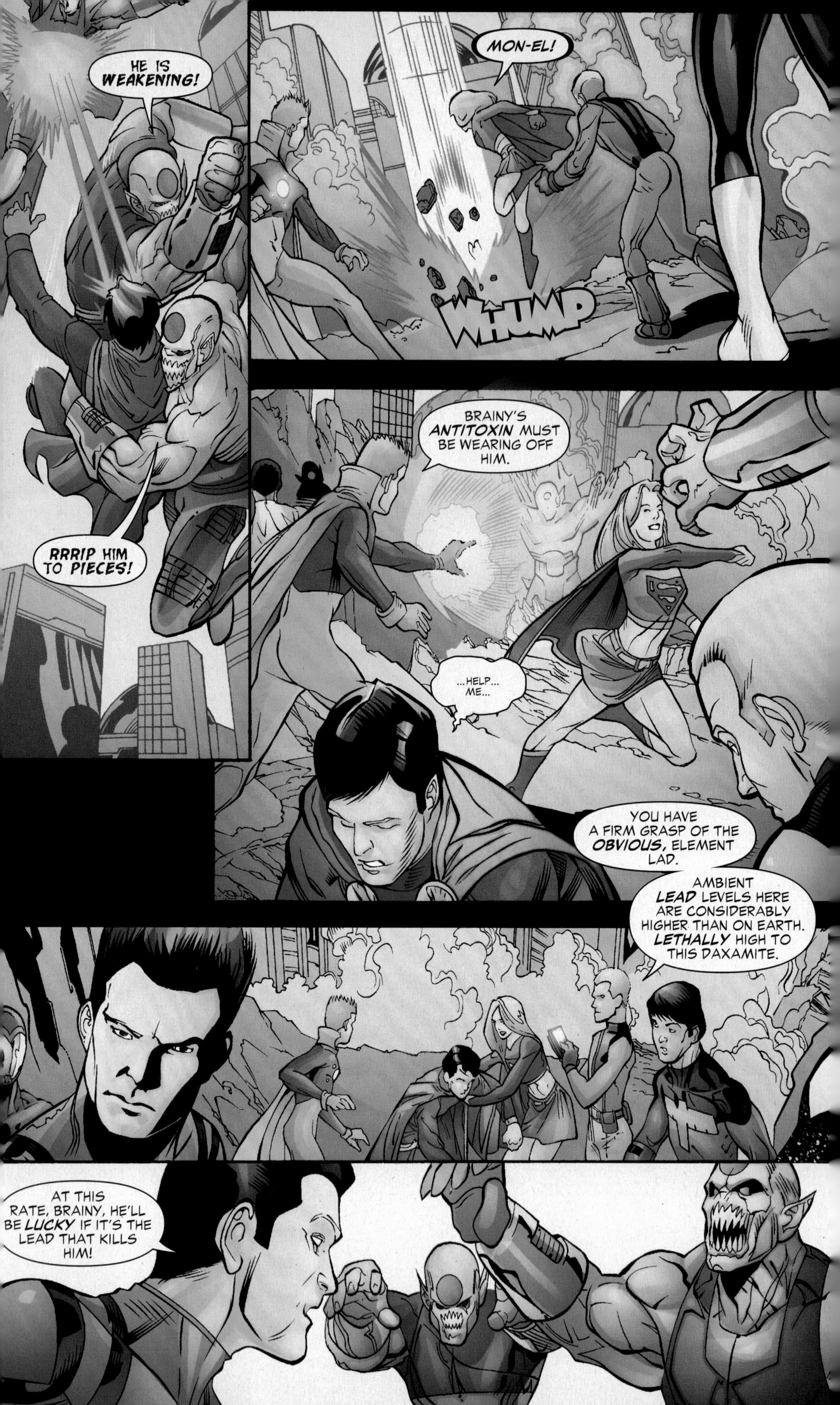
HE IS WEAKENING!
RRRIP HIM TO PIECES!
MON-EL!
WHUMP
BRAINY'S ANTITOXIN MUST BE WEARING OFF HIM.
...HELP... ME...
YOU HAVE A FIRM GRASP OF THE OBVIOUS, ELEMENT LAD.
AMBIENT LEAD LEVELS HERE ARE CONSIDERABLY HIGHER THAN ON EARTH. LETHALLY HIGH TO THIS DAXAMITE.
AT THIS RATE, BRAINY, HE'LL BE LUCKY IF IT'S THE LEAD THAT KILLS HIM!

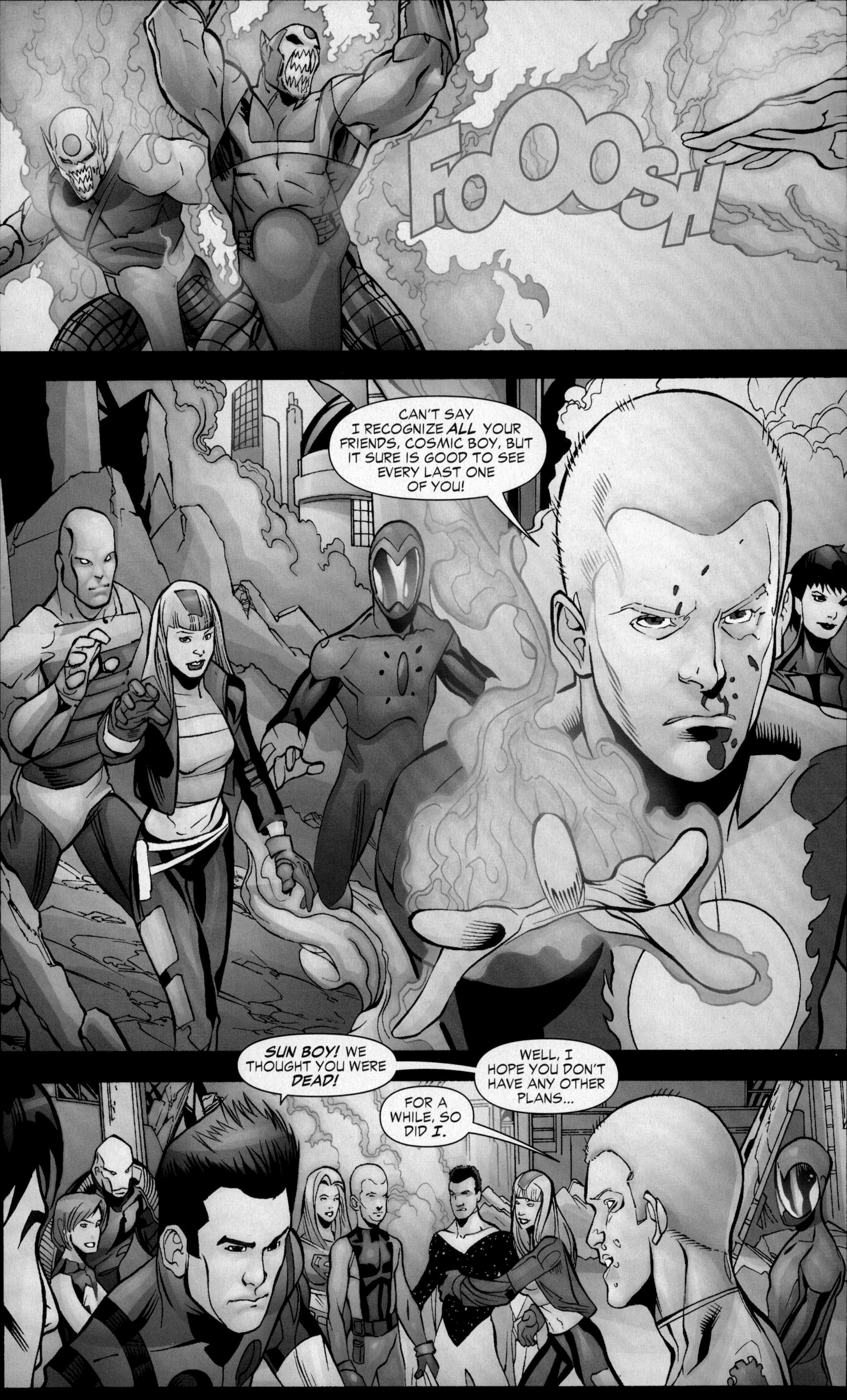
FOOOSH
CAN'T SAY I RECOGNIZE ALL YOUR FRIENDS, COSMIC BOY, BUT IT SURE IS GOOD TO SEE EVERY LAST ONE OF YOU!
SUN BOY! WE THOUGHT YOU WERE DEAD!
FOR A WHILE, SO DID I.
WELL, I HOPE YOU DON'T HAVE ANY OTHER PLANS...

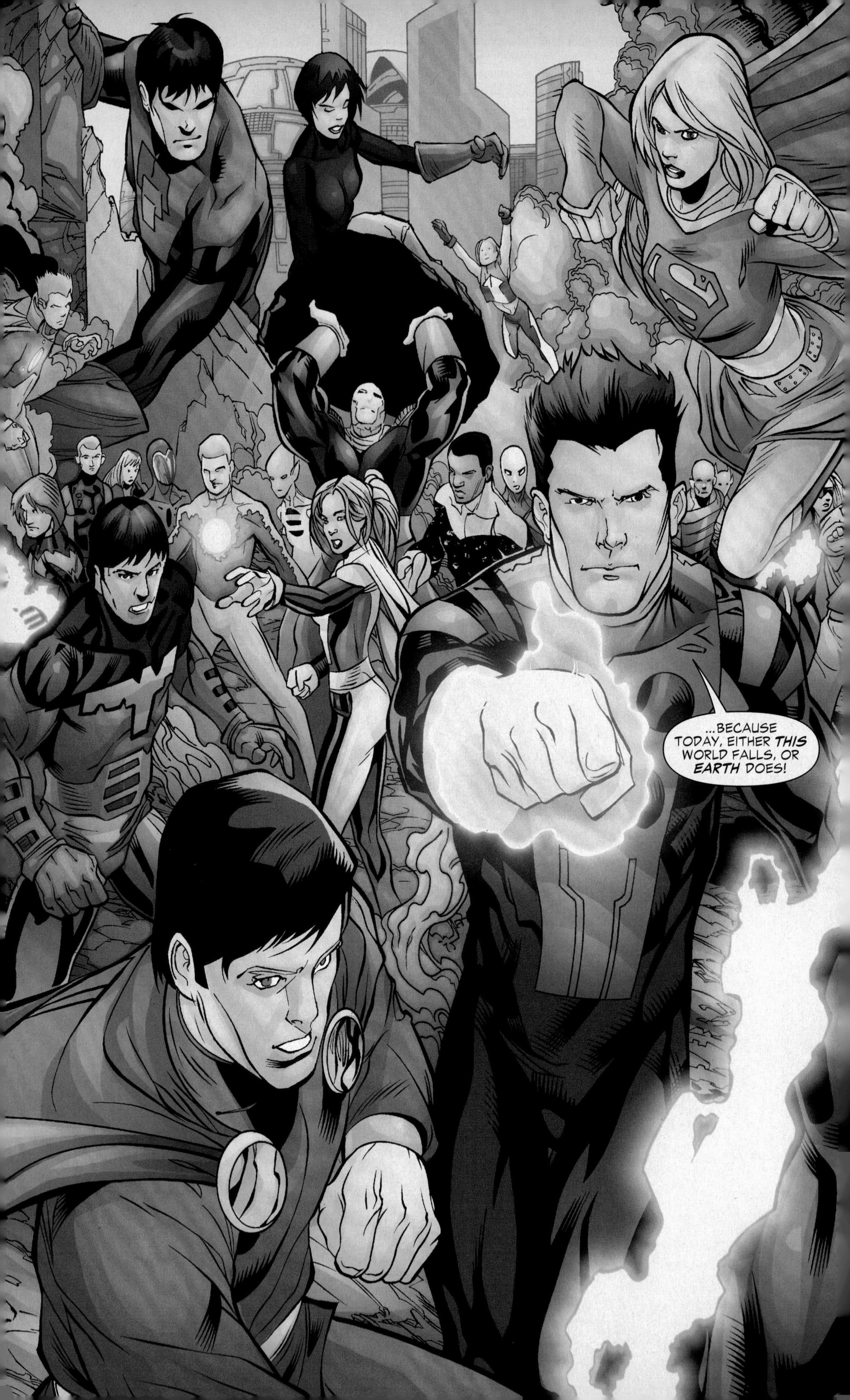
...BECAUSE TODAY, EITHER THIS WORLD FALLS, OR EARTH DOES!

SUPERGIRL & THE LEGION OF SUPER-HEROES #30

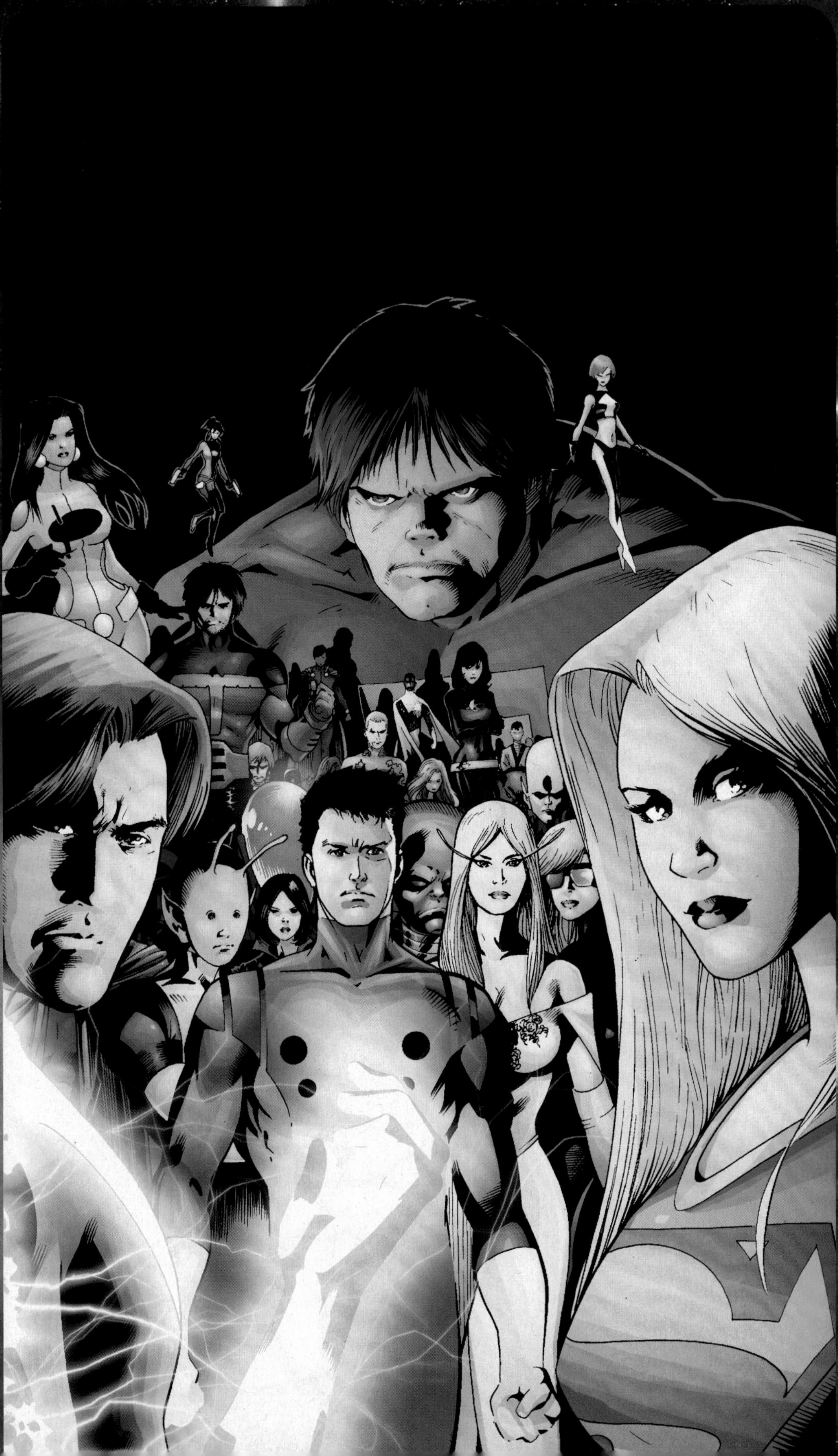

CHAPTER 5

Mark Waid Writer
Barry Kitson Penciller
Mick Gray & **Jimmy Palmiotti** Inkers
Barry Kitson & **Nathan Eyring** Cover

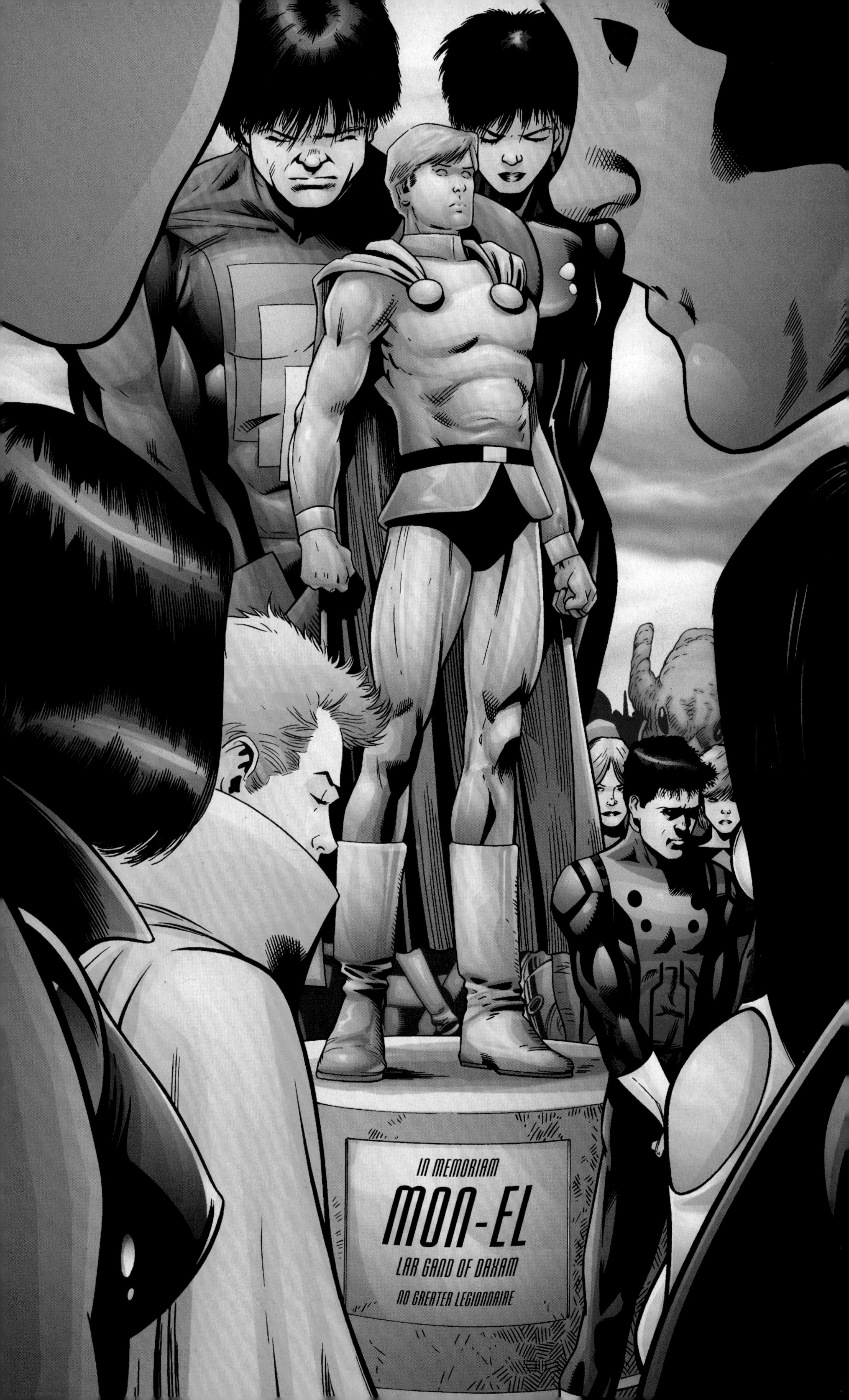
IN MEMORIAM
MON-EL
LAR GAND OF DAXAM
NO GREATER LEGIONNAIRE

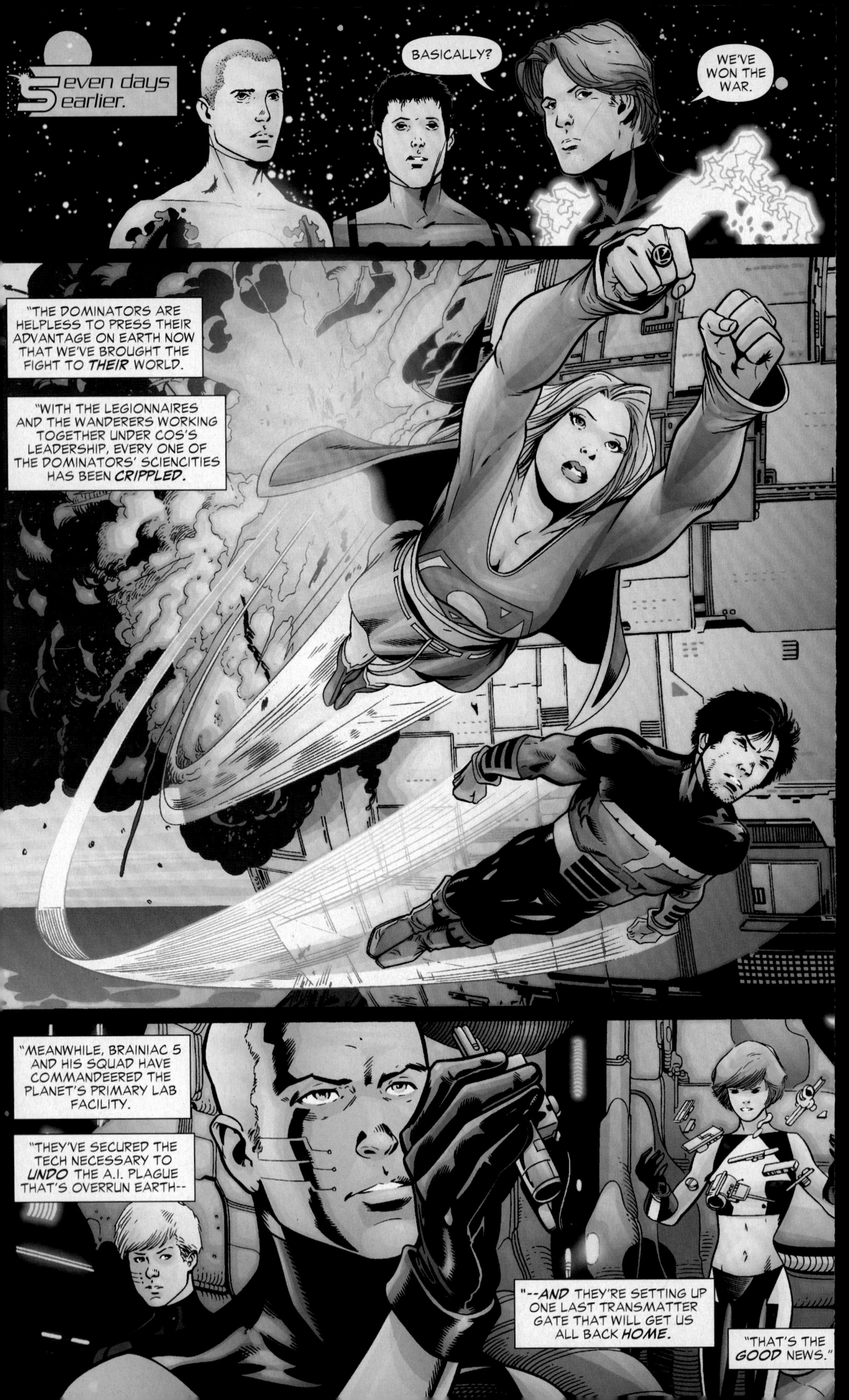
Seven days earlier.
BASICALLY?
WE'VE WON THE WAR.
"THE DOMINATORS ARE HELPLESS TO PRESS THEIR ADVANTAGE ON EARTH NOW THAT WE'VE BROUGHT THE FIGHT TO THEIR WORLD.
"WITH THE LEGIONNAIRES AND THE WANDERERS WORKING TOGETHER UNDER COS'S LEADERSHIP, EVERY ONE OF THE DOMINATORS' SCIENCITIES HAS BEEN CRIPPLED.
"MEANWHILE, BRAINIAC 5 AND HIS SQUAD HAVE COMMANDEERED THE PLANET'S PRIMARY LAB FACILITY.
"THEY'VE SECURED THE TECH NECESSARY TO UNDO THE A.I. PLAGUE THAT'S OVERRUN EARTH--
"--AND THEY'RE SETTING UP ONE LAST TRANSMATTER GATE THAT WILL GET US ALL BACK HOME.
"THAT'S THE GOOD NEWS."

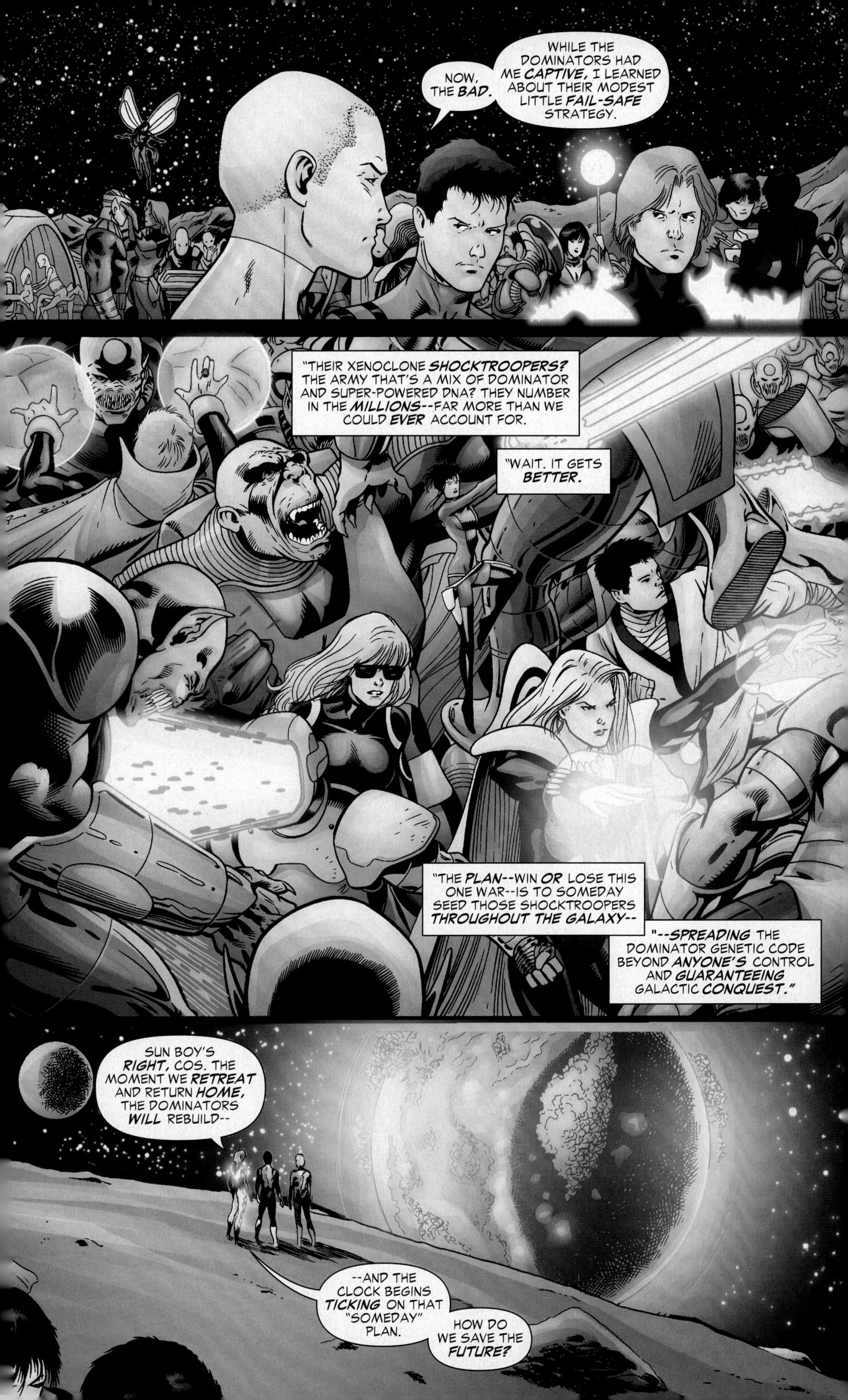
NOW, THE BAD.
WHILE THE DOMINATORS HAD ME CAPTIVE, I LEARNED ABOUT THEIR MODEST LITTLE FAIL-SAFE STRATEGY.
"THEIR XENOCLONE SHOCKTROOPERS? THE ARMY THAT'S A MIX OF DOMINATOR AND SUPER-POWERED DNA? THEY NUMBER IN THE MILLIONS--FAR MORE THAN WE COULD EVER ACCOUNT FOR.
"WAIT. IT GETS BETTER.
"THE PLAN--WIN OR LOSE THIS ONE WAR--IS TO SOMEDAY SEED THOSE SHOCKTROOPERS THROUGHOUT THE GALAXY--
"--SPREADING THE DOMINATOR GENETIC CODE BEYOND ANYONE'S CONTROL AND GUARANTEEING GALACTIC CONQUEST."
SUN BOY'S RIGHT, COS. THE MOMENT WE RETREAT AND RETURN HOME, THE DOMINATORS WILL REBUILD--
--AND THE CLOCK BEGINS TICKING ON THAT "SOMEDAY" PLAN.
HOW DO WE SAVE THE FUTURE?

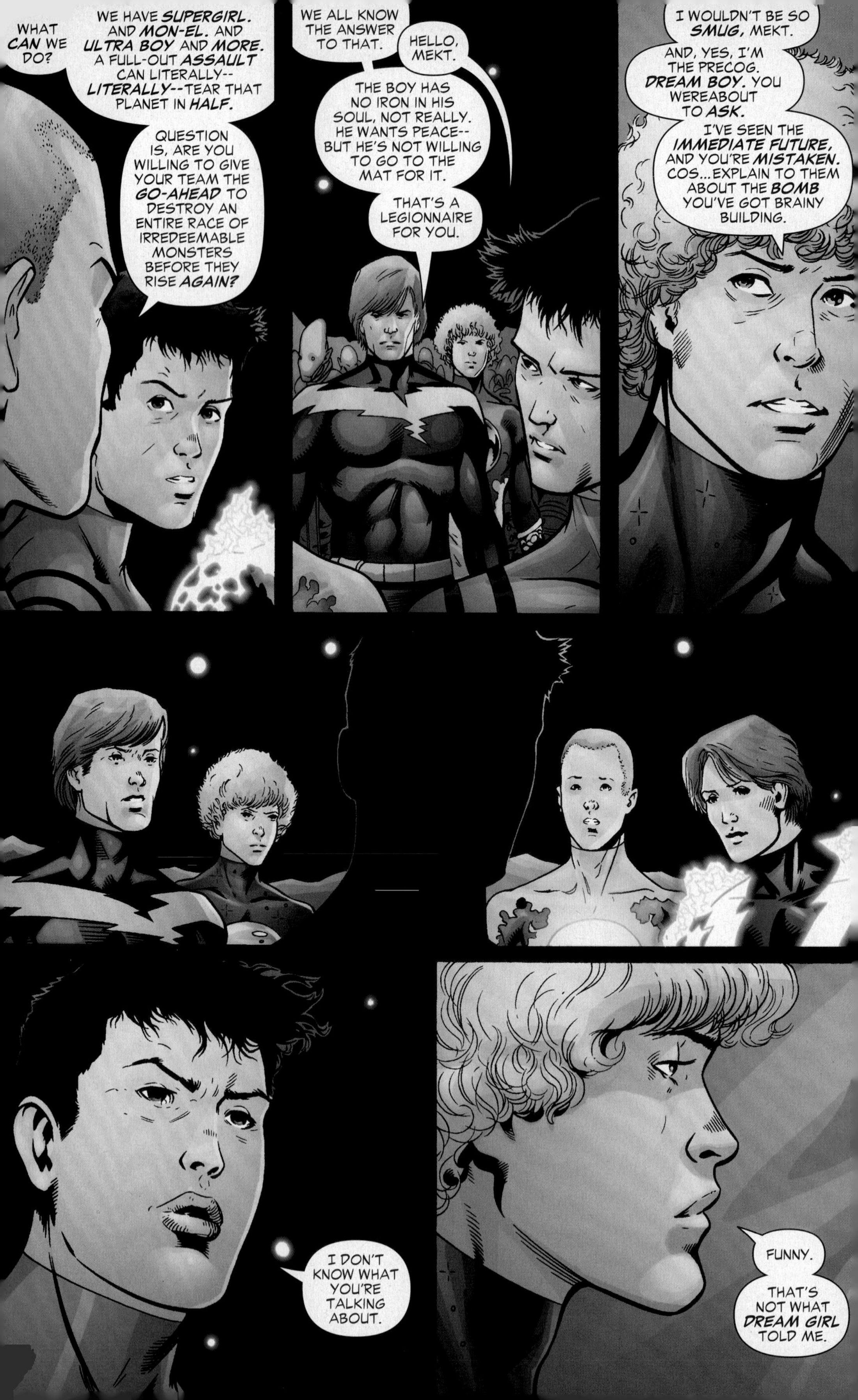
WHAT CAN WE DO?
WE HAVE SUPERGIRL. AND MON-EL. AND ULTRA BOY AND MORE. A FULL-OUT ASSAULT CAN LITERALLY-- LITERALLY--TEAR THAT PLANET IN HALF.
QUESTION IS, ARE YOU WILLING TO GIVE YOUR TEAM THE GO-AHEAD TO DESTROY AN ENTIRE RACE OF IRREDEEMABLE MONSTERS BEFORE THEY RISE AGAIN?
WE ALL KNOW THE ANSWER TO THAT.
HELLO, MEKT.
THE BOY HAS NO IRON IN HIS SOUL, NOT REALLY. HE WANTS PEACE-- BUT HE'S NOT WILLING TO GO TO THE MAT FOR IT.
THAT'S A LEGIONNAIRE FOR YOU.
I WOULDN'T BE SO SMUG, MEKT.
AND, YES, I'M THE PRECOG. DREAM BOY. YOU WEREABOUT TO ASK.
I'VE SEEN THE IMMEDIATE FUTURE, AND YOU'RE MISTAKEN. COS...EXPLAIN TO THEM ABOUT THE BOMB YOU'VE GOT BRAINY BUILDING.
I DON'T KNOW WHAT YOU'RE TALKING ABOUT.
FUNNY.
THAT'S NOT WHAT DREAM GIRL TOLD ME.

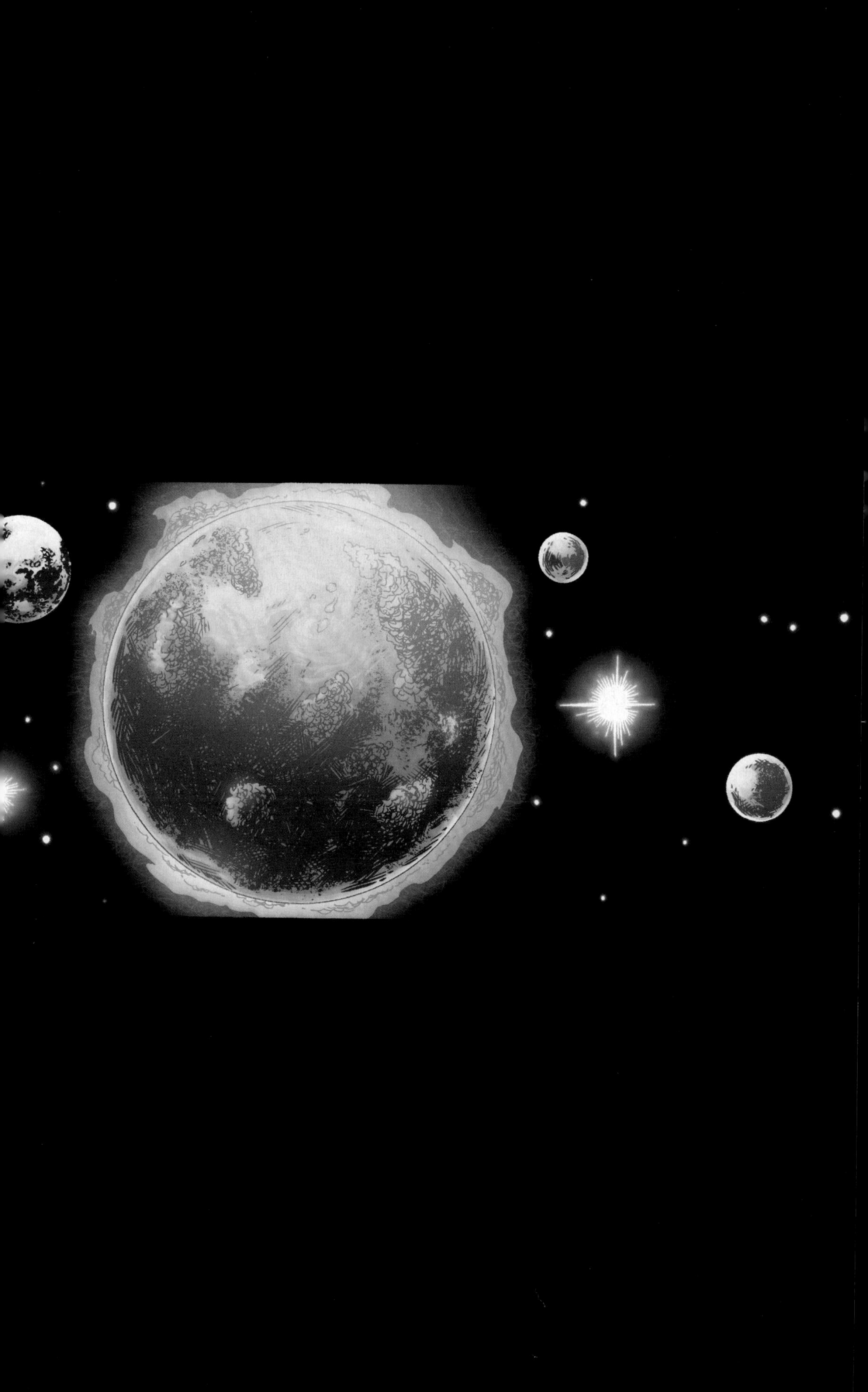

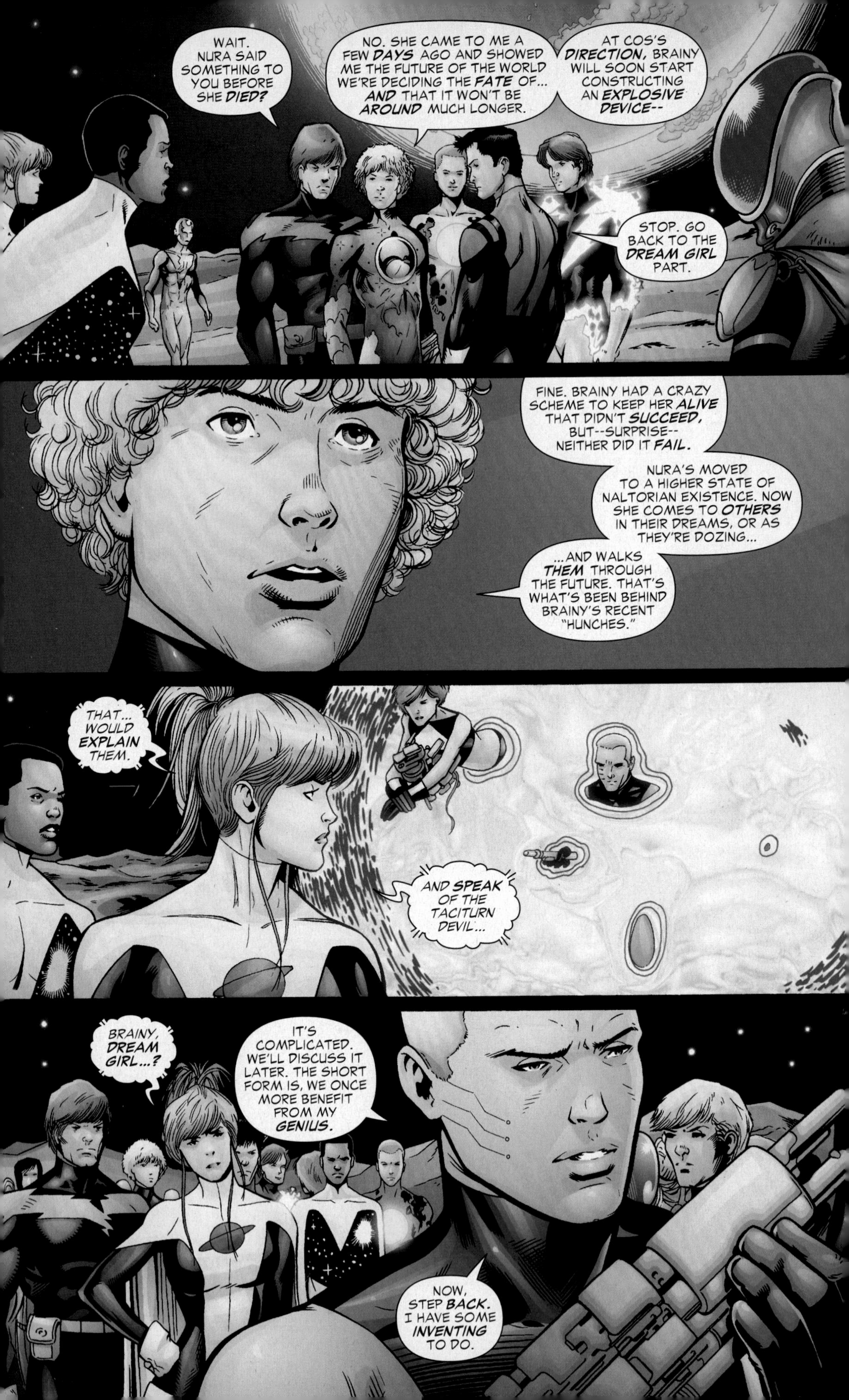
WAIT. NURA SAID SOMETHING TO YOU BEFORE SHE DIED?
NO. SHE CAME TO ME A FEW DAYS AGO AND SHOWED ME THE FUTURE OF THE WORLD WE'RE DECIDING THE FATE OF... AND THAT IT WON'T BE AROUND MUCH LONGER.
AT COS'S DIRECTION, BRAINY WILL SOON START CONSTRUCTING AN EXPLOSIVE DEVICE--
STOP. GO BACK TO THE DREAM GIRL PART.
FINE. BRAINY HAD A CRAZY SCHEME TO KEEP HER ALIVE THAT DIDN'T SUCCEED, BUT--SURPRISE-- NEITHER DID IT FAIL.
NURA'S MOVED TO A HIGHER STATE OF NALTORIAN EXISTENCE. NOW SHE COMES TO OTHERS IN THEIR DREAMS, OR AS THEY'RE DOZING...
...AND WALKS THEM THROUGH THE FUTURE. THAT'S WHAT'S BEEN BEHIND BRAINY'S RECENT "HUNCHES."
THAT... WOULD EXPLAIN THEM.
AND SPEAK OF THE TACITURN DEVIL...
BRAINY, DREAM GIRL...?
IT'S COMPLICATED. WE'LL DISCUSS IT LATER. THE SHORT FORM IS, WE ONCE MORE BENEFIT FROM MY GENIUS.
NOW, STEP BACK. I HAVE SOME INVENTING TO DO.

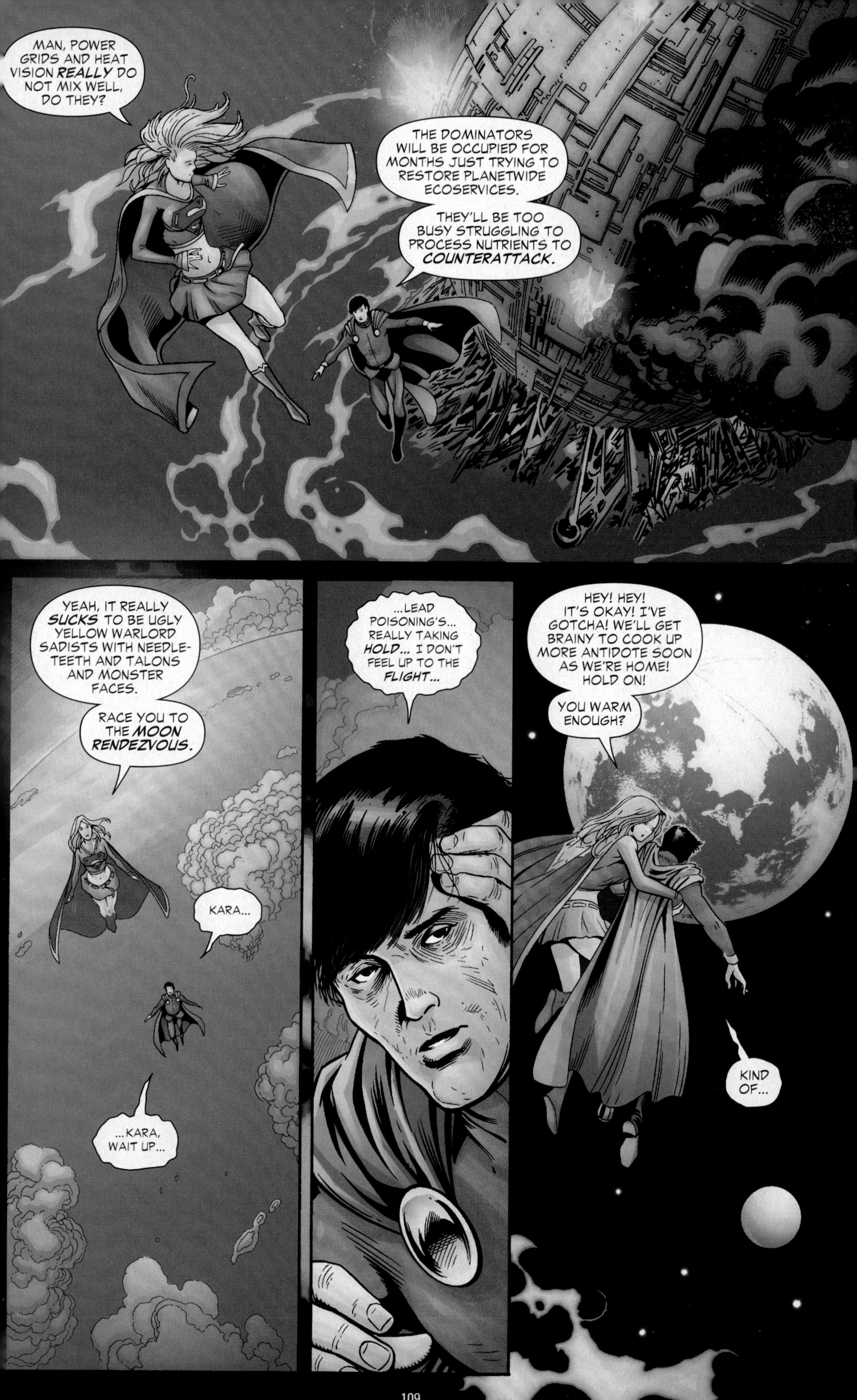

MAN, POWER GRIDS AND HEAT VISION REALLY DO NOT MIX WELL, DO THEY?
THE DOMINATORS WILL BE OCCUPIED FOR MONTHS JUST TRYING TO RESTORE PLANETWIDE ECOSERVICES.
THEY'LL BE TOO BUSY STRUGGLING TO PROCESS NUTRIENTS TO COUNTERATTACK.
YEAH, IT REALLY SUCKS TO BE UGLY YELLOW WARLORD SADISTS WITH NEEDLE-TEETH AND TALONS AND MONSTER FACES.
RACE YOU TO THE MOON RENDEZVOUS.
KARA...
...KARA, WAIT UP...
...LEAD POISONING'S... REALLY TAKING HOLD... I DON'T FEEL UP TO THE FLIGHT...
HEY! HEY! IT'S OKAY! I'VE GOTCHA! WE'LL GET BRAINY TO COOK UP MORE ANTIDOTE SOON AS WE'RE HOME! HOLD ON!
YOU WARM ENOUGH?
KIND OF...

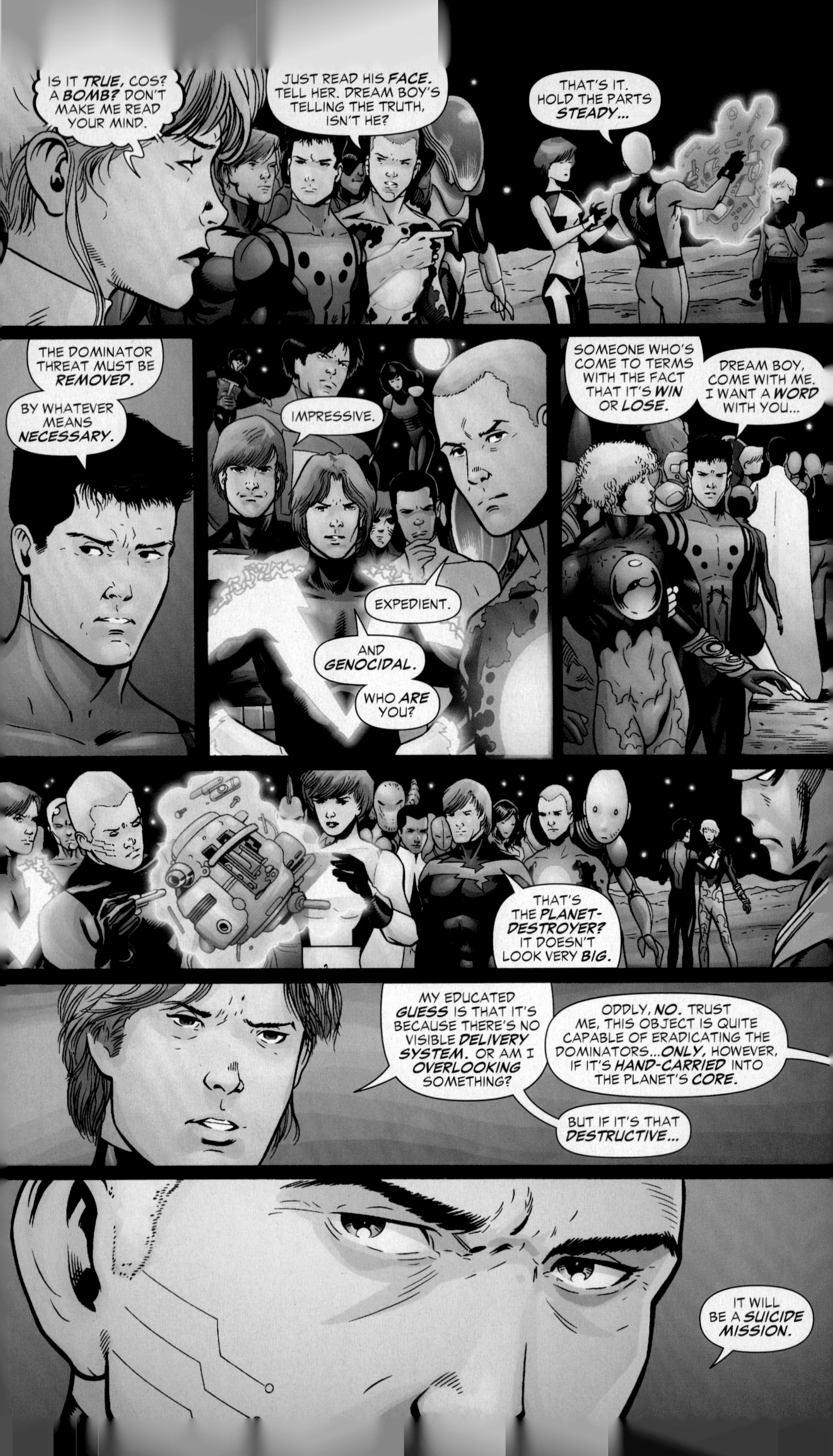
IS IT TRUE, COS? A BOMB? DON'T MAKE ME READ YOUR MIND.
JUST READ HIS FACE. TELL HER. DREAM BOY'S TELLING THE TRUTH, ISN'T HE?
THAT'S IT. HOLD THE PARTS STEADY...
THE DOMINATOR THREAT MUST BE REMOVED.
BY WHATEVER MEANS NECESSARY.
IMPRESSIVE.
EXPEDIENT.
AND GENOCIDAL.
WHO ARE YOU?
SOMEONE WHO'S COME TO TERMS WITH THE FACT THAT IT'S WIN OR LOSE.
DREAM BOY, COME WITH ME. I WANT A WORD WITH YOU...
THAT'S THE PLANET-DESTROYER? IT DOESN'T LOOK VERY BIG.
MY EDUCATED GUESS IS THAT IT'S BECAUSE THERE'S NO VISIBLE DELIVERY SYSTEM. OR AM I OVERLOOKING SOMETHING?
ODDLY, NO. TRUST ME, THIS OBJECT IS QUITE CAPABLE OF ERADICATING THE DOMINATORS...ONLY, HOWEVER, IF IT'S HAND-CARRIED INTO THE PLANET'S CORE.
BUT IF IT'S THAT DESTRUCTIVE...
IT WILL BE A SUICIDE MISSION.

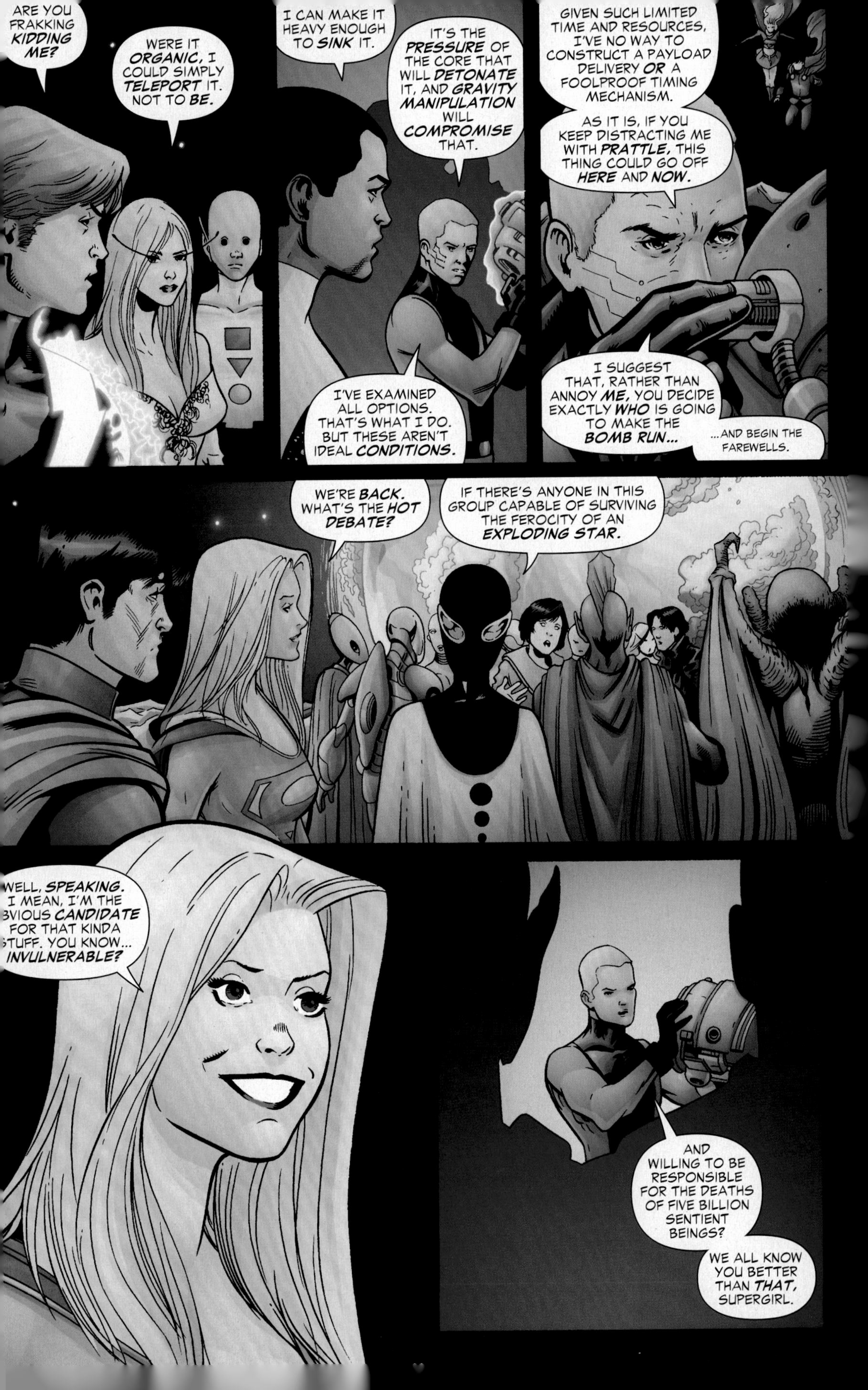

ARE YOU FRAKKING KIDDING ME?
WERE IT ORGANIC, I COULD SIMPLY TELEPORT IT. NOT TO BE.
I CAN MAKE IT HEAVY ENOUGH TO SINK IT.
IT'S THE PRESSURE OF THE CORE THAT WILL DETONATE IT, AND GRAVITY MANIPULATION WILL COMPROMISE THAT.
I'VE EXAMINED ALL OPTIONS. THAT'S WHAT I DO. BUT THESE AREN'T IDEAL CONDITIONS.
GIVEN SUCH LIMITED TIME AND RESOURCES, I'VE NO WAY TO CONSTRUCT A PAYLOAD DELIVERY OR A FOOLPROOF TIMING MECHANISM.
AS IT IS, IF YOU KEEP DISTRACTING ME WITH PRATTLE, THIS THING COULD GO OFF HERE AND NOW.
I SUGGEST THAT, RATHER THAN ANNOY ME, YOU DECIDE EXACTLY WHO IS GOING TO MAKE THE BOMB RUN...
...AND BEGIN THE FAREWELLS.
WE'RE BACK. WHAT'S THE HOT DEBATE?
IF THERE'S ANYONE IN THIS GROUP CAPABLE OF SURVIVING THE FEROCITY OF AN EXPLODING STAR.
WELL, SPEAKING. I MEAN, I'M THE BVIOUS CANDIDATE FOR THAT KINDA STUFF. YOU KNOW... INVULNERABLE?
AND WILLING TO BE RESPONSIBLE FOR THE DEATHS OF FIVE BILLION SENTIENT BEINGS?
WE ALL KNOW YOU BETTER THAN THAT, SUPERGIRL.

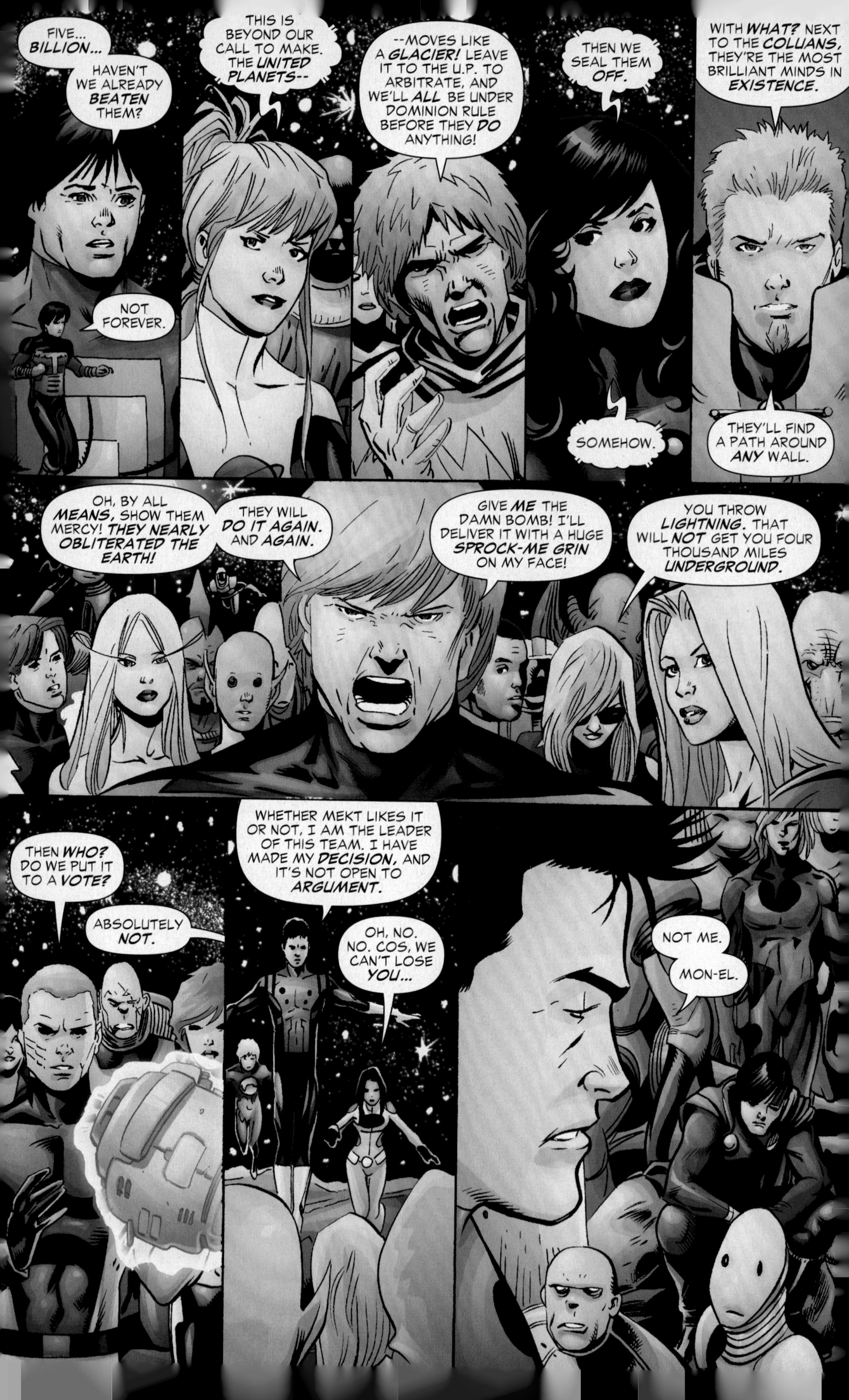
FIVE... BILLION...
HAVEN'T WE ALREADY BEATEN THEM?
NOT FOREVER.
THIS IS BEYOND OUR CALL TO MAKE. THE UNITED PLANETS--
--MOVES LIKE A GLACIER! LEAVE IT TO THE U.P. TO ARBITRATE, AND WE'LL ALL BE UNDER DOMINION RULE BEFORE THEY DO ANYTHING!
THEN WE SEAL THEM OFF.
SOMEHOW.
WITH WHAT? NEXT TO THE COLUANS, THEY'RE THE MOST BRILLIANT MINDS IN EXISTENCE.
THEY'LL FIND A PATH AROUND ANY WALL.
OH, BY ALL MEANS, SHOW THEM MERCY! THEY NEARLY OBLITERATED THE EARTH!
THEY WILL DO IT AGAIN. AND AGAIN.
GIVE ME THE DAMN BOMB! I'LL DELIVER IT WITH A HUGE SPROCK-ME GRIN ON MY FACE!
YOU THROW LIGHTNING. THAT WILL NOT GET YOU FOUR THOUSAND MILES UNDERGROUND.
THEN WHO? DO WE PUT IT TO A VOTE?
ABSOLUTELY NOT.
WHETHER MEKT LIKES IT OR NOT, I AM THE LEADER OF THIS TEAM. I HAVE MADE MY DECISION, AND IT'S NOT OPEN TO ARGUMENT.
OH, NO. NO. COS, WE CAN'T LOSE YOU...
NOT ME.
MON-EL.

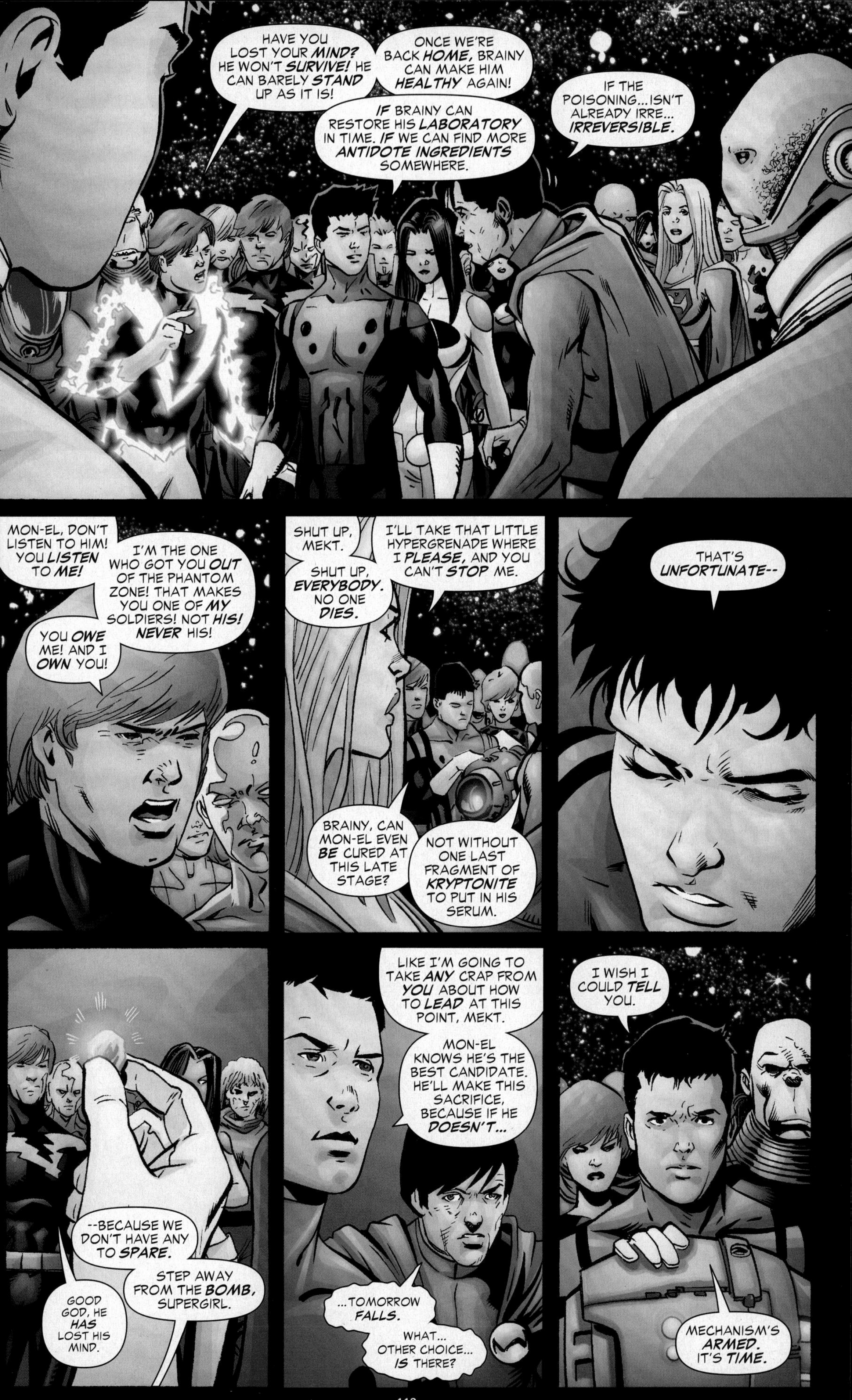

HAVE YOU LOST YOUR MIND? HE WON'T SURVIVE! HE CAN BARELY STAND UP AS IT IS!
ONCE WE'RE BACK HOME, BRAINY CAN MAKE HIM HEALTHY AGAIN!
IF BRAINY CAN RESTORE HIS LABORATORY IN TIME. IF WE CAN FIND MORE ANTIDOTE INGREDIENTS SOMEWHERE.
IF THE POISONING...ISN'T ALREADY IRRE... IRREVERSIBLE.
MON-EL, DON'T LISTEN TO HIM! YOU LISTEN TO ME!
I'M THE ONE WHO GOT YOU OUT OF THE PHANTOM ZONE! THAT MAKES YOU ONE OF MY SOLDIERS! NOT HIS! NEVER HIS!
YOU OWE ME! AND I OWN YOU!
SHUT UP, MEKT.
I'LL TAKE THAT LITTLE HYPERGRENADE WHERE I PLEASE, AND YOU CAN'T STOP ME.
SHUT UP, EVERYBODY. NO ONE DIES.
BRAINY, CAN MON-EL EVEN BE CURED AT THIS LATE STAGE?
NOT WITHOUT ONE LAST FRAGMENT OF KRYPTONITE TO PUT IN HIS SERUM.
THAT'S UNFORTUNATE--
--BECAUSE WE DON'T HAVE ANY TO SPARE.
STEP AWAY FROM THE BOMB, SUPERGIRL.
GOOD GOD, HE HAS LOST HIS MIND.
LIKE I'M GOING TO TAKE ANY CRAP FROM YOU ABOUT HOW TO LEAD AT THIS POINT, MEKT.
MON-EL KNOWS HE'S THE BEST CANDIDATE. HE'LL MAKE THIS SACRIFICE, BECAUSE IF HE DOESN'T...
...TOMORROW FALLS.
WHAT... OTHER CHOICE... IS THERE?
I WISH I COULD TELL YOU.
MECHANISM'S ARMED. IT'S TIME.

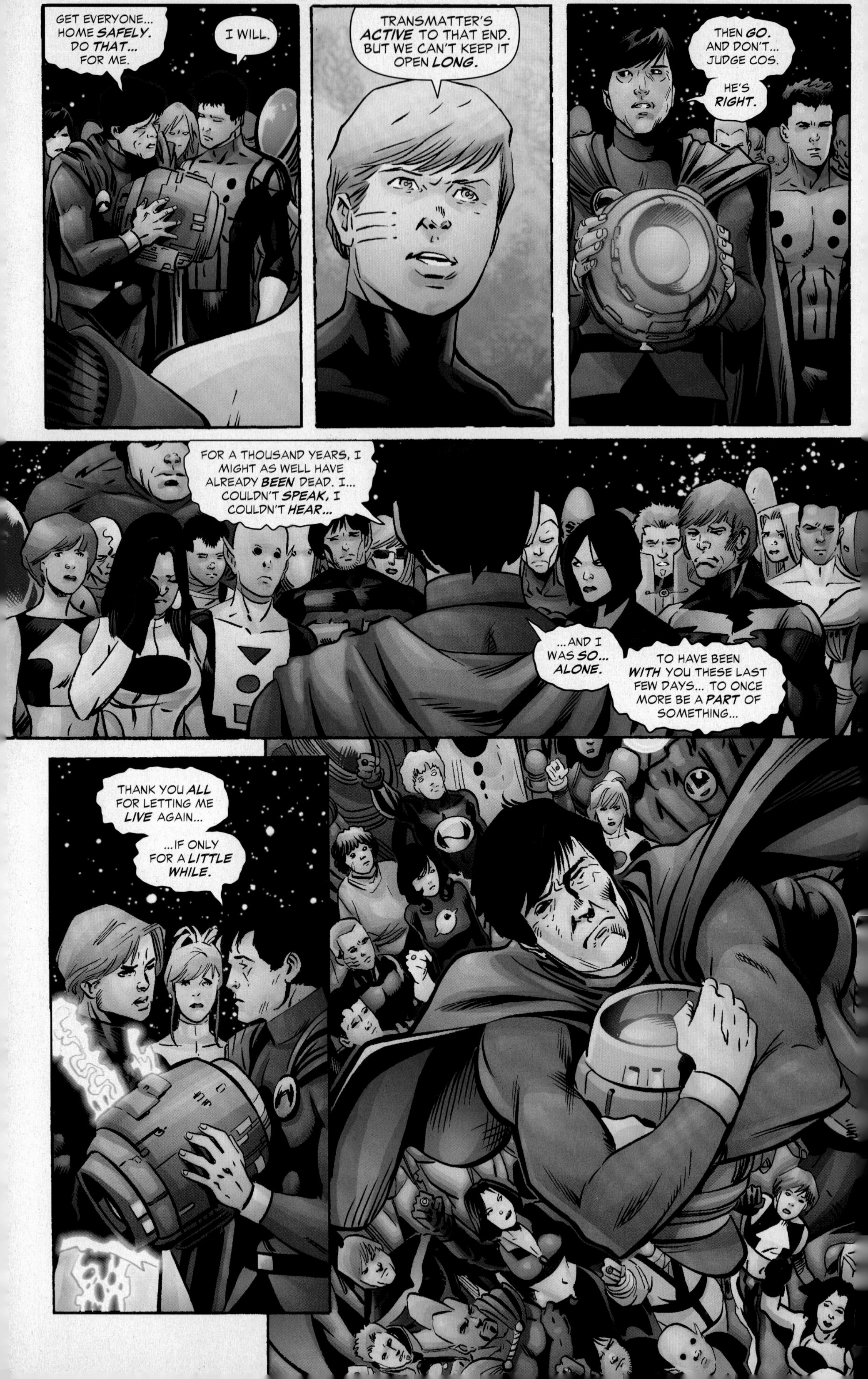
GET EVERYONE... HOME SAFELY. DO THAT... FOR ME.
I WILL.
TRANSMATTER'S ACTIVE TO THAT END. BUT WE CAN'T KEEP IT OPEN LONG.
THEN GO. AND DON'T... JUDGE COS.
HE'S RIGHT.
FOR A THOUSAND YEARS, I MIGHT AS WELL HAVE ALREADY BEEN DEAD. I... COULDN'T SPEAK, I COULDN'T HEAR...
...AND I WAS SO... ALONE.
TO HAVE BEEN WITH YOU THESE LAST FEW DAYS... TO ONCE MORE BE A PART OF SOMETHING...
THANK YOU ALL FOR LETTING ME LIVE AGAIN...
...IF ONLY FOR A LITTLE WHILE.

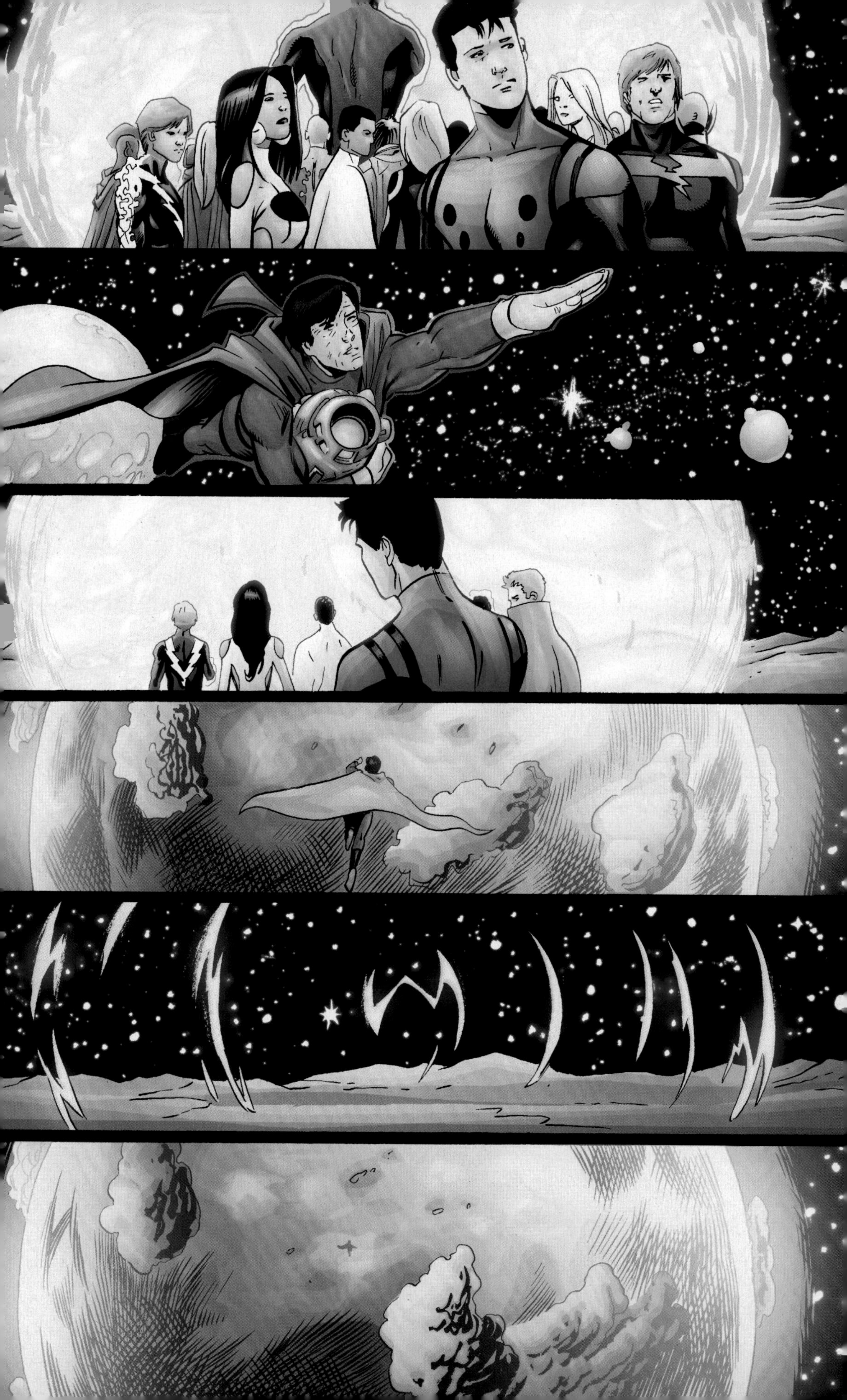

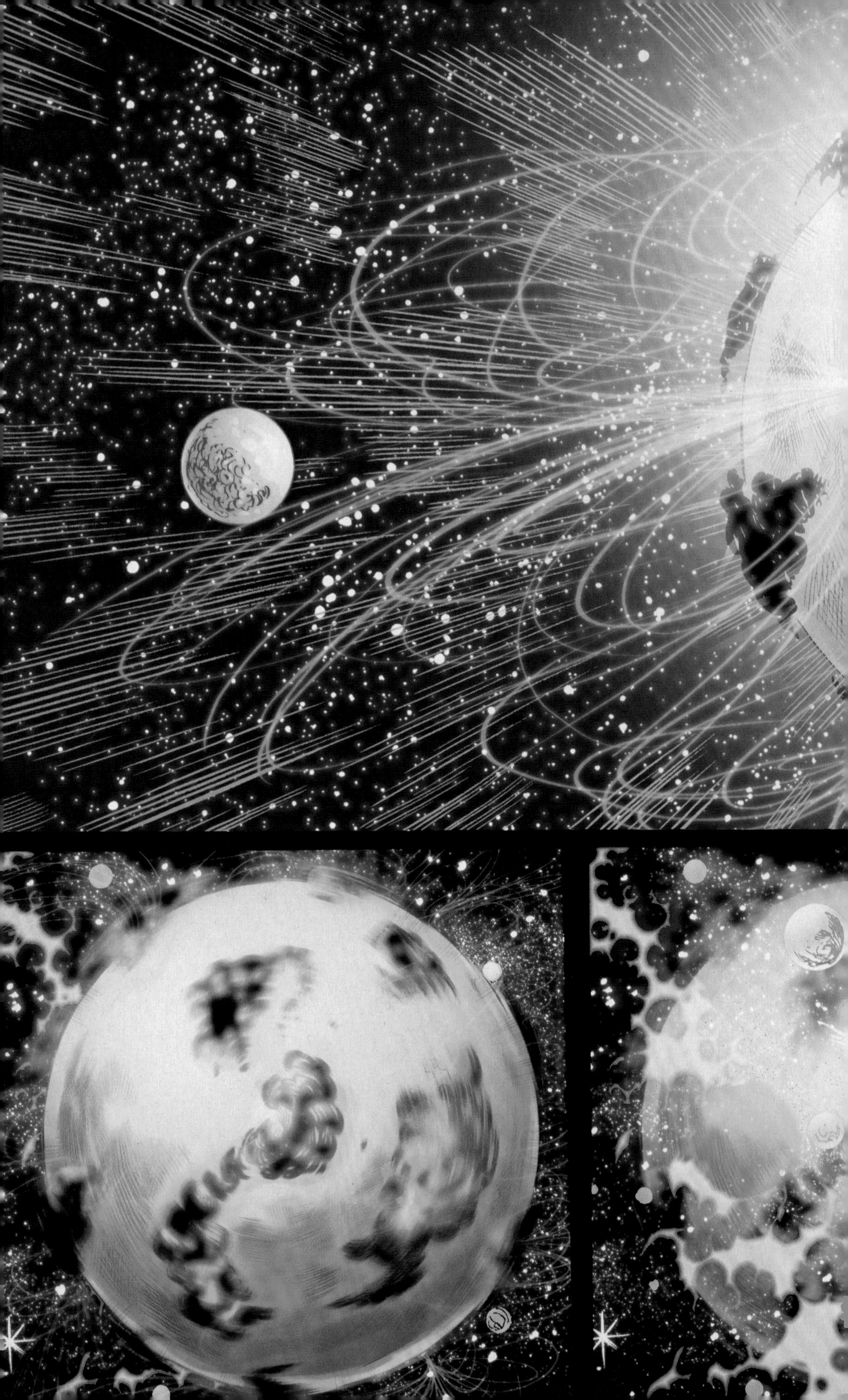

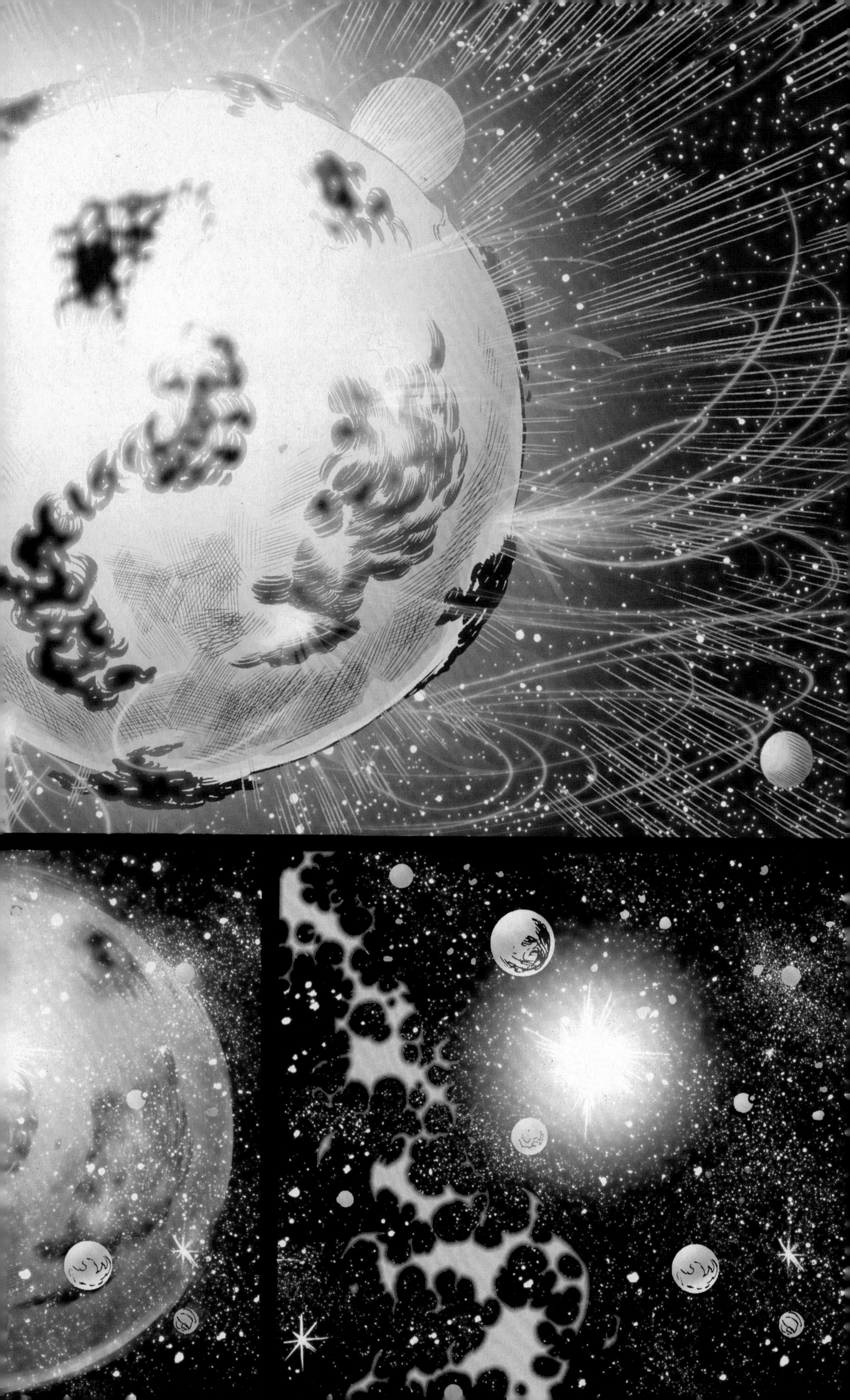

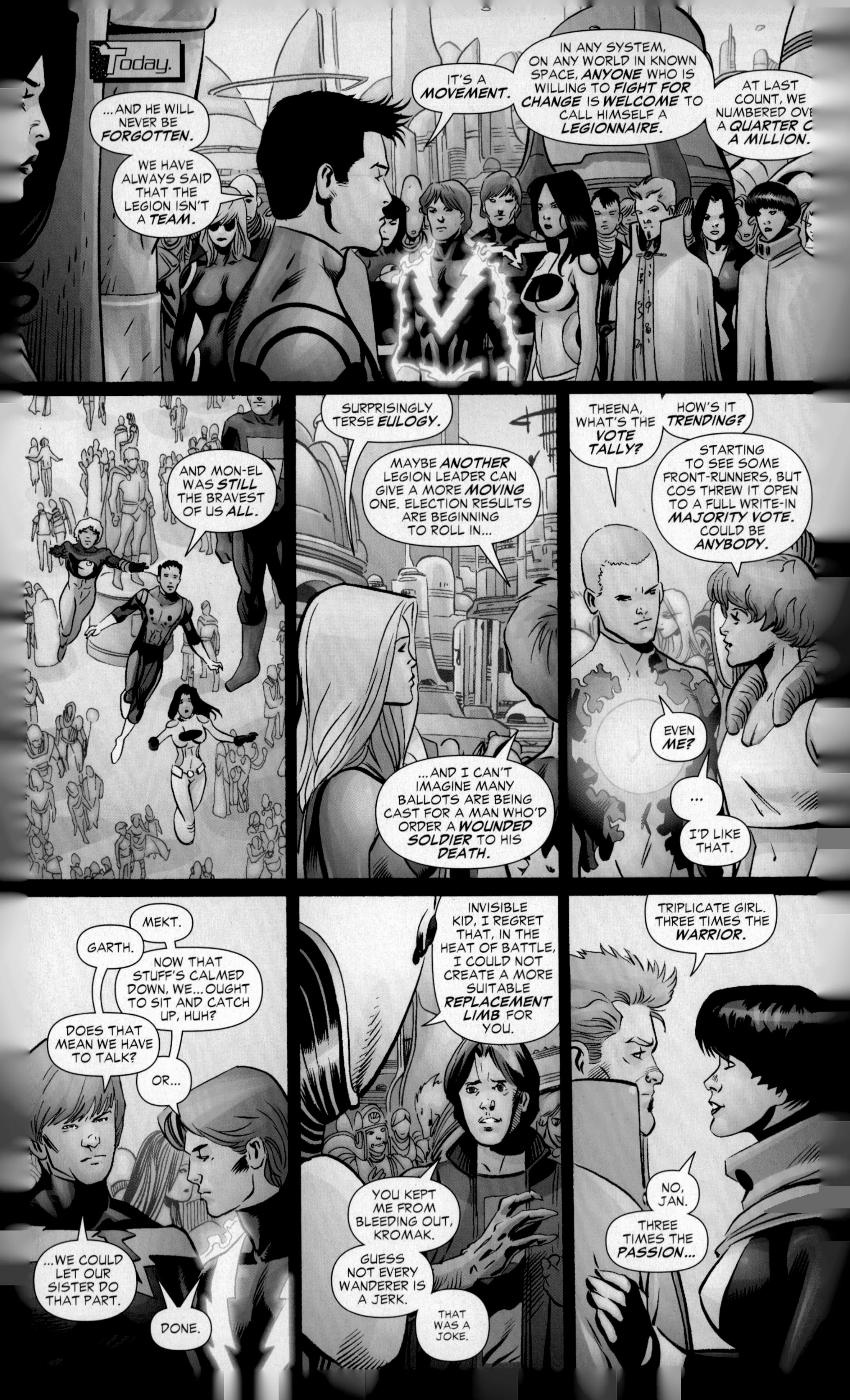
Today.
...AND HE WILL NEVER BE FORGOTTEN.
WE HAVE ALWAYS SAID THAT THE LEGION ISN'T A TEAM.
IT'S A MOVEMENT.
IN ANY SYSTEM, ON ANY WORLD IN KNOWN SPACE, ANYONE WHO IS WILLING TO FIGHT FOR CHANGE IS WELCOME TO CALL HIMSELF A LEGIONNAIRE.
AT LAST COUNT, WE NUMBERED OVE A QUARTER O A MILLION.
AND MON-EL WAS STILL THE BRAVEST OF US ALL.
SURPRISINGLY TERSE EULOGY.
MAYBE ANOTHER LEGION LEADER CAN GIVE A MORE MOVING ONE. ELECTION RESULTS ARE BEGINNING TO ROLL IN...
...AND I CAN'T IMAGINE MANY BALLOTS ARE BEING CAST FOR A MAN WHO'D ORDER A WOUNDED SOLDIER TO HIS DEATH.
THEENA, WHAT'S THE VOTE TALLY?
HOW'S IT TRENDING?
STARTING TO SEE SOME FRONT-RUNNERS, BUT COS THREW IT OPEN TO A FULL WRITE-IN MAJORITY VOTE. COULD BE ANYBODY.
EVEN ME?
...
I'D LIKE THAT.
GARTH.
MEKT.
NOW THAT STUFF'S CALMED DOWN, WE...OUGHT TO SIT AND CATCH UP, HUH?
DOES THAT MEAN WE HAVE TO TALK?
OR...
...WE COULD LET OUR SISTER DO THAT PART.
DONE.
INVISIBLE KID, I REGRET THAT, IN THE HEAT OF BATTLE, I COULD NOT CREATE A MORE SUITABLE REPLACEMENT LIMB FOR YOU.
YOU KEPT ME FROM BLEEDING OUT, KROMAK.
GUESS NOT EVERY WANDERER IS A JERK.
THAT WAS A JOKE.
TRIPLICATE GIRL. THREE TIMES THE WARRIOR.
NO, JAN.
THREE TIMES THE PASSION...

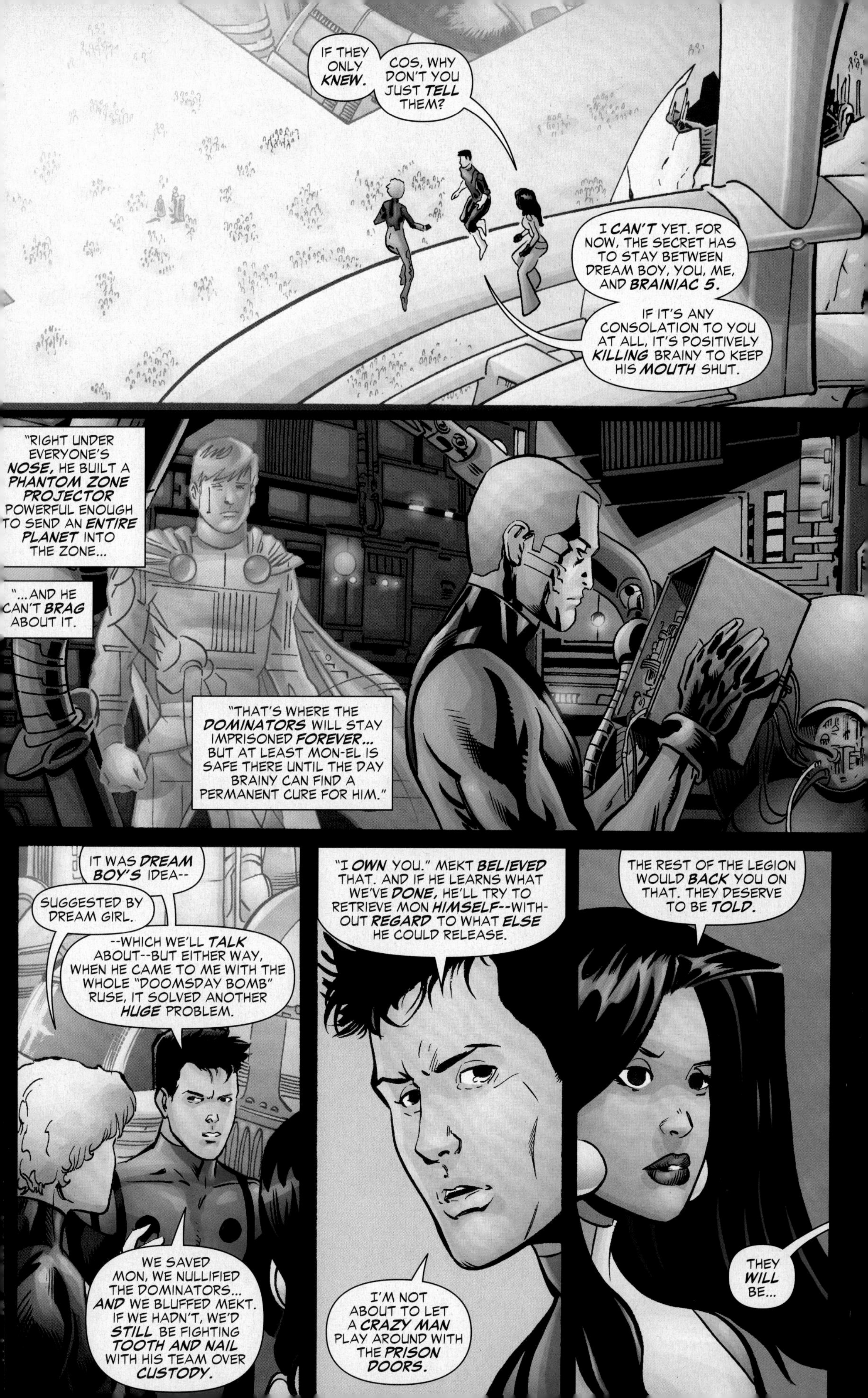
IF THEY ONLY KNEW.
COS, WHY DON'T YOU JUST TELL THEM?
I CAN'T YET. FOR NOW, THE SECRET HAS TO STAY BETWEEN DREAM BOY, YOU, ME, AND BRAINIAC 5.
IF IT'S ANY CONSOLATION TO YOU AT ALL, IT'S POSITIVELY KILLING BRAINY TO KEEP HIS MOUTH SHUT.
"RIGHT UNDER EVERYONE'S NOSE, HE BUILT A PHANTOM ZONE PROJECTOR POWERFUL ENOUGH TO SEND AN ENTIRE PLANET INTO THE ZONE...
"...AND HE CAN'T BRAG ABOUT IT.
"THAT'S WHERE THE DOMINATORS WILL STAY IMPRISONED FOREVER... BUT AT LEAST MON-EL IS SAFE THERE UNTIL THE DAY BRAINY CAN FIND A PERMANENT CURE FOR HIM."
IT WAS DREAM BOY'S IDEA--
SUGGESTED BY DREAM GIRL.
--WHICH WE'LL TALK ABOUT--BUT EITHER WAY, WHEN HE CAME TO ME WITH THE WHOLE "DOOMSDAY BOMB" RUSE, IT SOLVED ANOTHER HUGE PROBLEM.
WE SAVED MON, WE NULLIFIED THE DOMINATORS... AND WE BLUFFED MEKT. IF WE HADN'T, WE'D STILL BE FIGHTING TOOTH AND NAIL WITH HIS TEAM OVER CUSTODY.
"I OWN YOU." MEKT BELIEVED THAT. AND IF HE LEARNS WHAT WE'VE DONE, HE'LL TRY TO RETRIEVE MON HIMSELF--WITHOUT REGARD TO WHAT ELSE HE COULD RELEASE.
I'M NOT ABOUT TO LET A CRAZY MAN PLAY AROUND WITH THE PRISON DOORS.
THE REST OF THE LEGION WOULD BACK YOU ON THAT. THEY DESERVE TO BE TOLD.
THEY WILL BE...

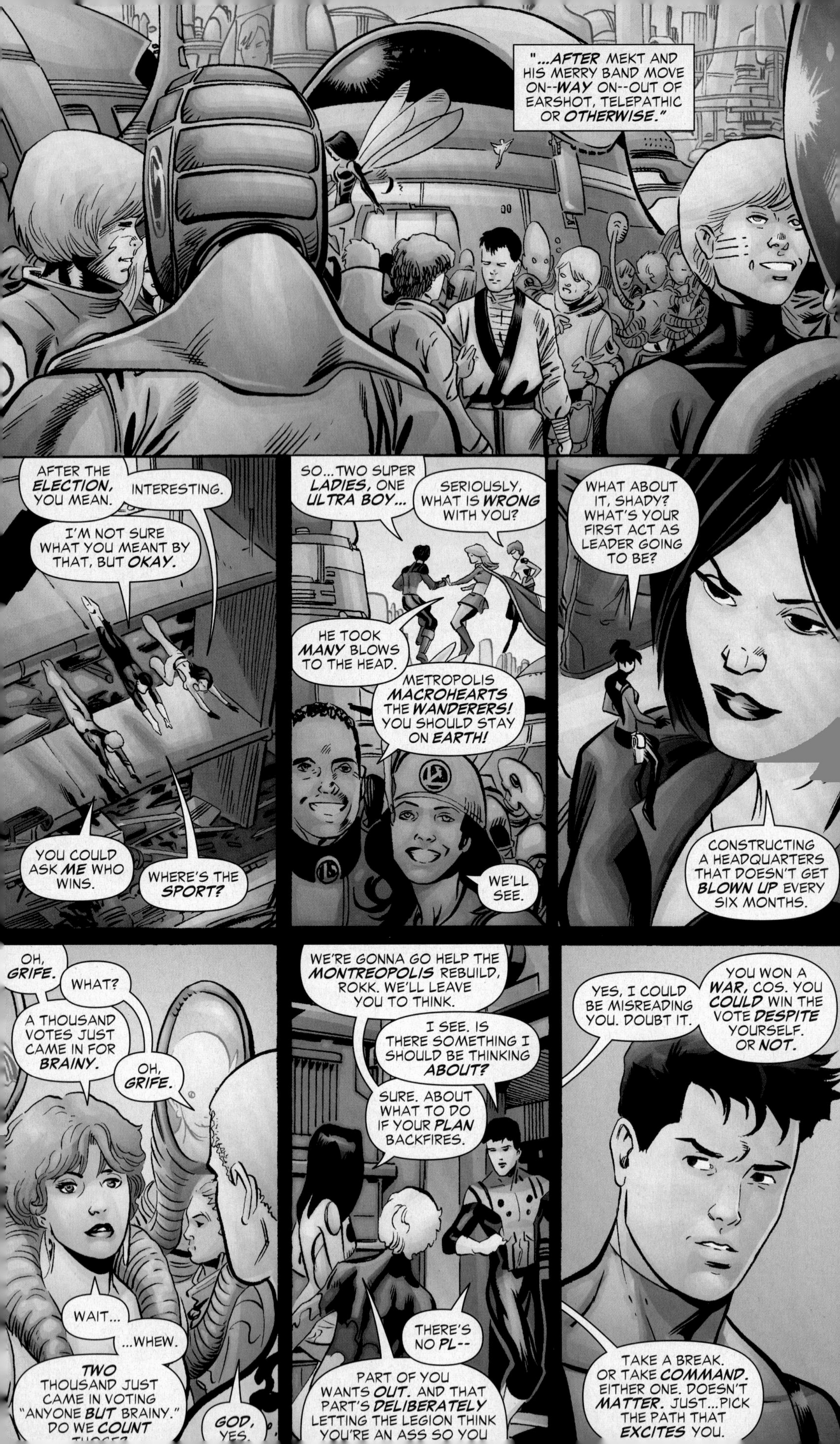
"...AFTER MEKT AND HIS MERRY BAND MOVE ON--WAY ON--OUT OF EARSHOT, TELEPATHIC OR OTHERWISE."
AFTER THE ELECTION, YOU MEAN.
INTERESTING.
I'M NOT SURE WHAT YOU MEANT BY THAT, BUT OKAY.
YOU COULD ASK ME WHO WINS.
WHERE'S THE SPORT?
SO...TWO SUPER LADIES, ONE ULTRA BOY...
SERIOUSLY, WHAT IS WRONG WITH YOU?
HE TOOK MANY BLOWS TO THE HEAD.
METROPOLIS MACROHEARTS THE WANDERERS! YOU SHOULD STAY ON EARTH!
WE'LL SEE.
WHAT ABOUT IT, SHADY? WHAT'S YOUR FIRST ACT AS LEADER GOING TO BE?
CONSTRUCTING A HEADQUARTERS THAT DOESN'T GET BLOWN UP EVERY SIX MONTHS.
OH, GRIFE.
WHAT?
A THOUSAND VOTES JUST CAME IN FOR BRAINY.
OH, GRIFE.
WAIT...
...WHEW.
TWO THOUSAND JUST CAME IN VOTING "ANYONE BUT BRAINY." DO WE COUNT
GOD, YES.
WE'RE GONNA GO HELP THE MONTREOPOLIS REBUILD, ROKK. WE'LL LEAVE YOU TO THINK.
I SEE. IS THERE SOMETHING I SHOULD BE THINKING ABOUT?
SURE. ABOUT WHAT TO DO IF YOUR PLAN BACKFIRES.
THERE'S NO PL--
PART OF YOU WANTS OUT. AND THAT PART'S DELIBERATELY LETTING THE LEGION THINK YOU'RE AN ASS SO YOU
YES, I COULD BE MISREADING YOU. DOUBT IT.
YOU WON A WAR, COS. YOU COULD WIN THE VOTE DESPITE YOURSELF. OR NOT.
TAKE A BREAK. OR TAKE COMMAND. EITHER ONE. DOESN'T MATTER. JUST...PICK THE PATH THAT EXCITES YOU.

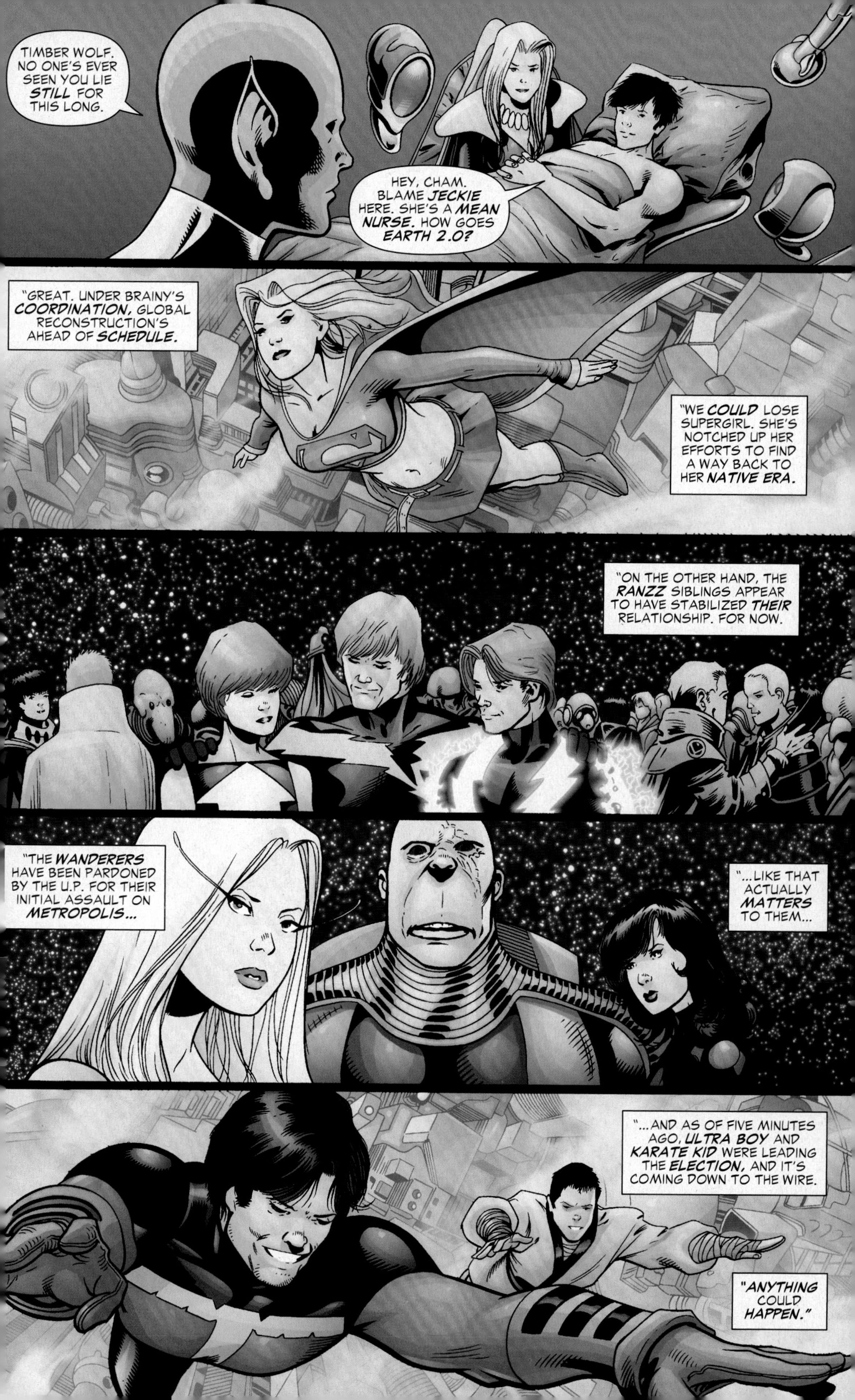
TIMBER WOLF. NO ONE'S EVER SEEN YOU LIE STILL FOR THIS LONG.
HEY, CHAM. BLAME JECKIE HERE. SHE'S A MEAN NURSE. HOW GOES EARTH 2.0?
"GREAT. UNDER BRAINY'S COORDINATION, GLOBAL RECONSTRUCTION'S AHEAD OF SCHEDULE.
"WE COULD LOSE SUPERGIRL. SHE'S NOTCHED UP HER EFFORTS TO FIND A WAY BACK TO HER NATIVE ERA.
"ON THE OTHER HAND, THE RANZZ SIBLINGS APPEAR TO HAVE STABILIZED THEIR RELATIONSHIP. FOR NOW.
"THE WANDERERS HAVE BEEN PARDONED BY THE U.P. FOR THEIR INITIAL ASSAULT ON METROPOLIS...
"...LIKE THAT ACTUALLY MATTERS TO THEM...
"...AND AS OF FIVE MINUTES AGO, ULTRA BOY AND KARATE KID WERE LEADING THE ELECTION, AND IT'S COMING DOWN TO THE WIRE.
"ANYTHING COULD HAPPEN."

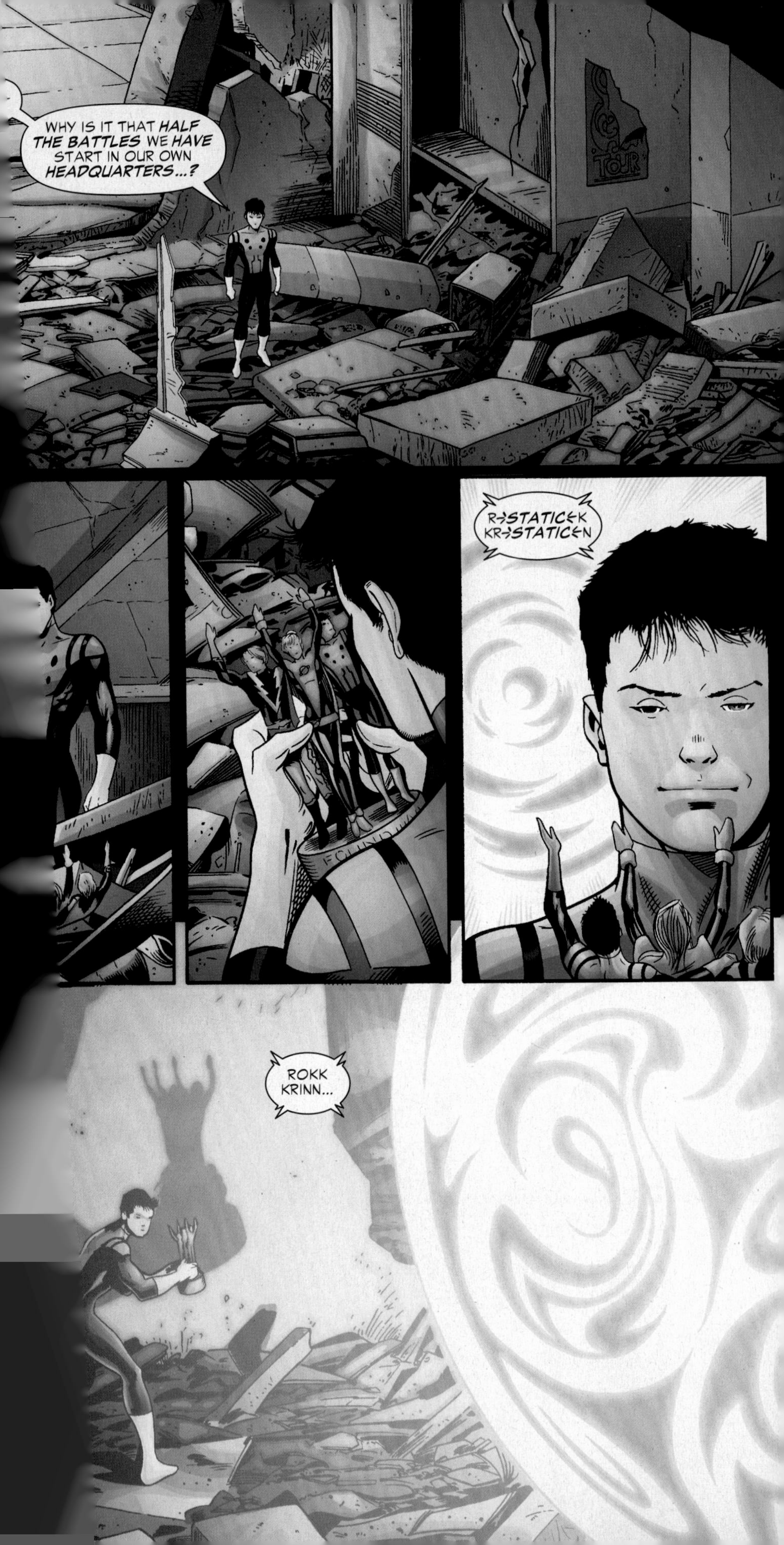
WHY IS IT THAT HALF THE BATTLES WE HAVE START IN OUR OWN HEADQUARTERS...?
R-STATIC-K KR-STATIC-N
ROKK KRINN...

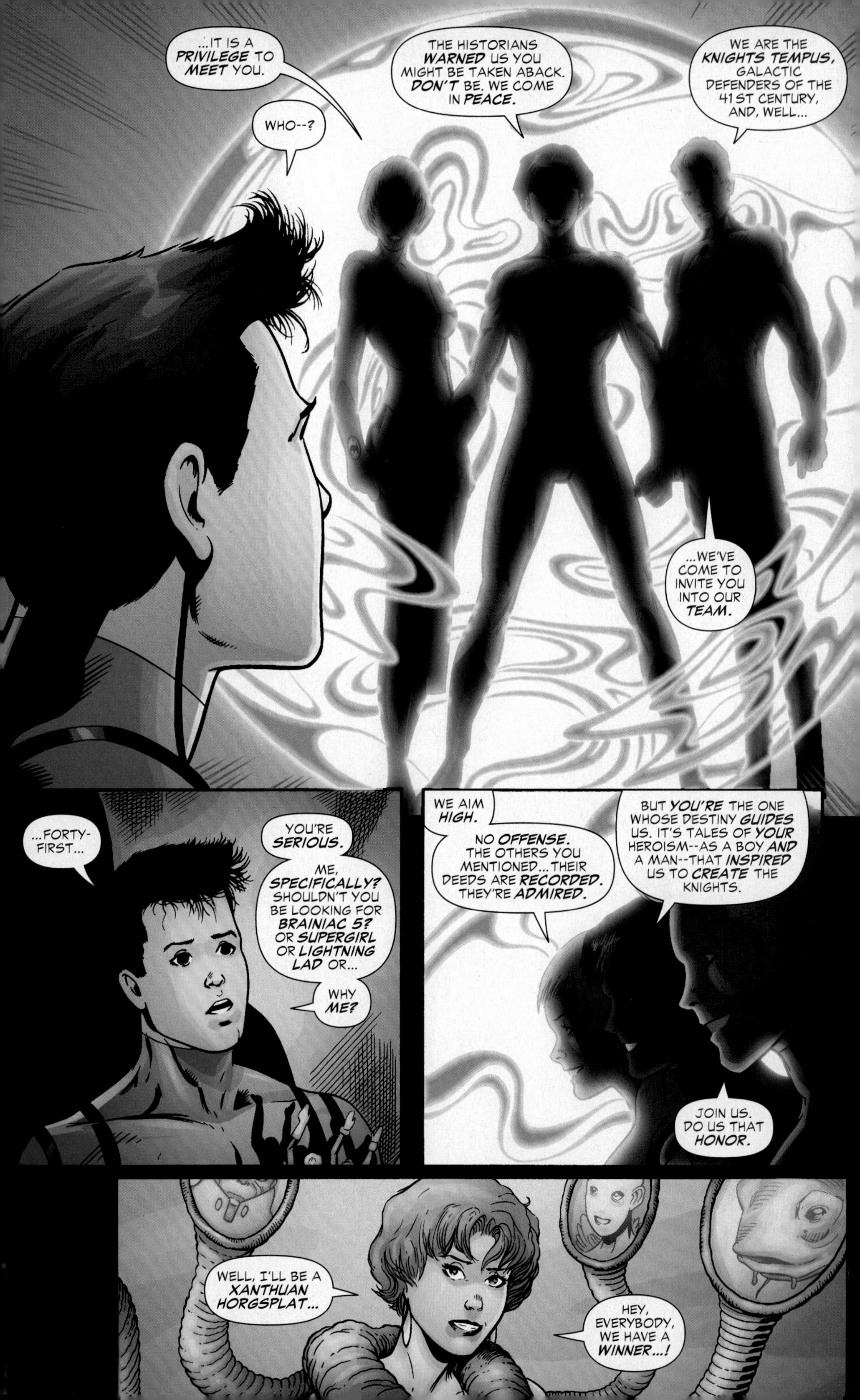
...IT IS A PRIVILEGE TO MEET YOU.
WHO--?
THE HISTORIANS WARNED US YOU MIGHT BE TAKEN ABACK. DON'T BE. WE COME IN PEACE.
WE ARE THE KNIGHTS TEMPUS, GALACTIC DEFENDERS OF THE 41ST CENTURY, AND, WELL...
...WE'VE COME TO INVITE YOU INTO OUR TEAM.
...FORTY-FIRST...
YOU'RE SERIOUS.
ME, SPECIFICALLY? SHOULDN'T YOU BE LOOKING FOR BRAINIAC 5? OR SUPERGIRL OR LIGHTNING LAD OR...
WHY ME?
WE AIM HIGH.
NO OFFENSE. THE OTHERS YOU MENTIONED...THEIR DEEDS ARE RECORDED. THEY'RE ADMIRED.
BUT YOU'RE THE ONE WHOSE DESTINY GUIDES US. IT'S TALES OF YOUR HEROISM--AS A BOY AND A MAN--THAT INSPIRED US TO CREATE THE KNIGHTS.
JOIN US. DO US THAT HONOR.
WELL, I'LL BE A XANTHUAN HORGSPLAT...
HEY, EVERYBODY, WE HAVE A WINNER...!

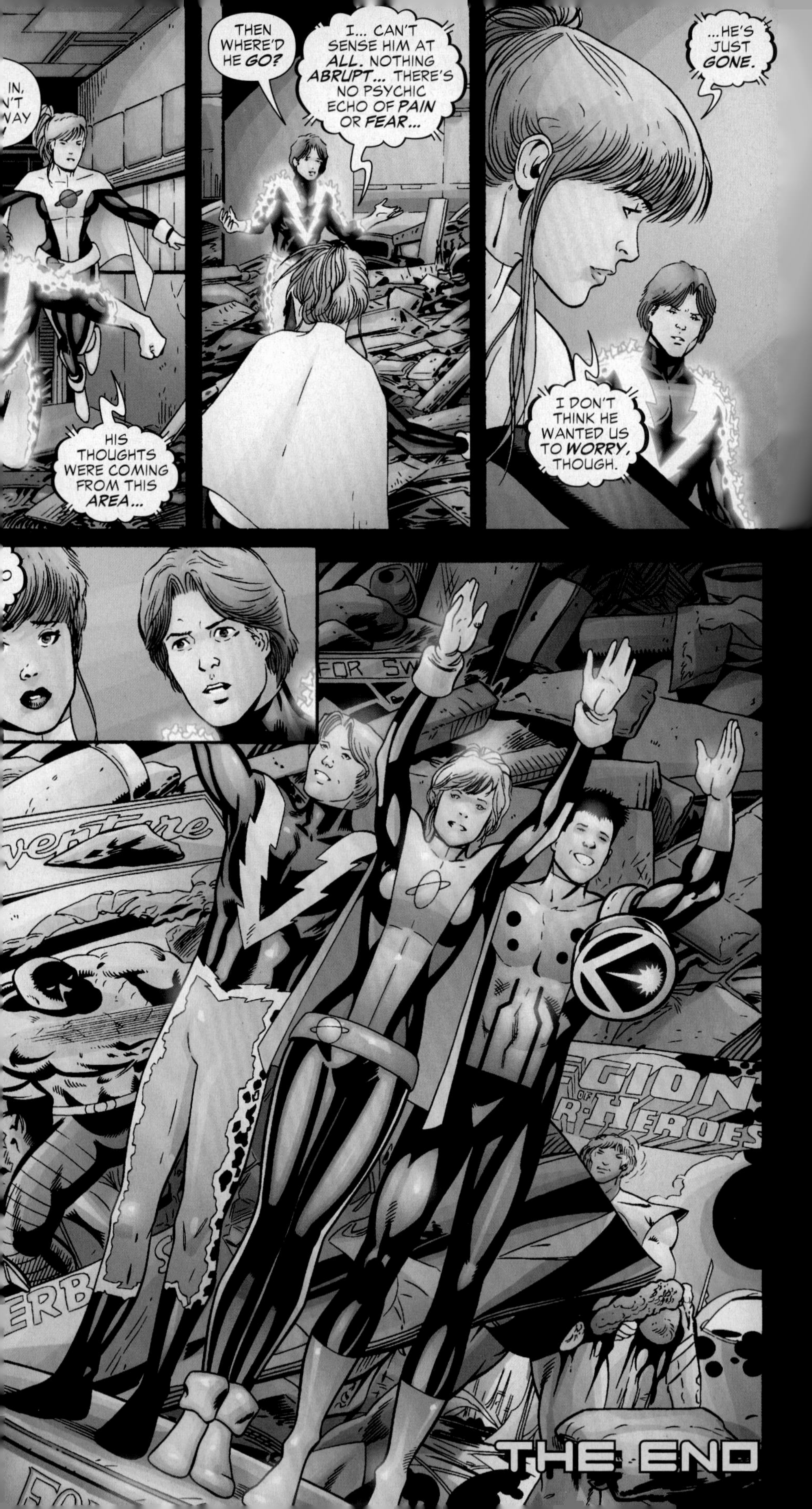
HIS THOUGHTS WERE COMING FROM THIS AREA...
THEN WHERE'D HE GO?
I... CAN'T SENSE HIM AT ALL. NOTHING ABRUPT... THERE'S NO PSYCHIC ECHO OF PAIN OR FEAR...
...HE'S JUST GONE.
I DON'T THINK HE WANTED US TO WORRY, THOUGH.
THE END

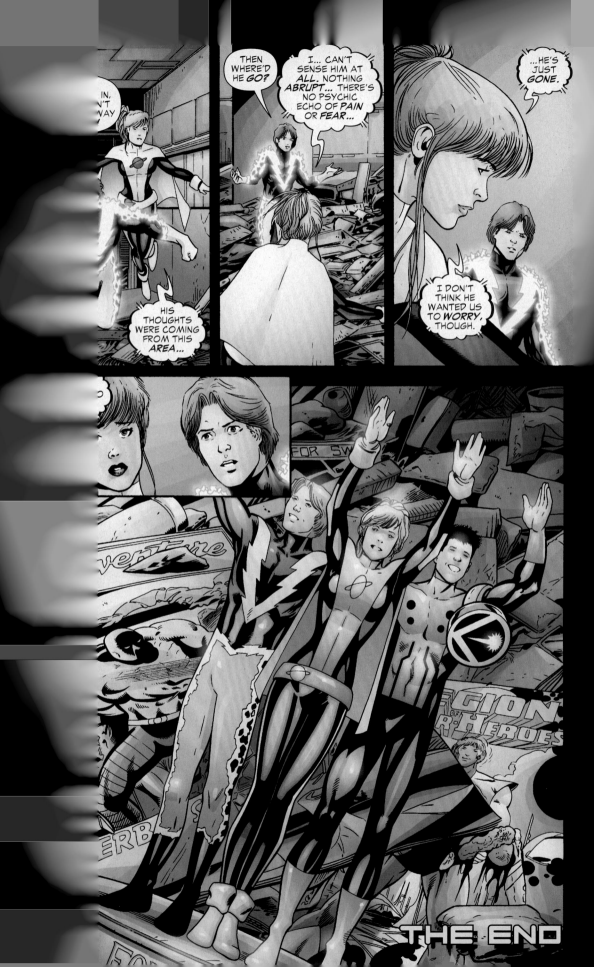

THE END IS ONLY THE BEGINNING!

AND DON'T MISS THESE OTHER GREAT TITLES FEATURING BATMAN!

BATMAN: WAR GAMES ACT ONE

**BILL WILLINGHAM
ED BRUBAKER
PETE WOODS**

THE BATMAN CHRONICLES VOLUME 1

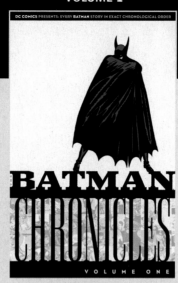

**BOB KANE
BILL FINGER**

BATMAN: THE DARK KNIGHT STRIKES AGAIN

**FRANK MILLER
LYNN VARLEY**

BATMAN: DARK VICTORY

**JEPH LOEB
TIM SALE**

BATMAN: HUSH VOLUME 2

**JEPH LOEB
JIM LEE
SCOTT WILLIAMS**

BATMAN: THE GREATEST STORIES EVER TOLD

**BOB KANE
NEAL ADAMS
FRANK MILLER**

SEARCH THE GRAPHIC NOVELS SECTION OF
www.DCCOMICS.com
FOR ART AND INFORMATION ON ALL OF OUR BOOKS!

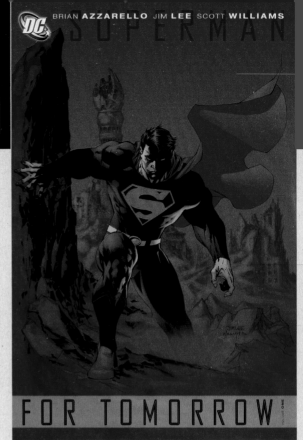
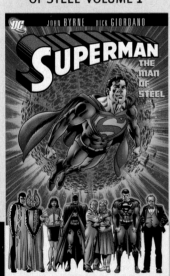
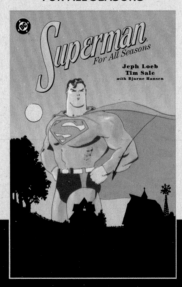